Transpacific Convergences

D0707567

STUDIES IN UNITED STATES CULTURE

Grace Elizabeth Hale, series editor

Series Editorial Board

Sara Blair, University of Michigan
Janet Davis, University of Texas at Austin
Matthew Guterl, Brown University
Franny Nudelman, Carleton University
Leigh Raiford, University of California, Berkeley
Bryant Simon, Temple University

Studies in United States Culture publishes provocative books that explore U.S. culture in its many forms and spheres of influence. Bringing together big ideas, brisk prose, bold storytelling, and sophisticated analysis, books published in the series serve as an intellectual meeting ground where scholars from different disciplinary and methodological perspectives can build common lines of inquiry around matters such as race, ethnicity, gender, sexuality, power, and empire in an American context.

Transpacific Convergences

Race, Migration, and Japanese American Film Culture before World War II

Denise Khor

The University of North Carolina Press CHAPEL HILL

© 2022 The University of North Carolina Press
All rights reserved
Set in Merope Basic by Westchester Publishing Services

Manufactured in the United States of America
The University of North Carolina Press has been a member of the
Green Press Initiative since 2003.

Complete Library of Congress Cataloging-in-Publication Data is available at
https://lccn.loc.gov/2021054804.

ISBN 978-1-4696-6796-6 (cloth: alk. paper)
ISBN 978-1-4696-6797-3 (pbk.: alk. paper)
ISBN 978-1-4696-6798-0 (ebook)

Cover illustration: International Theatre in Los Angeles, 1907. Courtesy of
Seaver Center for Western History Research, Los Angeles County Museum
of Natural History.

Chapter 4 was previously published in a different form as "'Filipinos Are the
Dandies of the Foreign Colonies': Race, Labor Struggles, and the Transpacific
Routes of Hollywood and Philippine Films, 1924–1948," *Pacific Historical
Review* 81, no. 3 (2012): 371–403.

For my family

Contents

Illustrations and Maps

MAPS

Author's Note

A substantial part of this book is derived from research conducted in historical archives of Japanese American materials. In direct quotes and as appropriate, this book preserves the conventions in the source materials. Modified Hepburn romanization without macrons is otherwise applied in the book. While the book discusses many individuals who were born in Japan and led transnational lives in the United States, it generally follows the name order convention observed in the English-language archive: given name before surname. Certain Japanese proper nouns do not have uniform English translations in the historical documents. I have adopted the English that appears most commonly in the archive or else the translation closest to the Japanese where the Japanese naming is consistent. While every effort has been made to match Japanese film titles mentioned in the English-language historical documents to titles of known films in Japanese-language databases, some titles have eluded confirmation due to variations that make the films difficult to identify or else because data about the films were not found.

Introduction

A photograph of the Fuji Kan in Los Angeles displays film posters and advertising banners hanging under a whimsical facade of Japan's iconic Mount Fuji. It is a brightly lit marquee, and the building itself appears nestled between storefronts, restaurants, and a bustling boulevard. Fuji Kan was first built in 1925 at 324 East First Street, in the heart of Los Angeles's Little Tokyo. It was among at least four theaters operated by Japanese in Los Angeles before World War II. At the Fuji Kan, the latest films from Japan were projected on-screen. Often these films were accompanied by musical instrumentation and a *benshi*, who provided live narration or commentary. It was the benshi with whom audiences identified and whom they longed for, their names publicized in local papers as prominently as the film titles and stars. Fuji Kan employed a cadre of benshi, each of whom brought his or her own style and performance to a given film show. Such dynamics made the filmic experience contingent, variable, and differentiated. While it was true that audiences in Los Angeles could now view the same films as audiences in Tokyo, the live performative elements at the Fuji Kan presented a view of cinema at once localized and irreproducible.

Operating at a pivotal time for Japanese in the United States, the Fuji Kan was more than a venue for commercial entertainment. When they moved across the cities and towns on the Pacific coast, many Japanese confronted a color line stretching from housing restrictions to the spaces of public accommodation. Against these exclusions, the Fuji Kan was something of a refuge, an untethered space that catered to its audiences. Throughout the decades, Japanese-owned theaters in the United States served a multiplicity of usages. Beyond offering film shows, they served as places of gathering, assembly, and collectivization. In conjunction with film screenings, they often held performances, lectures, sermons, rallies, community gatherings, or fund-raisers. Often located in urban centers, these spaces were even reconfigured at crucial moments to serve the barer necessities of housing and sustenance.

Even the screen at the Fuji Kan projected a plenitude of media across varying format, content, and genre. American feature films were the standard fare in the earliest days. When films from Japan began to be exhibited more

Photograph of Los Angeles's Fuji Kan in 1939. Courtesy of Los Angeles
Public Library.

regularly in the mid-1920s, they were most often coupled with short features
ranging from travelogues, educational or industrial shorts, and, as the
Sino-Japanese War escalated, propaganda films. Additionally, the Fuji
Kan on several occasions exhibited *local films*, depicting views of the neighborhood and commercial streets as well as community activities, such as
swimming competitions and judo matches. Showing local views and
recognizable places, these films appealed to audiences' desires for self-
recognition or "seeing oneself on the screen."[1] For Japanese excluded from
political participation in the United States (as determined by law until
1952), local films presented the audience with an alternative form of public
affirmation and recognition.

Providing a central gathering place for many Japanese, the Fuji Kan drew
together an ever-widening public. Junko Ogihara was among the first to write
about the theater and the film culture of Japanese in Los Angeles in the article "The Exhibition of Films for Japanese Americans in Los Angeles during
the Silent Film Era" (1990). The early days of the theater were influenced by
the city's fluctuating population. "'[Japanese] families rolled in from the out-
lying farms in their Model T's' to dine and shop in Little Tokyo," according

to one account, "[and] ended the night at the Fuji-kan, the local movie house showing Japanese silent films, complete with a silver-tongued benshi with shamisen accompaniment."[2] Like the city itself, the Fuji Kan was tied to migration and the growing cycles of agricultural fields, its audiences expanding and contracting with the centripetal movements characteristic of the developing Pacific coast of the early twentieth century. Fuji Kan served its multiplicitous audience for decades until its closure during World War II. It would reemerge after the war as the Linda Lea Theatre in 1945 and Kinema Theatre in 1955.

From its earliest years, the Fuji Kan offers us a glimpse of the radical heterogeneity within American film historiography. It tells the story of film circulation moving multidirectionally across the Pacific, of ephemeral exhibition practices during and beyond the silent era, and of alternative film publics and contexts taking shape in the United States throughout the early twentieth century and beyond. *Transpacific Convergences* explores this multifaceted history by tracing an alternative public sphere of film practice and possibility for Japanese in the United States before World War II. Drawing on original archival research, *Transpacific Convergences* moves beyond dominant film industries and nationalizing contexts to reenvision the transnational and global dimensions *within* the historiographies of U.S. film and media. Even in the first decades of the American film industry's development, films were being made by Japanese in the United States. Their early film production efforts, as well as their independently established production studios, were not entirely without precedent but shared varying traits with the emergent race film industry. Japanese films were also coming to the United States and circulated by U.S.-based benshi and across nontheatrical exhibition sites. Tracing these developments across the shifting technologies of the cinema, I go on to look at the impact of the sound transition as it reshaped Japanese participation in the film industry as well as the context of independent film production and exhibition. From across the Pacific and beyond, the routes of Japanese film culture moved ever expansively as Japanese theater owners also catered to Filipino audiences and their desires to view Filipino films. Taken together, *Transpacific Convergences* illuminates a plurality of filmmaking and filmgoing practices in the United States in the first half of the twentieth century.

I use the term *transpacific convergence* not to name or describe a particularized region or even a movement; rather, it is a heuristic for rethinking the terms of film historicism and historiography. As Jennifer M. Bean in *Silent Cinema and the Politics of Space* (2014) notes, it is the historicist logic of

European and North American modernity that shapes early cinema's discourse of itself. This conceptual legacy not only "artificially bifurcates [the study of cinema] into Western and non-Western spheres, but also obfuscates a view of the rest of the world as anything other than a space to be conquered or developed." This lingering historicism has shaped the field's assumptions about cinema's technological and industrial modernity and has situated the major film industries of France, Germany, Russia, and especially the United States as the center, presuming all else as periphery. Looking to the formative moments in the New Film History, Bean notes, "however paradoxically, a particularly powerful means of forestalling critical interrogation emerged as a somewhat oblique and unintended consequence of revisionist approaches to early film history." The study of early cinema's orientation toward Euro-American modernity has obfuscated and provincialized the multifarious responses to early cinema's "arrival" across the globe.[3] In (dis)orienting this historicist logic, *Transpacific Convergences* illuminates uneven and disjunctive features of cinema's relationship to modernity. Beyond widening the historiography, the book follows the routes of film circulation and exchange to trace a counterpublic for national film industries and dominant film cultures.

Transpacific Convergences tells a story of emergence, a cinema by Japanese in the United States during a transformative period. Between the years 1908 and 1917, U.S. film systems of representation, production, and distribution began consolidating into what David Bordwell and Kristin Thompson famously outlined as the classical Hollywood system. Scholarship demarcates these pivotal early years by the changes to film style (particularly the development of continuity editing and narrative storytelling), the shift from single-reel to multiple-reel formats, and the demise of the smaller storefront theaters reliant on changing programs and short films. These were also the years that American film studios began consolidating in southern California and gave rise to the industry we now know as Hollywood. In *American Cinema's Transitional Era: Audiences, Institutions, Practices* (2004), Charlie Keil and Shelley Stamp argue that the so-called transitional period did not merely pave the way for rationalization and a major studio system of mass production; rather, the era and the industry were marked by considerable instability and volatility. "The sheer diversity of representational, institutional and exhibition practices that coexist at this moment of transition," according to Keil and Stamp, "point as much to the eventual shape that Hollywood filmmaking would assume in the classical era as to other possibilities and other models lost in the wake of consolidation and standardization that marked the studio era."[4] *Transpacific Convergences* charts the emergence of a cinema within and beyond this formative period. Moving across several major eras in film history, from the earlier nickelodeon period (1905 to the early 1910s) to the introduction of synchronized sound (1927 to 1930) and until the end of World War II and the changes to the studio system, it locates a cinema emerging over and against the rise of the dominating studio system and the assimilative power of its consolidation.

At the same time, *Transpacific Convergences* also tells an ensuing story of foreclosure. The early film production efforts by Japanese in the United States were short-lived; their films had inadequate channels for circulation and distribution. Companies were often stymied by lack of adequate capital and limited access to technology. These challenges were exacerbated as the sound transition transformed the institution of the cinema. Alongside the devastating effects of World War II and the mass removal of Japanese Americans to concentration camps, the fullest possibilities of this earlier era were not to materialize. Within this view, *Transpacific Convergences* traces a cinema that would ultimately not come to be. Calling for a "film history as media archaeology" approach, Thomas Elsaesser looks to contemporary digital media as a mode to rethink film historicism and the "idea of historical change itself and what we mean by inclusion and exclusion, horizons and boundaries, emergence and transformation."[5] This approach means examining the change and continuity of media images, cultures, and practices beyond a teleological conception of film history. *Transpacific Convergences* charts these divergent and disjunctive trajectories to unsettle a successive and linear conception of film history. It traces a cinema no longer present and illuminates a past made available only across its relics, fragments, and archival traces. In so doing, *Transpacific Convergences* calls for a reimagining of the U.S. media past, not only of what that history is but also how and by what means it is told.

Reenvisioning Asian American Media Pasts

The years 2019 and 2020 mark a pivotal moment for Asian American film and media as such founding media arts organizations as Visual Communications (VC), Asian CineVision (ACV), and Center for Asian American Media (formerly known as the National Asian American Telecommunications Association [NAATA]) celebrated key anniversaries alongside the fifty years since Asian American studies centers and departments were established at U.S. universities. To recognize and reflect upon this legacy and its implications for the future, a cluster of projects and productions were organized. The

Japanese American National Museum held an exhibition *At First Light: The Dawning of Asian Pacific America*, featuring an opening plenary with core Visual Communications founders Robert Nakamura, Duane Kubo, Alan Ohashi, and Eddie Wong.[6] The long-awaited documentary series *Asian Americans* was also released for public television. Chronicling the history of Asian Americans (including its filmmaking), the five-part docuseries was produced by the documentary filmmaker Renee Tajima-Peña, who herself was a founding member of NAATA.[7] Other key events included the screening series *My Sight Is Lined with Visions: 1990s Asian American Film and Video*, featuring the work and contributions of experimental filmmakers.[8] Importantly adjoining these wide-ranging projects was *Film Quarterly*'s two-part symposium and special dossier "Asian American Film at Fifty." Featuring contributing articles, the issue was guest edited by Brian Hu and B. Ruby Rich. In their introduction, Hu and Rich called attention to the important founding moments and institutions of Asian American cinema, from its genesis in the panethnic political organizing of the Asian American movement to the radical struggles for decolonization and ending the American war in Vietnam. Yet even as these events reflected on and celebrated these founding and originating histories, they also encouraged new lines of inquiry and new objects of study to emerge. For instance, Hu and Rich look to UCLA's Visual Communication's initial impetus to produce and circulate visual education materials to highlight the importance of the original multimedia and nontheatrical contexts in Asian American film and media history.[9] Other contributing scholars like Josslyn Luckett revisit the student productions from Ethno-Communications to elucidate the largely unrecognized filmmaking efforts of Asian American women as well as their interconnections with the LA Rebellion (African American independent filmmaking at UCLA in the 1970s).[10] These new and developing efforts represent a multitude of ways to begin rethinking Asian American media pasts.

By looking to the first half of the twentieth century, *Transpacific Convergences* aims to reorient Asian American film and media history in several important ways. First, I reveal an earlier, longer, and more expansive history of Asian American independent filmmaking. Well before 1968, Japanese in the United States produced their own films and established what I would describe as an aspirational cinema based in the politics of racial uplift and respectability. Filmmakers also made a range of films during the period when the advent of synchronized sound transformed the institution of the cinema. In refocusing the lens on this earlier filmic era, the very terms *Asian American* and *independent* require considerable redefinition. Established long be-

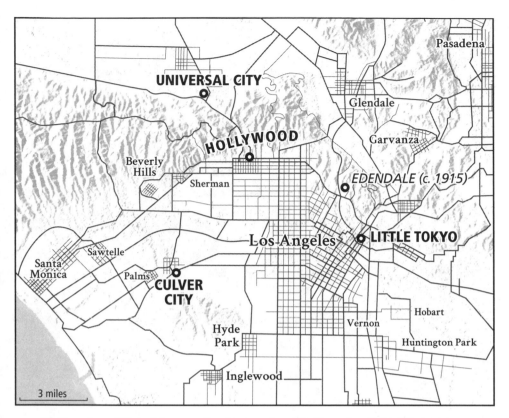

The location of Little Tokyo was far closer to the early film colony Edendale (present day Echo Park) than the Hollywood studios. Source: Auto Road Map of Los Angeles and Vicinity (Rand McNally, 1926). Cartography by Erik Steiner.

fore the usage of this term, the cinema of the early period was neither self-consciously Asian American nor similarly politicized by the radical and revolutionary movements that gave rise to post-1968 filmmaking.[11] While these filmmaking endeavors were independent from the dominant film industry in both the United States and Japan, their relationship to major film institutions was not necessarily, or self-avowedly, oppositional. In reorienting the earlier era, I suggest these earlier filmmaking productions and practices may be understood within geographies of *proximity* and *circulation*.

The earliest film companies established by Japanese were all located in and around the city of Los Angeles. These developments were shaped by the formation of Los Angeles's Little Tokyo and its geographical relationship to the emerging film industry. Los Angeles had become a particularly vibrant hub

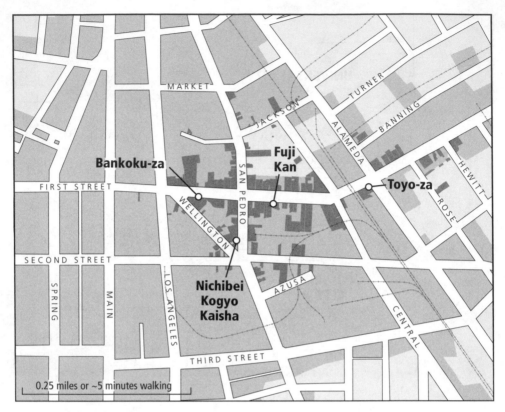

Map of film businesses in Little Tokyo, Los Angeles. Sources: Map of Congested District of Los Angeles (Sanborn, 1920) and Little Tokyo Japanese Businesses 1940 (japantownatlas.com). Cartography by Erik Steiner.

for the 130,000 Japanese who arrived in the continental United States and Hawaii by the time the first West Coast film studio was established in Edendale in 1908. The early film colony was in the northwest region of the historic downtown, only a few miles from the burgeoning Japanese district in the East First Street area. This neighborhood grew as many Japanese arrived in Los Angeles from San Francisco. In addition to the great 1906 earthquake, Northern California had become considerably less amenable with the segregation of Japanese students by the San Francisco School Board, an incident that catalyzed the 1908 Gentlemen's Agreement, and the stronger presence of white trade unions and anti-Japanese nativism. The population of Japanese in Los Angeles was doubled in 1907 and became the largest in the continental United States by the end of World War I. Consequently, Los Angeles's Little Tokyo emerged as a thriving commercial and residential hub and as a major artery of transit.

This physical proximity was especially central to the early production companies established during the period when Hollywood was emerging as a major studio system. Even as these Japanese-led companies were peripheral to the developing industry, they still relied on, or were influenced by, developments and resources emanating from that industry, creating what David James refers to as "minor cinemas." Some company founders gained prior experience working in the margins of the industry, while others relied on the industry for personnel or other creative or tangible materials.[12] Of course, Hollywood itself also made use of its locality, turning its geographical location into an invaluable asset. Not only did the earliest film pioneers and the emerging Los Angeles film companies utilize the favorable climate conditions, but they also benefitted from the open shop status of Los Angeles and the city's shifting and growing demographic population. In writing about Mexican film culture and Hollywood, Colin Gunckel further notes that the very consolidation of the industry was shaped by the efforts to preserve an image of Los Angeles as a "white spot," its actual racialized populations serving as a foil against which images of white Los Angeles were constructed.[13]

While situated at the margins of emerging Hollywood, the cinemas of this earlier period were simultaneously shaped by the circulation of people, culture, and film across the Pacific. Moving within and between the dominant film industries in the United States and Japan, participants of these earlier film cultures were influenced at varying scales by the developments and connections to the Japanese film industry. Aaron Gerow notes that film producers and studios in Japan had long envisioned an overseas market for its films. During a period in which American and European filmmakers were producing films set in Japan, Japanese filmmakers conversely imagined the "dream of export" as the "standard by which Japanese motion pictures could be recognized as a cinema."[14] Even though Japan never realized these ambitions to cultivate a substantial international market, Japanese producers and distributors in the United States were influenced by these dynamics as they sought opportunities and possibilities within and between the major industries on both sides of the Pacific. Japan had a particularly robust domestic film industry. Unlike other parts of the world, U.S. film studios were unable to seize control of Japan's film market due to the reorganization of the film industry and trade protections. According to Hiroshi Kitamura, Japan responded to the "Hollywoodization" of the world after World War I by strengthening and consolidating their film industry into a vertically integrated system. This allowed the industry to vastly increase their production output and ensure a domestic market. Moving multidirectionally across the

Pacific, Japanese who had work experience in Hollywood, including several who participated in the film cultures explored in this book, also circled back to the Japanese film industry to enhance these developments with adaptations of Hollywood filmmaking techniques and practices.[15]

These transpacific movements were a key part of the early film cultures in the United States. As I explore in the following chapters, some of the early production studios sought audiences not in the United States but instead looked overseas toward distribution markets in Japan. The impact of the sound transition in Japan also influenced the circulation of Japanese films in the United States. The industry's continual production of silent films during this period prolonged the silent-era exhibition practices in the United States. These transpacific interconnections complicate the center-periphery model of national cinema yet also challenge the later notion of a self-realized cinema "by, for, and about Asian Americans." In chronicling an earlier filmic history, *Transpacific Convergences* considers the overlapping and entangled circuits of transpacific exchange. Building from work by scholars like Laura Isabel Serna, it takes a historicized approach to studying circulation across borders.[16] Looking at a geography of varying scales, the book foregrounds the interface of the local and the national to historicize a phenomenon largely understood as a contemporary outcome of globalization and borderless flows. These reworkings of a historized transpacific film culture also elaborate on the ways Asian American cinema and media can be rethought within a shifting historiography of Asian Americans (and Japanese Americans more specifically) reconceptualized globally and via engagements "between two empires."[17]

Second, scholarship on Asian American film and media has tended to focus on bad screen objects and the ideological production of negative images and stereotypes. This tendency reflects the field's concern and perhaps overinvestment in Hollywood and the "culture industries" as a center of production. Within this view, post-1968 independent Asian American cinema seems merely reactive, a negative screen by which filmmaking is either resistant or complicit. But new studies of Anna May Wong, Sessue Hayakawa, and Philip Anh have complicated this way of viewing the relationship of Asian Americans to the history of Hollywood by exploring the complex negotiation of individual film stars with screen images, the star system, and industry casting and production practices.[18] While these important studies shed light on a myriad of strategies deployed by Asians and Asian Americans to adapt, resist, and keep working in the industry, they also refocus our gaze at Hollywood itself. *Transpacific Convergences* moves further afield to consider a multiplicity of film publics and a wider range of participation in the cinema. In her now seminal book *Migrating to the Movies: Cinema and Black Urban Modernity* (2005), Jacqueline Stewart looks beyond the dominant screen culture to consider the overlapping Black film publics in shaping the rise of American cinema. Criticizing a sole focus on the systematic objectification of Blackness in American popular culture, Stewart shows how some "accounts unwittingly replicate the marginalization of Blackness that characterizes minstrelsy and the dominant cinema by obscuring the roles African Americans have played as subjects of their own history with mass culture." In reorienting the study of Black images, Stewart brings into view not only early Black film exhibition and production efforts but also the relationship between cinema and Black migration to northern cities, especially in the formation of Black urban cultures in the early twentieth century.[19]

This book aims to similarly widen and complicate the relationship of Asian Americans to the institution of the cinema. *Transpacific Convergences* emphasizes the multidimensional aspects of the cinema, or what Rick Altman refers to as "cinema as event." This formulation moves beyond film as text. Highlighting the interchange between projection and reception, Altman calls for a study of cinema focused on multiplicity, instability, mediation, and materiality. Such an approach registers cinema as a constellation of events rather than a unified chain of images. It makes possible the recognition of the live and performative aspects of the cinema, the disunity of film as a material object, and the intermediality of the cinema and its viewing publics.[20] Building on these conceptions, *Transpacific Convergences* works to expand the objects, sites, and foci of filmic inquiry; in so doing, the book recognizes Japanese Americans as themselves participants in the emerging and changing film publics of the early twentieth century.

Finally, *Transpacific Convergences* looks across racialized historiographies and illuminates a multilayered historicity. While at the periphery of the studio system, the early Japanese filmmaking of the 1910s shares a border with the race film industry and African American film culture of the early twentieth century. Early Japanese film producers were similarly motivated by discourses of racial uplift, and the systems of alternative filmmaking and exhibition also reveal a historical point of overlap. From the use of Spanish words by Japanese benshi in California to the patronage of Japanese-owned theaters by Filipino filmgoers, the points of convergence and interracial encounter can become visible in the ephemeral archival fragments even when they are obscured within the dominant historiography. In looking to the study of cinema and media studies (and especially early cinema studies), comparative race and intersectional approaches remain limited. Daniel Bernardi's edited collection *The Birth of Whiteness: Race and the Emergence of U.S. Cinema* (1996) continues to be one of few exceptions. Written over two decades ago, Bernardi noted then that film studies tended to ignore race altogether or take a singular racial group approach that elides the "historical, theoretical, and critical work on the meaning of race that these groups share."[21] More recent comparative scholarship includes Allyson Nadia Field and Marsha Gordon's *Screening Race in American Nontheatrical Film* (2019) and Joshua Glick's *Los Angeles Documentary and the Production of Public History, 1958–1977* (2018). Though the work remains emergent in cinema and media studies, comparative and intersectional approaches have abounded for the past decade in the interdisciplinary field of ethnic studies (so much so that the field has reached its own abnegation). Nevertheless, ethnic studies scholars have led the way, chronicling and critiquing over a century of Afro-Asian encounter and beyond, from W. E. B. Du Bois's declaration of Japan as "champion of the colored races" to the identification with Black power by Asian American activists in the 1960s and 1970s and beyond.[22]

With its intertwined relationships to the LA Rebellion and the revolutionary filmmaking of Third Cinema, post-1968 Asian American independent filmmaking has a "family of resemblance" within this earlier era of film production and exhibition.[23] As Renee Tajima-Pēna, Glen Mimura, and the recent work by Josslyn Luckett have shown, filmmaking practitioners and foundational media arts programs like Ethno-Communications worked collaboratively across racialized communities and made work shaped by multiracial coalition building and Third World anticolonial solidarity.[24] While the post-1968 period differs considerably, as I have indicated, this earlier period's interconnections to the race film industry and African American filmgoing publics (as well as other sites of convergence and divergence) illuminate an intriguing line of continuity. In rethinking the many pasts of Asian American film history, the book ultimately hopes to reimagine its many possible futures.

On Lost Films and Writing Film Pasts

I first learned of early Japanese filmmaking in the United States in a footnote. As if breathing a life into existence, Yoshio Kishi briefly referenced the presence of two early studios called the Japanese American Film Company and the Yamato Graph Motion Picture Company in the now classic Asian American film anthology *Moving the Image: Independent Asian Pacific American Me-*

dia Arts (1999).[25] Unbeknownst to me then, these two film companies produced some of the earliest known film productions by Japanese Americans. As I would later discover, most of these early films no longer exist. Films of this era were made of nitrate celluloid, a highly flammable chemical material. With their vulnerability to combustion and deterioration, many early films were destroyed. Over 80 percent of American silent-era films have been irretrievably lost. Early films made by Asian Americans were even less likely to survive. Produced outside the commercial industry and subject to racialized marginalization, early films by Asian Americans often eluded institutional preservation efforts. Excavating the history of these lost films has enabled my writing the history of early Asian American filmmaking.

Many of the films included in *Transpacific Convergences* are *lost films*, or films with no existing print. This book takes up the problem of "writing film histories without films" by widening the archive and expanding methodological approaches. Eric Smoodin has argued that the archival turn can potentially enlarge the horizons of cinema studies, opening possibilities for new directions and new historiographies. "Films themselves," according to Smoodin, "might have a modest place and none of the singular importance that marked the discipline for so long."[26] Indeed, it is in part the field's privileging of extant films that has long shaped the scholarly writing on American film history. In shifting the objects of study and expanding the archives, *Transpacific Convergences* brings into view an alternative historiography, indeed a counterarchive of filmmaking practice and possibility.

I approach the study of lost films and ephemeral film practices as a primary rather than ancillary concern. Writing about the problem of lost, fragmentary, unreliable, and disappearing sources in the study of early African American filmmaking, Allyson Nadia Field has argued that "lost to us today, nonextant films nonetheless existed at a given time and place and functioned in particular contexts, had actual effects on specific audiences, and consisted of certain formal properties." Even if the actual print no longer exists, excavating the context of production, exhibition, and accounts of reception can provide important insight into ephemeral film practices and on the formal qualities of the films themselves. Source materials may provide information on the length or format of films as well as narrative elements, whereas other editing and compositional features may be less easy to discern given the surviving evidence. To consider any of these aspects of lost or incomplete films, according to Field, requires us to "look beyond the screen" and to the broader culture of the time.[27] Wherein an actual print may not exist, the archives may provide insight into how films may have been formally constituted and how ephemeral film practices may have been enacted, regardless of whether we can currently see it.

Existing archives make it possible to consider lost films and reconstruct lost film histories, yet they also present historiographical and methodological challenges. The archival turn in cinema studies has been enhanced by the availability of digital resources, such as Eric Hoyt's Media History Digital Library (MHDL), an indispensable resource for my research.[28] However, as Rob King importantly notes, whereas previous generations of silent-era film historians depended on a handful of trade magazines whose primacy was tied to their availability on microfilm, the MHDL vastly expanded these holdings by digitizing scores of additional sources; but "what goes unchallenged in this process is the historiographical primacy of journals and fan magazines in the first place." "The website's very usefulness bespeaks an inevitable circularity," according to King. "Existing methodological protocols have prioritized certain categories or materials for digitization (trade and fan magazines), which in turn ensures the ongoing production of scholarship that, in drawing on those same general categories, thereby conforms to established methodological protocols." Beyond additive or supplemental, the effort to expand the archive must also engage epistemological concerns and the modes of knowledge production. As King further asserts, "a more expansive conception of the archive unsettles traditional hierarchies of documentation by forcing sanctioned categories into dialogue with the margins. Such an interpretive practice will, moreover, be dialogic twice over. Not only will it be attuned to archival objects that interrupts or disrupts business-as-usual historiography, but it will also examine those objects for traces of the counterhistories lurking beneath the official record."[29]

While this study utilizes traditional film history sources, including trade journals and sources from the Media History Digital Library, the most important archives for *Transpacific Convergences* come largely from underutilized media-related Asian American collections. First, I draw extensively from Japanese American print media.[30] By searching Japanese American newspapers, I was able to identify filmmakers, producers, studios, and film titles, many of which were completely unacknowledged in American cinema catalogs and film listings. Short articles or notices in the papers identified local screenings of Japanese films. Not only did these sources allow me to map the routes of Japanese film circulation in the United States, but they also enabled me to chronicle the work of the benshi, who exhibited and performed with the films. Japanese American journalists and film critics wrote about films and film viewings for local Japanese audiences and they also provided keen observations of Japanese participation in Hollywood and its film culture. Together with mainstream newspapers, both regional and national sources, Japanese American newspapers provided rich insight into early Japanese American film practices and public cultures.

The availability of Japanese American newspapers and other archival sources is itself a product of history and power. It was not until the 1970s and the emergence of the Asian American movement that alternative repositories for collecting the histories of Asian Americans was even conceivable. Japanese American newspapers were especially well preserved in collections because they were kept and used by U.S. military intelligence during the years leading up to World War II. Collected by the FBI as "raw data" on the "pro-Japan" sentiments of Issei, these sources served as justification for the surveillance, round-up, and mass incarceration of Japanese Americans.[31] While I consulted numerous microfiche collections, a significant portion of my print media sources come from the Hoji Shinbun Digital Archive, an open-access digital collection begun in 2017 by the Hoover Institution at Stanford University.[32]

Second, such manuscript collections as the Takeshi Ban Papers at the Japanese American National Museum also provided valuable materials. This collection was donated by descendants in 1996. Ban was a traveling film exhibitor and benshi who set up Japanese film shows across the continental United States. Ban kept journals of his work between the years 1933 and 1941. These materials provide invaluable insight into the operation of Japanese film exhibition and delineate the scope and scale of the showman's endeavors. Looking at Ban's business records, as well as his correspondence with Noboru Tsuda and Suimin Matsui, exposes the centrality of nontheatrical venues and a broader network of filmic activity. Letters between Ban and the famed W. E. B. Du Bois (held at the University of Massachusetts Amherst Library) document Ban's film work beyond mere commercial or entertainment purposes. Ban approached the cinema as a "race man," and his efforts to foster a viewing public illuminate his ideas about racial progress and uplift, as I explore in chapter 2.

Nonfilmic materials—including trade papers, collected oral histories, government documents, and ephemera—compose the bulk of my research archive. However, a singular film remains one of my most significant sources. I first discovered a print of *The Oath of the Sword* in 2016 at the George Eastman Museum (GEM) via its cataloging in the International Federation of Film Archives (FIAF) International Index. As far as I know, the film is the earliest

Asian American film with a surviving print. Made in 1914, the film was produced by a company in Los Angeles called the Japanese American Film Company. Its all-Japanese cast enact a story drawing on the conventional tropes of Madame Butterfly but also promulgate a vision of racial uplift and modernity not unlike better known race films of this era.

In preservation terms, *The Oath of the Sword* can be understood as an *orphan film*. In the early years of film preservation, the priority was to restore commercial releases from the major motion picture industry. The term *orphan film* designates films outside the domain of commercial preservation. It also means "motion pictures abandoned by its owner or caretaker" or lacking clear copyright or ownership. Writing about the expanding scholarly engagement with orphan films, Paul Moore further asserts that the term has been "deliberately left un-defined to include . . . the preservation of [any] films left on the margins."[33] Indeed, *The Oath of the Sword* was a classically orphaned film. The provenance of the donated print is not known. GEM records do not capture who donated the print and when. The original print was photochemically preserved in 1980 and reproduced as a 35 mm safety negative and print, which is the copy that I was able to initially view in 2016.

The materiality of the print shapes both preservation and the understanding of the film's historiographical significance. GEM received the original film material as a 35 mm incomplete, silent tinted nitrate print. *The Oath of the Sword* was originally produced as a three-reel narrative feature, although its original length remains unknown. GEM's surviving print was preserved in a slightly shortened version measuring 1,778 footage feet, still contained in three reels. As an incomplete film print, a critical part of recovering the film is using written materials to fill in the missing pieces. In the first chapter, I analyze the surviving film print materials against the coverage of the film in the trade press and in documentary evidence, such as the film's scenario and the production company's incorporation papers. Additionally, the incompleteness of *The Oath of the Sword* exemplifies the uncertain status of film as a material object. The fragility of nitrate and the practice of producing varied prints at this time means that early films of this sort can rarely be conceived as original, complete, or definitive. The possibility of recovering additional prints and in ongoing restoration work means that the status of an extant print can always change.

As of this writing, I am working on a National Film Preservation Foundation grant in collaboration with GEM and the Japanese American National Museum (JANM) to preserve and restore *The Oath of the Sword*.[34] The original nitrate has so significantly deteriorated that preservation efforts must utilize the safety negative, relying on the original nitrate only as a reference to restore the original tinting in the film. The restoration project will restore the original tinting to the film and yield a new print for storage at GEM and master digital materials to be held at JANM. My efforts here build upon a growing body of work in recovering pre-1968 Asian American films. Some of the most pioneering work has been done by Asian American filmmakers themselves. Arthur Dong discovered the only known existing material from *The Curse of Quon Gwon* (1916) while working on his documentary *Hollywood Chinese* (2007).[35] According to Jenny Kwok Wah Lau, Dong found two reels of the 35 mm original negative and a 16 mm print in the basement of the Chinese American Historical Society in San Francisco. The surviving material is held and preserved by the Academy Film Archive.[36] Other research on the emergence of early Chinese American filmmaking efforts have led to the recovery of scant archival material and surviving reels for the filmmakers James B. Leong and Joseph Sunn Jue.[37] The work of Esther Eng and lesser-known Chinese American filmmakers also comes to light through the work of the filmmaker S. Louisa Wei and scholar Danielle Seid.[38]

To date, far less has been recovered for early Japanese American feature filmmaking. A surviving print of Sessue Hayakawa's *The Dragon Painter* (1919) was located at GEM by Stephen Gong and has since been restored and digitized.[39] In recovering and preserving *The Oath of the Sword*, it is my hope that the film can be viewed by future audiences and scholars alike and that new public audiences will encounter the film within the new viewing spaces of museums, film festivals, and digital media. While the contemporaneous release of the film was limited, as I detail in the following chapters, it remains possible for the once lost film to reemerge under new flickering (pixelated) lights.

Transpacific Convergences

The book begins in 1902, with an early nickelodeon established by Japanese in Seattle, Washington; moves through the major developments in cinema, including the silent and sound eras and the rise of the studio system; and ends with changes in film culture in the 1940s and the devastating impact of World War II. It contains four chapters, each organized around film production, exhibition, and reception to tell a story of multiple overlapping film publics in the United States during the first half of the twentieth century. Chapter 1 explores early Japanese American independent filmmaking as it emerged over and against the development of early Hollywood. This chapter recovers the film production efforts of Japanese in the United States as an alternative system of film production and circulation. I emphasize early filmmaking endeavors by Japanese in the United States as a mode of filmmaking concerned with the optic of representing "the race." Early Japanese American film producers and companies developed further within the context of a collective response to growing anti-Japanese sentiment on the Pacific coast. Seizing the modern apparatus of the cinema, Japanese in the United States utilized filmmaking to address their concerns for racial progress, uplift, and respectability.

Even before Sessue Hayakawa established Haworth Pictures, filmmaking enterprises by Japanese burgeoned in California and beyond. As early as 1912, Japanese in Portland, Oregon, were making educational films that showcased the abundance of agricultural crops harvested by Japanese farmers in California as well as other successes of the immigrant pioneers. These efforts in early filmmaking envisioned a transpacific film enterprise from its inception as producers sought audiences not only in the United States but also in Japan. Building on these early efforts, the Japanese American Film Company in 1914 opened offices in the emerging filmmaking capital, Los Angeles, and produced *The Oath of the Sword*, a film I closely analyze, while the Fujiyama Film Company in 1916 followed suit and established a studio in nearby Redlands, California. Japanese working in Hollywood contributed to other early film efforts. Oriented by their geographic and professional proximity to the major studios, these early filmmaking enterprises charted a path in independent filmmaking while also envisioning a new cinema in which Japanese were behind the scenes and in front of the camera.

Chapter 2 charts the formation of an alternative network of film circulation and exhibition by Japanese in the United States. Upending the oft cited claim that Japanese cinema first appeared in the United States via the art house circuit of the 1950s, this chapter argues for Japanese cinema's American encounter in an earlier moment and across an expansive circuit of exchange by and for Japanese Americans. Whereas Japanese proprietors operated film theaters from the first start of the nickelodeon era and beyond, Japanese films were also often projected in nontheatrical exhibition venues. Across the United States, agricultural fields, abandoned warehouses, Buddhist temples, community halls, churches, and even people's backyards were converted into makeshift theaters to project and view Japanese films. By highlighting these nontheatrical contexts, I locate Japanese film exhibition as a *useful cinema* that extended beyond commercially or entertainment-oriented purposes.

This chapter also highlights the central role of the benshi in both performing alongside the film as well as serving as a film's distributor and exhibitor. Often it was the benshi who took the Japanese film on the road, moving from town to town with equipment and film print in hand. Working independently or in partnership with Nichibei Kogyo Kaisha in Los Angeles, the benshi retained significant control in promoting, projecting, and exhibiting film. While characteristic of silent era exhibition at large, these dynamics in Japanese film exhibition ensured an irreproducibility of the filmic experience even as industries moved toward increasing standardization. Underscoring the localized dimensions of film exhibition, the chapter follows the work of Takeshi Ban, a benshi and Japanese film exhibitor who traversed hundreds of exhibition sites in the United States with Japanese films. Motivated not only by profit, Ban crafted a film public based in religiosity and transpacific politics.

Chapter 3 explores the sound transition as it took place within and between the film industries of the United States and Japan. Across a rapidly changing industry, Japanese in Hollywood found themselves incorporated into the efforts of the major studios as they sought to recapture global audiences. The emergence of sound technology introduced the problem of Hollywood's nationalization—as film became audible not only of sound but also of national languages. Hollywood looked to Japanese working in the industry to engage the development of the new medium as translators, interpreters, foreign-language actors, and writers. Yet these changes in the film industry also reinforced and fortified the system of racialized casting and production practices. In the transition to sound, early Hollywood sound films reengaged the screen Orientalism of the silent era, animating and making audible a new field of racialized speech sounds and sonic effects.

The chapter also examines the residual practices of the silent era as they continued across multiple aspects of Japanese American participation in production and exhibition. It looks at the first and only independent Japanese-language film made in the sound transition in the United States, along with a handful of amateur films made in the silent medium by Japanese producers. Finally, I look at the continual circulation of Japanese silent films within the sound era and the persistence of the benshi, whose work seemed to gain momentum with the outbreak of war in the Asia Pacific and as Japanese war and propaganda films began their circulation in the United States. Between national contexts and across the sphere of production and exhibition, together these discordant aspects of Japanese film culture mark the sound era's audible divides.

Chapter 4 considers the non-Japanese and working-class participants in Japanese film culture in the United States. Filipinos, in particular, were a sizable patronage for Japanese-owned film theaters. Looking at the theaters catering to Filipino patrons, I situate a film viewing public consolidated in opposition to intra-Asian relations and the racialized labor politics of Depression-era California. Japanese owned venues, like the Lincoln Theatre, were located in Stockton's Filipino district and contributed to a Filipino public world centered in urban leisure and consumer participation. Drawing on Filipino print media sources, I consider the implications of Filipino presence in Japanese film culture in the United States not only as economically motivated but also as constituting the sorts of cross-racial and localized encounters not easily incorporated into a singular conception of cinema, national or diasporic.

Not only did Japanese own or operate filmgoing venues for Filipino patrons, but they also played a role in exhibiting some of the earliest films from the Philippines to be seen in the continental United States and Hawaii. Tracing the circulation of Filipino films in the 1930s and 1940s, this chapter chronicles the transpacific movements of early Tagalog talkies and their exhibition histories in Japanese-owned theaters. Whereas the bulk of films under consideration were produced within the industry based in the Philippine archipelago, I include within this circulation history a relatively unknown and no longer extant Filipino film made in San Francisco, California, in the early 1930s. Additionally, Filipino films were often exhibited in California as "midnight rambles," following a common practice of racial segregation prevalent in the South.

In the epilogue, I look at the eventual collapse of these multiple film publics. Many of the promoters and exhibitors of Japanese film were incarcerated in concentration camps during World War II. The film culture itself emerged as a target of federal scrutiny and investigation. Confiscating film reels as perceived propaganda material, U.S. authorities viewed the film cultures of Japanese in the United States as a part of the wartime Pacific theater. I conclude with a discussion of our contemporary media era and the implications of new histories of media pasts.

FUJI KAN NO LONGER EXISTS. The physical site of its former location is now a Citibank and flanked on both sides by parking garages. Between the 1950s and 1970s, Los Angeles's Little Tokyo, like so many American urban neighborhoods, confronted the devastating consequences of urban renewal. With affordable housing and commercial businesses demolished (in addition to the long-term impact of World War II and the mass incarceration of Japanese Americans), what remains of Los Angeles's Little Tokyo today is contained in nine square blocks. At present, there is no physical trace of the Fuji Kan, no reminder of its mark on the city, and virtually no recognition of its significance within the history of the cinema. Its presence is lost to us, much like the history in this book.

Transpacific Convergences recovers a history not easily reconstituted. Its forking pathways end soon after they begin. The routes of its travel require looking between and beyond the major film studios and dominant film cultures. It moves across borders and, at times, creates them. In telling the story of a lost film history, *Transpacific Convergences* reconsiders not only what that history entails but also the terms by which it is reimagined. Such a telling reveals a history of the cinema that has never been singular nor chronological. It is not led from the core to the periphery nor bounded by clear categories and designations. Instead, *Transpacific Convergences* illuminates a media past unfurled in its fragments. In mapping "alternative" and "marginal" film networks, routes, and practices, I do tell the story of the cinema, not of the history that would come to be but of the one that could have been.

CHAPTER ONE

Owned, Controlled, and Operated by Japanese

Racial Uplift and Japanese American Film Production,
1912–1920

> I neither drink liquor of any kind, nor smoke, nor play cards, nor
> gamble nor associate with any improper persons. My honesty and
> industriousness are well known among my Japanese and American
> acquaintances and friends. . . . So I have all confidence in myself
> that as far as my character is concerned, I am second to none.
>
> —TAKAO OZAWA, 1917

> Recalling my experiences in making this picture [*The Cheat* (1915)]
> brings to mind the opposition of my playing the role of the
> villainous Japanese stirred among those of my nationality in Los
> Angeles and throughout the country after the film was released.
> For portraying the heavy, as screen villains are called, as a Japanese,
> I was indignantly accused of casting a slur on my nationality.
>
> —SESSUE HAYAKAWA, in *Zen Showed Me the Way*

Takao Ozawa stood before the Supreme Court to declare that he deserved American citizenship. He first filed his petition in 1914 in Hawaii, and the case came before the United States Supreme Court three years later. In one of two legal briefs submitted to the court, Ozawa yearned to show that he was a reputable member of the community—a person of moral conduct, respectability, and public esteem. Leaders of the Pacific Coast Japanese Association Deliberative Council recognized that Ozawa represented the ideal public character for Japanese American citizenship. Ozawa was educated at the University of California, Berkeley. He was married, with a family. He spoke English and practiced Christianity. He was, as suggested in his brief, a person of exemplary moral character. He neither drank, smoked, gambled, nor "associated with any improper persons." After the case was referred to the Supreme Court, the Japanese Association undertook leadership in what they assumed was an ideal test case to advocate for the naturalization rights of all Japanese in the United States. In the 1922 landmark case, the United States Supreme Court ruled against Ozawa, which ultimately codified the status of the Japanese in the United States as "alien ineligible for citizenship" until the 1952 McCarran Act. The declarations made by Ozawa, nevertheless, demonstrated the growing concern among many Japanese Americans over their public presentation. As the Ozawa case made clear, at stake in the performance of respectability and propriety was nothing less than the worthiness to the full rights to American citizenship.

Throughout the 1910s and 1920s, Japanese Americans developed a racial politics of respectability and uplift as a strategy to advance their community's interests and well-being. As a part of a mounting tide for Japanese exclusion, "Keep California White" campaigns contributed to the election of anti-Japanese politicians while groups like the Asiatic Exclusion League and Native Sons of the Golden West agitated to halt all immigration from Japan. San Francisco passed segregation orders to exclude Japanese schoolchildren, and in 1907, the federal government reached an agreement to limit Japanese immigration. Even before the Supreme Court ruled against Takao Ozawa and barred citizenship for all Japanese in the United States, state legislatures approved laws restricting Japanese from owning property and marrying whites. In response to the escalating anti-Japanese agitation, Japanese American leaders mobilized to advocate for rights and community betterment. The Japanese Association, in particular, was initially established as a mutual aid society to coordinate social services and provide rotating credit, among other resources. However, as Yuji Ichioka notes, many of the Japanese Associations also attempted to serve as moral guardians over the community by promulgating varying practices of racial uplift.[1]

In some ways, Japanese American racial uplift converged with African Americans' race-centered campaigns to promote the advancement of "the race." Writing about Los Angeles in the interwar years, Scott Kurashige notes that both Black and Japanese American elites advanced models of racial uplift based in white notions of Progressive social reform. Leaders believed that maintaining the moral integrity of their communities was critical to not only making their own individual members virtuous and productive but also in demonstrating their races' overall fitness for citizenship. Organizations like the Japanese Association worked in coordination with the Japanese consulate (although the relationship was also at times fraught) to encourage acceptable behavior and norms. These shared models of racial uplift also advanced concepts of self-help and entrepreneurialism, which were important for both Black and Japanese American communities facing barriers to the labor market.[2]

At the same time, the efforts of Japanese in the United States to advance the race was profoundly shaped by Japanese imperial modernity. As Eiichiro

Azuma notes, racial uplift for Japanese Americans not only sought to repudiate exclusion but also to uphold the vision of Japan's ascendency as imperial nation-state. From the onset, Japan's modernization (known as the Meiji Restoration) sought to build a modern monarchy based on Western models. Not only were Japan's leaders motivated to signal to the West that Japan was not a candidate for colonization, but they were also actively engaged in their own imperialist practices.[3] Within this context, the campaigns for racial uplift in the United States converged on the imperialist ideology of Japan's honorary white status. At the crux of Ozawa's bid for respectability and citizenship, after all, was his claim of whiteness. Ozawa petitioned the Supreme Course for citizenship on the basis of several criteria: his good character, American acculturation, that Japanese were not Chinese (as the Chinese Exclusion Act in 1882 established Chinese as "aliens ineligible for citizenship"), and that his skin was ultimately white.[4]

It is worth noting that Japanese American racial uplift was itself a campaign over the *image* of the race. Leaders and advocates sought self-transformation; to not only reform but to remake the racial self. Calling for the banishment of gambling and prostitution, proponents of racial uplift sought to distinguish the respectable classes from laborers, who were often castigated for their "uncivilized" habits. Consulate officials even issued conduct guides for Japanese emigrating to the United States. Japanese were encouraged to adopt "modern" appearance and Western style clothing and bodily comportment while women were urged to avoid nursing babies in public.[5] Thus, Japanese American racial uplift was a sort of *screen* for shaping a public self. It was a project based in refashioning the *look* of the race. Within this vein, there was perhaps no better means to engage in such endeavors than the modern technologies of the camera. As early as 1900, Japanese in the United States were involved in such professions as photography. According to Peter Palmquist, commercial photographers of Japanese ancestry abounded in Seattle, San Francisco, Sacramento, Fresno, and Los Angeles. The numbers of Japanese listed as workers employed in a "Kodak store" in the 1910 census suggest that Japanese also joined in the era's craze in amateur photography.[6] As Amy Sueyoshi notes, many early twentieth-century photographs served to document Japanese adoption of Western-style clothing. These images often featured Japanese men and women donning Western-style suits and dresses and posing to signify whiteness and social respectability. The photographs reflect the optimistic belief in the permeable categories of "being American" as well as Japanese nationalism.[7]

Given its development as a far-reaching mass commercial industry, the cinema offered perhaps the most significant screen through which to refashion a public self and uplift the race. For Japanese Americans, cinema's association with modernity and its growing ubiquity made for an opportune canvas for self-fashioning and reimagining the look of racial progress. Many Japanese increasingly recognized the possibilities of the cinema as a surface for representing the race and charting a future in the United States. Against this backdrop, Japanese in the United States adapted their campaign for racial uplift and respectability to the American screen. In the year after Ozawa first filed his court case, the American film *The Cheat* (1915) was released amid an uproar in Japanese American communities. Community leaders and newspaper editors mobilized a campaign against the film and denounced the film's star, Sessue Hayakawa, as a "race traitor." These protests erupted across multiple sites and as a part of organizing campaigns in California and even reverberated across the Pacific Ocean to spur publicly expressed outrage in Hawaii and Japan. These campaigns also coincided with the more well-known protests by African Americans against the landmark film *The Birth of a Nation* (1915). Most significantly, amid these overlapping media campaigns, Japanese Americans established one of the first Asian American media advocacy organizations to call for new film images and roles for Japanese actors. The Japanese Photoplayers' Club of Los Angeles was founded in 1917 to foster the "dignity of the race" in motion pictures.

Recognizing the role of the screen image in shaping the possibilities for Japanese in the United States, the first companies and studios to support independent Japanese American filmmaking were formed. Drawing on extensive archival research in historical newspapers and the trade press, I uncover the initial forays into filmmaking by Japanese in the United States. Japanese established film production companies that worked independent from or adjacent to the major studio system. Sessue Hayakawa's Haworth Pictures, perhaps the most well-known of these film companies in the United States, was first established in 1918 and produced nineteen feature-length films. However, as this chapter reveals, Hayakawa's company was predated by several other independent and lesser known ventures. In 1912, Japanese in Portland, Oregon, a place known more for its strawberries than its filmmaking, established an independent film company called the Yamato Graph Motion Picture Company. Gravitating closer toward the hub of American filmmaking in Los Angeles, Japanese producers also established the Japanese American Film Production Company in 1914 and the Fujiyama Film Company in 1916. Other ventures were also developed, yet their appearances in the archive remain scant.

As filmmaking concerned with the optic of the race, these early Japanese American filmmaking enterprises coincided with many facets of the race film industry in the United States. Race filmmakers formed independent production companies and developed an alternative network of film production and exhibition by and for African Americans. Working mostly outside of Hollywood, race filmmakers like Oscar Micheaux capitalized on the major studios' disinterest in Black viewership and filmmaking. Between 1915 and the late 1940s, race filmmakers made over five hundred films that circulated across a sprawling network of independently operated theaters and exhibition venues. Typically featuring all-Black casts, race films were dynamic and varied but often, as Barbara Lupack describes, "portrayed uplift achieved through education, exposed and punished race betrayal, and revealed black aspiration."[8] Against this context, I explore the only surviving print of *The Oath of the Sword*, which I first located in 2016 in the George Eastman House Archives. Closely reading the extant materials, I argue that the film provided a double view for audiences: a familiar and recognizable Japan-themed melodrama, on the one hand, and an aspirational story built on the possibilities for racial uplift, respectability, and modernity, on the other.

The Campaign against *The Cheat* (1915)

In 1915, Paramount Pictures released *The Cheat*, a film directed by Cecil B. DeMille and featuring a relatively unknown actor at the time, Sessue Hayakawa. The Japan-born actor appeared in several earlier films, but *The Cheat* was his star vehicle and catapulted his extraordinary career. While American audiences praised and admired the acting of Hayakawa in *The Cheat*, the Japanese American community decried the rising star and generated a widespread campaign to ban the film. Debates over the film's representational politics, a political demand as modern as cinema itself, were played out in the major Japanese American newspapers. Many denounced the portrayal of Japanese treachery by Hayakawa. With the film's release and popularity, Japanese in the United States and elsewhere fiercely debated the portrayal of the race and the implications of these filmic representations at the height of the anti-Japanese movement in the United States. Some even disparaged Hayakawa himself, labeling the actor a "national disgrace" and "race traitor."

The Cheat features a wealthy socialite who misuses charity funds for a Wall Street investment. Upon losing all of her money, Edith Hardy turns to a Japanese art dealer, played by Sessue Hayakawa, for a financial loan. Her husband returns the squandered funds, but when she tries to give the money back, the villainous Hayakawa assaults the repentant Edith and brands her shoulder with a symbol of his ownership. The film was immensely successful and played upon popularized fears over white slavery and the "yellow peril." As Daisuke Miyao explains, film audiences and reviewers around the world were captivated by the Japanese actor for his embodiment of the art deco Orientalism in vogue during the early twentieth century. In contrast to the pantomime acting of the early silent era, Hayakawa's restrained expressionlessness was perceived as a breakthrough in acting style, even forming the basis of a modernist film art concept: *photogenie*.[9] *The Cheat* was also lauded as an innovation in cinematography, particularly in the use of lighting and the close-up shot. With his starring role in De Mille's celebrated film, Hayakawa would become an internationally famous matinee idol. However, the film's reception among Japanese and Japanese American audiences significantly contrasted with American and European approval and enthusiasm.

In Japanese American communities, the campaign against *The Cheat* was extensive as protests radiated from Los Angeles and moved through cities and towns throughout California. The Japanese American newspaper *Rafu Shimpo* launched a campaign against *The Cheat* upon the film's debut in Los Angeles on December 23, 1915. The newspaper criticized *The Cheat* for "distorting the truth of the Japanese people." "The film depicts Japanese people as outrageously evil," one critic argued. "This film would have a bad influence on people, living in places where there are not so many Japanese. They would come to think that the Japanese are extremely savage. The film destroys the truth of the Japanese race. It is unforgiveable for Japanese actors to appear in such a film, even for money."[10] In February, the Japanese Association of Southern California filed a formal petition with the Los Angeles City Council to ban the film from American theaters.[11] The *Rafu Shimpo* included a news story about this campaign every day for over a month. The Japanese Association in San Bernardino joined the *Rafu Shimpo* and the Los Angeles chapter in protesting *The Cheat*. The film was scheduled to debut in San Bernardino in January 1916 at the local opera house. The Japanese Association petitioned the board of censorship to ban the film on the grounds that "the film scene of a Japanese branding an American woman on the back with a branding iron would embitter the American people against Japan."[12] Similar protests were launched in Riverside and Santa Monica, California.[13]

Opposition to the film also traveled across the Pacific. In May, news of these protests reached Japanese in Hawaii. The island's newspaper *Hawaii*

JAPANESE SEEK TO HALT FILM 'THE CHEAT'

Censorship Board Sees the Opera House Picture and Approves It

Declaring that the film scene of a Japanese branding an American woman on the back with a branding iron would embitter the American people against Japan, the local Japanese association yesterday demanded the board of censorship halt the powerful picture-drama, "The Cheat," a Lasky production, scheduled for Sunday, Monday and Tuesday at the Opera House.

Coverage of the Japanese American mobilization against *The Cheat*. *San Bernardino Sun*, January 22, 1916, 5.

Shinpo issued a protest against the showing of the film at Liberty Theater in Honolulu. According to the paper, "The play is anti-Japanese in nature and we must make a strong protest against its exhibition in this city. While the picture was being shown at San Francisco, the Japanese Association of California orchestrated several protests. The play is performed so that people who attend the theater will experience hostile sentiments toward the Japanese. We believe it is necessary to make a protest against this exhibition."[14] The controversy over the film's exhibition even influenced reporting in Japan. According to Miyao, Hayakawa's films were denounced by the Japanese press as "anti-Japanese propaganda." The Japanese film magazine *Katsudo no sekai* decried the character in *The Cheat* as a "slave of carnal desire" and the actor Hayakawa as an "unforgiveable national traitor."[15] With such controversy, *The Cheat* never had a release in Japan despite its extraordinary commercial success in the United States and elsewhere.

The unsuccessful efforts by Japanese leaders to ban *The Cheat* coincided with a highly publicized national campaign against D. W. Griffith's *The Birth of a Nation*. Released in the same year as *The Cheat*, Griffith's film was adapted

Advertisement for *The Birth of a Nation* (also known as *The Clansman*). Rough translation from right to left: "See tonight, a scale size movie at 12 stupendous reels 'Clansman' in the setting of American Civil War—south generation talk. The cost of ticket is the same as always. At Hawaii theater." *Nippu Jiji*, April 24, 1924.

from Thomas Dixon's popular novel *The Clansman* (1905). Decrying its distortion of Reconstruction and celebration of white supremacy, critics of *The Birth of a Nation* launched a national campaign against the film, organizing direct action protests, advocating censorship, and lobbying local legislatures. The mobilization against the film was one of the first national campaigns by the National Association for the Advancement of Colored People (NAACP), which was only five years old when it filed a legal injunction to stop the film's premiere.[16] Black filmmakers also responded with alternatives to the controversial film. As Allyson Nadia Field details, filmmakers with Booker T. Washington's Hampton Institute produced a "screen record" with intertitles intended to intercut the film with messages of "Negro achievement." Additionally, these filmmakers produced a short epilogue called *The New*

Era intended to screen after the film and present a counterargument to *Birth's* anti-Black racism. Not surprisingly, these filmmaking efforts to include positive imagery could not successfully disarm *Birth's* filmic power and box office success.[17]

Similar to the efforts of African American protest against *The Birth of a Nation*, the campaign by the Japanese Association to ban *The Cheat* largely failed. In Los Angeles, the city council concluded that the film had already passed the National Board of Censors and "should not be barred because it might hurt the feelings of people of any particular race, as this procedure might result in barring a great portion of the films."[18] In San Bernardino, local censors made sure that "the actual burning of the flesh by the branding iron had been eliminated from the picture before the film arrived." City officials believed that this editing "somewhat mollified the Japanese association." The San Bernardino board had a special screening, and all agreed that "it was a wonderful film." Moreover, as one committee member put it, "while I can see no objection at all to the picture, if the Japanese object they should protest to their fellow countryman who does the acting."[19]

While city officials refused to ban the film, the motion picture studios may have been motivated by the organized protests to respond. Upon the rerelease of the film in 1918, the nationality of Hayakawa's character was changed. In this rerelease version, which is the only version now extant, Hayakawa's character transforms from Hishiru Tori (the Japanese art dealer) to Haka Arakau (a Burmese ivory merchant). The shift in the character's nationality was made by changes and embellishments to the intertitles.[20] Nevertheless, such superficial cosmetic changes by the studio continued to reveal Orientalist assumptions by conveying racial signifiers as interchangeable.

Cinema and the "Dignity of the Race"

The uproar over *The Cheat* sparked new developments and interventions by Japanese Americans as community leaders recognized the consequences of shifting public perception. The act of being seen, whether on the streets or the screen, gained in significance for many Japanese Americans whose lives had become more precarious with a concurrent surge in anti-Japanese agitation. Community leaders recognized the significance of moving pictures in inflaming racial sentiment and prejudice. In a 1920 Hawaiian newspaper article entitled "Race Problems and Moving Pictures," Yasutaro Soga noted, "In California, where an anti-Oriental atmosphere prevails, many motion picture films, having as their topic ostracism of colored race, have been man- ufactured." Soga lists not only De Mille's *The Cheat* but also a spate of recent films about villainous Chinese characters. "In places like Hawaii where the races of the East and West cooperate and make their living peacefully and harmoniously," Soga explains, "any act that incites racial feeling for purpose of making profits is unpardonable . . . [and] it does not make any difference which race is made the subject of such an act." Soga encourages readers to pay attention to film productions and to "stop patronizing questionable films which make their way into Hawaii."[21]

Later, when the controversial *The Birth of a Nation* debuted in Hawaii, crit- ics would decry the film and seek a court injunction to restrict its exhibition at the Hawaii Theatre. In the Japanese American press, the film was adver- tised yet also criticized in editorials for inciting racial hatred and animosity. Japanese American critics contended that "no medium controls people's pas- sions more than moving pictures" and that "racial prejudice among the white people still remains." For these reasons, filmgoers should not attend the show- ing of *The Birth of a Nation* or any film that "stirs racial prejudice." The editorial also noted that the example of the Japanese and their mistreatment in Califor- nia offered proof positive for the connection between acts of racial hatred and the negative projected images in the motion pictures. "That films appealing to racial prejudice affect popular mind is [proven] by the fact the films used in the agitation against the Japanese in California brought results."[22]

These concerns over the image of the race strongly reverberated in Los An- geles. In 1917, the Japanese Photoplayers' Club of Los Angeles was formed. The organization was a motion picture endeavor principally concerned with the project of racial uplift. The Japanese Photoplayers' Club not only con- demned bad objects of the screen but strongly advocated for positive and respectable portrayals of Japanese and Japanese Americans. According to extant records, the organization was established to prevent anti-Japanese films and "to see its members do not appear in productions reflecting [nega- tively] upon the Japanese race." Moreover, the Japanese Photoplayers' Club sought to protect the image of the Japanese and ensure the "dignity of the race be maintained in all pictures in which their countrymen appear."[23] This organized advocacy against disparaging filmic representation and Japanese participation in the film industry offers a longer and earlier view into "Asian American media activism," which has been understood as beginning in the civil rights era with the formation of organizations like the Oriental Actors of America in 1968, Brotherhood of Artists in 1970, and the Association of Asian/Pacific American Artists in 1976.[24]

The Japanese Photoplayers' Club was supported by the Japanese counsel, editors of several major Japanese-language newspapers, and the Japanese Association of Southern California, which had led the effort to ban *The Cheat* in Los Angeles. Working actors in Hollywood—Frank Tokunaga, Henry Kotani, and Goro Kino—led the organization. One founder was Yukio Aoyama, one of the most active Japanese actors in early twentieth-century Hollywood. Aoyama worked on at least sixty films, produced and directed films, and wrote film criticism for Japanese film magazines. Having first started on the stage with the Cherry Blossom Players in Chicago, Aoyama was among the cadre of Japanese actors who signed with Thomas Ince's early film production studio.[25] Like other Asian actors in Hollywood, Aoyama supplemented his income and used his clout in the industry to establish adjacent businesses. Throughout the mid-twentieth century, he operated the Oriental Costume Company in Santa Monica, California, which supplied costumes and decor for the major studios. The advertisements for the Japanese Photoplayers' Club in the trade press often appeared alongside the costume company, suggesting coterminous avenues that were used to facilitate Asian actors' participation in the American film industry.

The other founder of the Japanese Photoplayers' Club was none other than Sessue Hayakawa himself. The famed actor had become unsettled by the vocalized protests to his role in *The Cheat*. Hayakawa apologized in the *Rafu Shimpo* for "unintentionally offending the feelings of the Japanese people in the U.S." and vowed to "be careful not to do harm to Japanese communities."[26] Hayakawa was eager to remake his image in the Japanese immigrant community and even officially joined the Japanese Association in Los Angeles. In his memoir, the actor claimed that—in his view—even his wealth and fame were a responsibility to the race:

> I went "Hollywood" as the term is for another reason, too. An anti-Japanese feeling had begun to take hold in California. There was talk of legislation to prohibit Orientals from owning property, and eventually such a law was passed. . . . Such agitation angered me. So it was not just out of vanity and demand of social obligation that I acquire "Argyle Castle" as our mansion was promptly nicknamed. Defiantly, I was determined to show the Americans who surrounded me that I, a Japanese, could live up to their lavish standards. Along with the mansion I took up golf and become an avid player, frequently held poker parties—and frequently lost—and I purchased a number of

automobiles. At one time I had four: two Cadillacs, a Ford and a Pierce Arrow town sedan for all of which I paid something like $12,000.[27]

Hayakawa's celebrity was continually remade in fan magazines and news media of the early twentieth century. The stories of his lavish parties and expensive cars tantalized his female fans while reproducing Hayakawa's stardom as both constructed image and commodity. Hayakawa sought to usurp this star image as a testament to Japanese American refinement and respectability. For Hayakawa, the projected image of the elite "gentleman" was the purported antidote to the racial subjection of Japanese in the United States. Hayakawa's leadership in the Japanese Photoplayers' Club seemed to indicate his growing sense of race pride and a recognition of these representational politics in motion pictures. His role in the Japanese Photoplayers' Club also anticipated, or at the least predated, the formation of his own motion picture production company, Haworth Pictures Corporation, in 1918.

A Cinema of One's Own

The origins of Japanese American filmmaking were established a few years before the controversy over *The Cheat*. In 1912, Japanese in Portland, Oregon, established a company called Yamato Graph Motion Picture Company.[28] Toyoji Abe headed the film studio along with his associates Bungaro Takita and Kimbey Narusawa. These entrepreneurs envisioned a cinema not for entertainment and profit but for education and uplift. The films made by Yamato Graph promoted the advancements made by the race, particularly the contributions to agriculture and commerce made by Japanese farmers and business leaders. In establishing their own film company, Abe and his compatriots fostered a sense of autonomy and self-sufficiency. Their entrepreneurship made a cinema in which their own countrymen exercised control over the means of production. These ideas of autonomy and economic independence had taken shape over the past two decades and found expression in an earlier entrepreneurial experiment, one that coincidentally bore the same namesake.

Yamato Colony had been first established in 1906 by Kyutaro Abiko as a farm settlement colony. Abiko had envisioned the building of agricultural colonies and increasing Japanese landholdings as a way to promote the idea of permanent settlement. For Abiko, it was imperative for Japanese to cast off the image of itinerant laboring, to reinforce their economic base, and to improve their standards of living. He believed that "planting roots" and eliminating gambling and prostitution in their community would "deprive the exclusionists of any real substance in their anti-Japanese rhetoric."[29] Importantly, the building of agricultural settlements and cultivating farmlands were essential components of Japanese overseas expansion and imperialism. Eiichiro Azuma has argued that these immigrant efforts in agricultural cultivation constituted an "agrarian settler colonialism" modeled after New World "manifest destiny" and the settlement and conquest of the American West. Japan's earliest imperialist experimentations in the northern hinterlands of Hokkaido were focused on varying forms of agricultural development. The model of, and even the people involved with, Japanese agrarian colonization in the United States, including that of the Yamato Colony, would go on to influence other sites of Japan's colonial empire, such as Taiwan and Korea. These agricultural pursuits by Japanese in the United States reinforced and contributed to Japan's ascendance to global and imperial power.[30]

Abiko in 1906 purchased 3,200 acres of underdeveloped land in Livingston, California. He subdivided the land into 40-acre parcels and sold the tracts to Issei families. The colony in Livingston was entirely composed of landowning farmers. In ensuring self-sufficiency and autonomy, the Yamato Colony farmers formed their own agricultural cooperative to market their crops and purchase supplies. The colony had its own packing sheds and private railroad platform. Abiko also developed businesses in labor contracting, banking, and newspaper publishing.[31] Similar Japanese farm settlement experiments were conducted across California in Cortez, Dundee, Santa Ana, and Cressy. Japanese in Texas and Florida also established their own "Yamato Colony." Bolstered by these agricultural settlements, Japanese farming burgeoned across California and in the western regions of the United States. By 1920, Japanese farmers held 361,276 acres in California and produced crops valued at $67 million.[32]

The bounty of these agricultural pursuits was the subject of the Yamato Graph's films. No prints exist, but documentary evidence suggests that Yamato Graph's productions were solely nonfiction films. According to newspapers, the filmmakers for the Yamato Graph captured the strawberry fields in Oregon and Washington, the hog ranches in California, and the exceptionally successful farms under the control of Kinji Ushijima, otherwise known as George "the Potato King" Shima.[33] The films, which amounted to 12,000 feet, were intended to chronicle the outstanding advances in agriculture and commerce made by Japanese in the United States. The "pioneer spirit" of the Issei can be seen in the bounty of their crops and in the success of their ventures. These films represented the aspiration for permanent settlement, as envisioned by Issei leaders like Abiko. In another scene of the film, "the pretty sight of kindergarten children" is presented before the camera.[34] Indeed, the proponents of permanent settlement believed that in addition to landownership, the building of families was essential to changing the sojourner status of the Japanese. Abiko and others encouraged all men who became landowning farmers and merchants to summon wives from Japan and to settle in the United States and have a family.

The intended purpose of the Yamato Graph films was not amusement or profit but to facilitate, according to newspapers, "the campaign in education."[35] The Yamato Graph film producers hoped to show how "Japanese in Oregon, Washington, and California fight against tremendous odds" and the "magnitude of the effect of anti-Japanese laws and regulations."[36] Indeed, the Yamato Graph films were participating in a broader set of reform politics. The films were exhibited the same year California passed its first alien land laws, which restricted the agricultural holdings of Japanese immigrants. In the ensuing years, a full-fledged anti-Japanese movement would emerge, and fourteen states would pass legislation to limit Japanese landownership. Issei elites responded to the surge in anti-Japanese agitation with an organized effort to reform their community's image. In chronicling Japanese agricultural success and family formation, the Yamato Graph films presented a view of Japanese as permanent settlers. The Japanese were industrious and prosperous. Their family formation signaled their moral conduct and respectability. Such self-characterizations enabled elite Issei to draw lines of distinction between themselves and the lower classes, as well as "immoral" Chinese, who predominately lived in so-called bachelor societies. For some elite Japanese, these "undesirables" were most directly responsible for the white racism directed at all Japanese in the United States.

The Yamato Graph films end with a tragic scene of a small boat crossing the Pacific. Over a dozen Japanese emigres appear on board the vessel. "After a life-and-death struggle for nearly two months," the review described, "[the Japanese were] caught by American immigration officers and deported."[37] At the films' end, the images of bountiful harvests are halted by a scene of exclusion. The ending reads as a cautionary tale. The success and abundance achieved by individuals like George "the Potato King" Shima would be an unrealizable dream for others.

The Yamato Graph films were intended to circulate transnationally among Japanese in the United States as well as in Japan. According to Itakura Fumiaki, the films had a screening in San Francisco in 1913.[38] Additionally, newspapers reported that the Yamato Graph films were exhibited in Japan at nontheatrical venues such as the YMCA. Regarding their screening in Japan, the films were sent with the "Home Visiting Party" and exhibited with a display of "Japanese merchandise, foodstuffs, and sundry goods by the Japanese in America."[39] The extrafilmic presentation of these agricultural products highlighted the significance of agricultural commodities and, more broadly, of capitalized productions of the Japanese in the United States. Similar kinds of films depicting Japanese American agricultural work were also on display in Japan's Overseas Expansion Exhibition, held in Tokyo in 1919.[40]

These nonfiction films depicting scenes of Japanese American commerce and agricultural endeavors contributed to a vision of Japanese American immigration and settlement as integral to Japanese imperial modernity. Importantly, the films appeared to bolster the imperial state's educational campaign for overseas Japanese. Toward this end, Yamato Graph's films were likely a sort of instructional or pedagogical filmmaking. Intended for neither amusement nor profit, the films served a broader educational function. As scholars have noted, educational cinema had a wide range of purposes, production modes, and exhibition contexts. They composed a large component of the media landscape despite their marginalization within film scholarship.[41] While scholars have primarily focused on the 1920s when a discourse of documentary filmmaking emerged, these earlier forms of educational filmmaking, like those of Yamato Graph, suggest the scope of educational cinema to be expansive.

The Yamato Graph Motion Picture Company was led by Toyoji Abe, who presided as the company's founder and president. Abe was born in Yamagata Prefecture in 1880. After obtaining a college education in Japan, he emigrated first to Seattle and then settled in Portland in 1906. In the same year Abe established Yamato Graph Motion Picture Company, he returned to Japan and married Yuka. They had six children, all born in the United States. His son would later become an U.S. Army sergeant. The Abe family joined the many other Japanese families who settled in the region. Near to Portland, Hood River developed into a distinctive region with landowning farming families who sought to build a "permanent settlement."[42] Realizing the ideals presented in the Yamato Graph films, the Japanese farm communities in Oregon gradually changed from single male laborers to immigrant families, as leaders encouraged "planting roots" and the immigration of women from Japan.

As an educated, family-oriented Issei, Abe was a respected and prominent member of the Japanese American community. His foray into the business of motion pictures was only a short departure from his longtime career as a newspaper editor and publisher. Upon first arriving in Seattle in 1905, he be-

Photograph of Yamato Graph Motion Picture founder Toyoji Abe, circa 1909.
Courtesy of Yasui Family Collection, Densho: The Japanese American
Legacy Project.

came the editor of the *Asahi News*, a Japanese-language newspaper that was also known for its publication of fiction and poetry by members of the local Japanese community. In 1907, he took over the *Oregon News* (*Oshu Shinpo*), a newspaper read mostly by Japanese laborers throughout the western United States. Abe changed this paper to *Oregon Daily News* (*Oshu Nippo*), which published daily and would become the primary Japanese-language paper of Oregon. Abe also established a printing company called Oregon Press Company (Oshu Insatsujo) and later relocated to San Francisco and took over *New World News* (*Shin Sekai Asahi Shinbun*) in 1935.[43]

Abe's movement from film production to news journalism illustrates the linkages between these two industries. Not only did early film function as a form of reportage, but Abe's role in both contributed to building the Japanese American community and uplifting the race. Throughout his life, Abe was an active member of the Portland Japanese Association and the Japanese Association of Oregon.[44] In some ways, Abe's trajectory mirrored the career of race film pioneer William D. Foster, who wrote for the *Chicago Defender* and later moved into filmmaking, establishing the Foster Photoplay Company in Chicago in 1910. While Abe left no records detailing his vision of the Yamato Graph Motion Picture Company, his film studio appeared to be part of his mission as a "race man" and leader in the Japanese American community.

Success and Striving in *The Oath of the Sword* (1914)

In 1914, *Moving Picture World* boldly announced a new filmmaking venture to join the "Los Angeles film colony." They declared the Japanese American Film Company to be the "first company in America to be owned, controlled and operated by Japanese."[45] Based in Los Angeles, the film studio was incorporated in 1913 by seven businessmen and fourteen stockholders, all of whom were of Japanese descent and all of whom held equal part shares in the company. The company had a greater capitalization than its earlier predecessor Yamato Graph Motion Picture Company, making the venture grander than the Portland enterprise.[46] In newspaper articles and promotional bills, the Japanese ownership of the studio was often highlighted and emphasized. "Every cent of this was subscribed by Japanese business men," an article relayed, "and every bit of managerial work will be directed by members of the same race." Featured prominently in the article was a dashing photograph of the company's president, Kimura Numamoto.[47]

The company first began producing educational and industrial pictures, similar to the nonfiction actualities made by Yamato Graph. In 1914, how-

Japanese-American Film Company

Organization Numbers Forty Japanese Players and Is Located at Los Angeles—Has Made Many Successful Pictures.

ONE of the most interesting trade announcements of the week chronicles the entry of a new producing company into the field. And as this is the first company in America to be owned, controlled and operated by Japanese, many will be glad to know details of this latest addition to the Los Angeles film colony.

The Japanese-American Film Co. had $200,000.00 paid into their treasury before they started business. Every cent of this was subscribed by Japanese business men, and every bit of the managerial work will be directed by members of the same race. They are fortunate in having secured Sawyer, Inc., to market their films.

The company brought

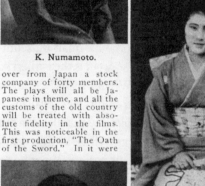

K. Numamoto.

over from Japan a stock company of forty members. The plays will all be Japanese in theme, and all the customs of the old country will be treated with absolute fidelity in the films. This was noticeable in the first production, "The Oath of the Sword." In it were

Miss Hisa Numa.

no kisses or other demonstrations such as America is accustomed to. The heroine does not go down to the boat to see her fiance embark for America—because it would not be the correct thing to do in Japan. And just as painstaking are the directors in every other detail—costuming and scenic settings, which are all beautiful.

For over two years they have been producing commercial, educational and industrial features, which had a large circulation in Japan. It is planned to make dramatic pictures in Japan during part of each year, and also in Hawaii, where a great proportion of the villages are Japanese, and the weather is usually sunny. The president of the corporation is K. Numamoto, and the secretary is J. Takata.

Tomi Morri.

Prominent members of the company are Miss Hisa Numa, leading woman, who is 20 years old. She has been featured in motion pictures and is a great favorite among the Japanese people. Mr. Tomi Morri, leading man, is 30 years old, and is a star of the Japanese legitimate stage in Japan, and has been with Broncho Film Co. for the past two seasons. Miss Kohano Akashi plays character leads, and Mr. Jack Y. Abbe juvenile 'eads.

Article featuring producers and cast of *The Oath of the Sword*. Moving Picture World, October 17, 1914, 314.

JAPANESE AMERICAN FILM CO.

(Operated and Controlled by Japanese)

PRESENT THEIR FIRST PHOTODRAMA, IN THREE PARTS

"THE OATH OF THE SWORD"

PLAYED BY A MARVELLOUS AGGREGATION OF THE GREATEST JAPANESE
ACTORS, WITH SCENIC SETTINGS SO SUMPTUOUS THAT THEIR MAGNIFI-
CENCE BAFFLES DESCRIPTION—SOMETHING ABSOLUTELY NEW AT LAST!

SAWYER SAYS:
"Never in my life have I seen such a wonderful three-reeler as this. 'The Oath of the Sword' is the Sensation of the Century. It has a real punch—it grips and thrills you. It is a masterpiece—Take my word for it."

(Signed)   A. H. SAWYER.

THRILLING!   **VIVID!**   **AWE-INSPIRING!**

Advertisement for *The Oath of the Sword. Moving Picture World*, October 10, 1914, 139.

ever, the company shifted course and produced an ambitious three-reel narrative feature called *The Oath of the Sword*. As I have detailed in the introduction, the only existing print of the film is held in the George Eastman Museum in Rochester, New York. As far as I know, *The Oath of the Sword* is the earliest surviving film made by Japanese in the United States. When I visited the archive in 2016, neither the film's provenance nor production credits were available. In addition, the print itself was—and remains—incomplete, with unknown missing footage. These nonextant parts of the film print, as well as the fragmentary nature of the archive, remind us that early films of this period cannot be conceived as original or definitive, as it is always possible to recover better prints, missing reels, and other findings in the archive and beyond. But the very existence of such a print, of what might very well be the earliest Asian American independent film, merits a careful, even if speculative, reading.

As a production from the United States, *The Oath of the Sword* resembles and draws on the conventions of similarly themed American films and productions of the era. The film's most obvious intertexts are Giocomo Puccini's opera *Madame Butterfly* and a set of "Japan films" that proliferated with an emerging Japanophilia of the time. As Gregory Waller notes, a spate of films capitalizing on the public fascination with Japan emerged after 1908 and remained notable well into the 1910s. Waller also notes that the industry produced a considerable range of films thematically using Japan, which included both fiction and nonfiction films (scenic pictures, travelogues, industrial shorts, etc.).[48] Included among these productions were melodramas involving ill-fated lovers and romances, especially between white and Japanese characters. Sessue Hayakawa rode a wave of success with this genre, not only via *The Cheat* but also in earlier productions like *A Relic of Old Japan* (1914), *The Wrath of the Gods* (1914), and *The Typhoon* (1914). *The Oath of the Sword* can be seen as a part of this Japan-focused melodrama genre, as Nick Browne suggests.[49]

The film begins in coastal Japan and with a nostalgic and picturesque scene of makeshift fishing boats on the seashore. Audiences are introduced to the setting by an intertitle card that reads, "Home of Hisa." The film's temporal and spatial narrative are structured by intertitle cards indicating the movement between Japan and the United States and by the lapse of time in the protagonist's American sojourn and return home. The plot revolves around a tragic romance unfolding on both sides of the Pacific. The film tells the story of two young lovers separated as the ambitious young man, Masao, leaves his beloved Hisa to study abroad in the United States. Unable to cope with her solitude, Hisa betrays Masao and marries a white American ship captain. Upon Masao's return to Japan and the discovery of her presumed infidelity, Hisa fulfills "the oath of the sword" (*katana*) and commits suicide. Following the trope of Madame Butterfly in which a tragic interracial romance ends with suicide, the character Hisa in *The Oath of the Sword* is the "undone" Japanese woman. She is bound to tradition and to the male figures in her life: the young Masao she vows to love, the father she dutifully serves, and the American husband she ultimately marries. In the end, Hisa fulfills her "duty," a seemingly tragic yet inevitable destiny, by ending her life. As Browne notes of the genre more generally, the undoing of the Japanese woman would become a dominant fictional representation of Japan and Japaneseness in the Western imagination.[50]

To signify Japanese authenticity, the shots and camera views in *The Oath of the Sword* utilize objects, costumes, and decor associated with Japan. The film's opening in coastal Japan shifts to the domestic setting of Japanese home life. The interior domestic spaces for each character are ornamented with the display of silk screens, teacups and rice bowls, and calligraphy pens. The Japanese setting remains stationary in the film, an unchanging same even upon Masao's return years later. The objects marking Japanese space signal a notion of Japan as ahistorical or nostalgic. The sacred sword constantly appears in the scenes with Hisa, its presence tying her to a symbol of her duty and honor. Writing about Hayakawa's early films such as *O Mimi San* (1914), Daisuke Miyao argues that the films emphasize the "picturesque" and the "nostalgic pursuit of authenticity." Objects, settings, and things come to signify *Japonisme*, the image of Japan as cultural refinement in European modernist art and style. Beyond the screen, the use of Japonisme during this period of cinema, according to Miyao, also became a means of reshaping the medium of filmmaking

Film stills from *The Oath of the Sword*. Courtesy George Eastman Museum.

Film still from *The Oath of the Sword*. Courtesy George Eastman Museum.

itself. In utilizing the cultural refinement of Japonisme, American producers sought to dissociate the cinema from its "vulgar" working-class origins and appeal to a purportedly more cultivated middle-class audience.[51]

These dynamics can also be seen in *The Oath of the Sword* as producers sought to promote, as one reviewer described, a film of "unusual merit." In advertising campaigns, the film was described with "scenic settings so sumptuous that their magnificence baffles description."[52] Other critics highlighted the film's "real Japanese settings" and "all the customs of the old country treated with absolute fidelity."[53] Indeed, these aspects of the "picturesque" in *The Oath of the Sword* were especially pronounced in marking the film as noteworthy. As one contemporaneous reviewer put it:

> Apparently the story is the least important part of the picture. It is merely the vehicle through which we get glimpses of the inner life and modes of thought of the Japanese and around which has been built up an extremely attractive and fascinating portrayal of Japanese manners and customs, their home life, their fisheries, their betrothal and marriage customs, and lastly their peculiar code of honor. . . .

According to the Anglo-Saxon ideas the story leaves much to be desired, but as a portrayal of Japanese life and thought, the picture is educational of distinct and unique value.[54]

While *The Oath of the Sword* reproduces predictable conventions, I want to argue that the film also makes possible a double view. Produced at the height of the anti-Japanese movement and by a company "owned, controlled and operated by Japanese," the film develops the main character, Masao, as a "New American." Migrating from Japan to California, Masao is remade as an educated and modern subject. He is a success at the American university, a well-dressed gentleman who gains the respect of his American peers. He is also a star athlete who performs the ideals of white American masculinity. Masao's accomplishments, and acculturation writ large, signaled something of a wish fulfillment of Japanese imperial modernity. In presenting Masao as a worthy representative of the race, *The Oath of the Sword* also heralds a diverging set of intertexts and mode of address.

Although the more well-known films by Oscar Micheaux were produced after *The Oath of the Sword*, I suggest that the race film industry provides a useful comparative optic by which to understand this film. Typically featuring all-Black casts, race films were produced and circulated within an alternative network for African American audiences. Most race films were made between the years 1915 and 1952, although places like the Tuskegee and Hampton Institutes began to produce industrial and sponsored films as early as 1909 and 1913. These early race films from Tuskegee and Hampton promoted the idea of education as a vehicle for racial progress and in so doing established an important basis for the race film industry.[55] While I am not suggesting that *The Oath of the Sword* was itself a race film, I am suggesting that this aspect of race films as "uplift cinema" provides a countervailing intertext for the film.

In *The Oath of the Sword*, the story is set into motion by migration. Masao leaves the provincial fishing village in coastal Japan for study in the United States. Forcing Masao to leave behind his lover, this departure is cast against the pull of Western modernity, its arrival awash on the shores of Japan. Written by the American writer Edwin M. La Roche, the scenario was published in *Moving Picture Magazine* in 1915. It narrated the scene as follows: "'The old days of our fathers,' [Masao] said, 'are dying, Hisa, my beloved one, and the brains and commerce of the white man are fast crowding us out. For many months I have studied of their books, and the deep thirst of knowledge has fastened upon me.'"[56] Structured by Masao's movement from Japan to the United States, the film locates the West, with its Euro-American commerce and knowledge, as the site for modernity and progress. Importantly, this theme of migration and modernity is also recurrent in early race films, according to Jacqueline Stewart. Films such as *The Realization of a Negro's Ambition* (1916) cast Black progress as achievable within narratives of westward migration. Micheaux himself set a number of his films, including *The Homesteader* (1919), in the wide-open spaces of the U.S. West. For Micheaux, the South and even the North provided inadequate opportunities for racial progress. Instead, these ambitions were to be sought elsewhere. Stewart suggests early race filmmakers, utilizing narratives of migration and patriotism in many of their films, echoed the popular race rhetoric of the period to create alternative narratives "defining and asserting the 'Americanness' of the Negro."[57]

Set against Japan's imperial modernity, we can read *The Oath of the Sword* as a kind of narrative of migration and racial achievement and progress. Indeed, the character Masao, in coming to the United States for education, exemplifies the then popular discourses of modernity and Japanese emigration. Students were among the first arrivals from Japan to the United States at the start of the twentieth century. Both emigration to the United States and achievement of Western-style education were central facets of Japan's modernization. As Azuma notes, a popular "success boom" swept Japanese society in the mid-1890s, and emerging ideas of "striving and success" were popularized by circulating stories of self-made white men such as Andrew Carnegie, Theodore Roosevelt, and John D. Rockefeller. Importantly, this ideology of mobility and modernity, as Azuma notes, "was often worded in the familiar language of 'extending national power' . . . [and] catered to the aspirations of students to work their way through school in the American West."[58]

The ideal of work and study in the United States signaled, and indeed bolstered, Meiji Japan's quest for modernization and colonial expansion. That is to say, the student emigrant and the discourse of "success and striving" were mutually constituted within the ideology of Japan's imperial nationalism. During this period, young men left Japan for many reasons, including deferment of military enlistment when Japanese conscription laws changed. As students in the United States, moreover, many Japanese found themselves working in menial occupations. It was common for a Japanese student laborer, *dekasegi-shosei*, to work as a domestic servant, or houseboy, in white American households. This work was not only low wage but also signaled gendered labor and feminization. As Yuji Ichioka notes, "A school boy's job was associated with the work of lower class women . . . [and] when described in deprecating terms, the job was referred as *gejo hoko* or maid-servant's work, which made it analogous to the tasks female domestics performed in Japan."[59]

In the United States, Irwin Wallace's literary column "Letters of a Japanese Schoolboy" popularized this figure of the Japanese student laborer in 1907 by creating the character Hashimura Togo. These columns would become enormously popular and were reprinted over a quarter century in *Collier's*, *Good Housekeeping*, the *American Magazine*, *Sunset*, *Life*, and the *New York Times*. They were also reprised in several book publications and film productions, including *Hashimura Togo* (1917), starring Sessue Hayakawa.[60] According to Donald Kirihara, the character Togo tapped into the accommodationist strategy advanced by Japanese American communities during the nativist period. While the column was created by the Scotch-Irish writer Wallace under a pseudonym and the character communicated in stereotypical pidgin English, Togo was generally a sympathetic figure portraying the struggles of a new immigrant in an unfamiliar culture and earnestly working hard to survive.[61] It can be argued that the character diverged from the yellow peril stereotype and the menacing figure portrayed in *The Cheat*.

In *The Oath of the Sword*, the character Masao was also a "Japanese schoolboy." The filmic portrayal of Masao, however, appears as an idealized version of dekasegi-shosei and without the trappings of servitude and the caricature of Wallace's Hashimura Togo. The filmic character Masao was a student but decidedly not a laborer. Masao arrives in the United States and becomes a popular student on the campus of the University of California, Berkeley. In the first scene at the university, Masao is surrounded by a group of his American peers as the intertitle reads, "Masao has made many friends." While in Japan he wore "traditional" Japanese clothes, he appears in California dressed in a Western suit, standing at the center, akin among peers. Masao's self-presentation signals not only assimilation with the American students but also a class symmetry. Unlike Togo and the many dekasegi-shosei, the well-dressed body of Masao appeared unmarked by the signs of domestic and gendered labor. Indeed, no scenes depict, or even suggest, that Masao had ever been a worker while at the University of California campus.

To further underscore his social distance from dekasegi-shosei, Masao is presented as a superior student athlete who embodies twentieth-century ideals of white American masculinity. Whereas Irwin's Togo appears as a physically weak pacifist, Masao conveys masculine prowess via collegiate athletics and the visual display of his masculine body. In a sequence set on the university campus, Masao works out in the college gym and demonstrates the art of jiujitsu to his classmates. As the camera focuses on his lean and muscular body, Masao wrestles and overpowers his opponents. He later becomes a star athlete and champion, racing against his competitors in a track-and-

THE COLLEGE GIRLS TRY TO LIONIZE MASAO

Trade press image from *The Oath of the Sword*. *Motion Picture Magazine*,
January 1915, 90.

field competition and victoriously crossing the finish line, as the awed spectators joyously cheer. In the scenario by La Roche, the scene was intended to signal that "Masao was the lion of the hour."[62]

While Irwin's Togo was servile, Masao in contrast was "one of the boys," gaining acceptance and admiration from his American peers. His athleticism signaled conventional American and Japanese forms of manhood and virility. On campus, Masao was presented as an object of desire. Among his American admirers were white female students, one of whom offers Masao a flower as a symbol of her affection. The upstanding Masao, however, politely refuses her sexual attention. Masao's athletic achievements garner public attention and accolade. The camera intercuts the scene with a news headline, "The U.C. having a Japanese student Masao who is looked upon as a coming champion." Masao's triumphs are presented as a form of Japanese national pride. Throughout the film, the ideology of "success and striving" is signaled in national terms. In Masao's dorm room, for instance, the national flag of Japan hangs on the wall alongside decor bearing the University of California insignia.

It is worth noting that this wish fulfillment of Japanese imperial modernity is placed not within the female character Hisa but in Masao and his performance of white American manhood. In this way, the film illuminates the gendered assumptions of the racial uplift project. Ultimately, Masao is the one portrayed as a worthy representative of modern imperial Japan. Presenting a double view, *The Oath of the Sword*'s incorporation of the Madame Butterfly trope appears crossed by the "opportunity narrative." Writing about Micheaux's *Within Our Gates* (1920), Jane Gaines argues that the old race melodrama is reworked in the film; sentimentality is replaced by post-Reconstruction concerns with education, respectability, community, and opportunity.[63] Through the migration narrative and the character Masao's self-transformation, *The Oath of the Sword* refutes nativist perceptions of Japanese unassimilability. Counterposed against the pitiable Hisa and the docile Togo of Irwin's imagination, Masao in contrast emerges as the ideal subject of Japanese immigrant reformist campaigns. In the effort to purge "undesirable" characteristics and represent the race in civilized and modern terms, reformers called for acculturation to middle-class American norms, urging compatriots to eschew Japanese customs and adopt Western-style dress, bodily comportment, and living standards. In *The Oath of the Sword*, Masao represents this form of racial uplift as an ideal of a modern Americanized Japanese subject.

Representing "the race" in *The Oath of the Sword* also entailed utilizing an all-Japanese cast. Producers promoted the film as the "first Jap production" made in the United States, and in which "all the principal characters are Japanese and played by eminent Jap actors."[64] Another newspaper headline described the film as "Jap Films by Jap Actors."[65] This casting practice was one of the central objectives of the Japanese American Film Company. As one critic noted, "[The Japanese American Film Company has] taken up the production of comedies and dramas in which Americanized Japanese will play all parts . . . because of the demand in Japan for 'Japanese actors who impersonate correctly the Japanese.'"[66] Charting a diverging path in the film industry, the Japanese American Film Company sought to emphasize its casting as contributing to the film's realism.

Paramount Pictures produced a filmic adaptation of *Madame Butterfly* (1915) in the same year that *The Oath of the Sword* was released. Directed by Sidney Olcott, the film cast the white actress Mary Pickford in the role of Cho-Cho San, a fifteen-year-old Japanese geisha. Deploying a long-standing practice from the stage, the film was one of the initial feature films of the silent era to use "yellowface."[67] Against these emerging industry casting practices, *The Oath of the Sword* was promoted as a sort of embodied verisimilitude, with Japanese actors playing Japanese characters. Whereas the film's director was white (likely an American named Frank Shaw), the film's featured actors and supporting cast were all working Japanese actors. Hisa was played by a young actress of the same name, Hisa Numa, who was purportedly "a great favorite among the Japanese people." Appearing as Masao, Tomi Morri was a recognized stage actor from Japan and player for an American company called Broncho Film. Also, among the film's cast was Yutaka Abe, who was later "discovered" by Thomas Ince after his work on *The Oath of the Sword*. He would find considerable work in the American film industry, including a role in one of the earliest Chinese American independent films, *Lotus Blossom* (1921), by James B. Leong and his Los Angeles–based Wah Ming Motion Picture Company. Leaving for Japan in 1925, Abe would become influential in shaping the future direction of Japanese cinema as a proponent of "pure film" and in pushing the Japanese film industry to adopt Hollywood-style film techniques and practices. Abe is credited with directing some sixty-six films in Japan, including Japanese nationalist propaganda films during World War II and the commercially successful *The Makioka Sisters* (1950). Working in the industry at a pivotal time, Abe had a storied career on both sides of the Pacific, exemplifying the era's porous borders between independent filmmaking and the major studios as well as the industries in the United States and Japan.

Hollywood's Periphery

Other new film production companies also surfaced in the wake of the controversy over *The Cheat*. The Hollywood actor Sojin Kamiyama attempted to establish a company called the Diana Film Company in 1919. Also located in Los Angeles, the company was supposedly capitalized at $200,000 and employed as star actress Uraji Yamakawa, who was also married to Kamiyama. The venture, however, never materialized. According to newspapers, the couple abandoned their film production efforts and moved to Tacoma, Washington, to pursue careers in journalism before resuming later careers in the film industry.[68] In the same year, another Japanese American film production company was proposed. Led by Eddies Young, the new film production company, capitalized at $60,000, intended to employ both Japanese and American actors. "The new company will use some of the most charming and picturesque regions of Japan," according to the article, "and it is believed that this undertaking will advertise Japan to the world to a degree that has never before been presented."[69] Neither of these companies, Diana Film Producing Company nor Eddie Young's company, seemed to last. It is unlikely any films by these companies were ever produced.

More notable among these early ventures was the Fujiyama Feature Film Company. Established in 1916, the studio was located a short distance from Los Angeles in Redlands, California. The company intended to expand northward and build a second studio in Fresno, although no evidence suggests that these plans for a second site ever materialized.[70] Like its predecessors, Fujiyama Film Company was noteworthy as a company producing films with Japan themes, settings, and actors. As the Los Angeles critic Grace Kingsley noted, "Fuji Yama is the name of a unique motion picture enterprise with Los Angeles capital behind it. The object of the company is the filming of pictures of Japan where it considered that a fresh and fertile field exists, not only as regards subject matter, but also for a new type of picture entirely [with] Japanese actors [in the] leading roles."[71]

Fujiyama Feature Film Company intended to produce their first film on the subject of the Japanese empire in Korea. It was to be a twelve-reel feature in which "only Japanese people will appear as players," although it is unclear if this film was ever made.[72] The company's subsequent production, however, was filmed and released with much greater success and fanfare. The film was a ten-reel feature called *Nami-Ko* (1917) starring Matsu Matsumoto, an actress who formerly worked for the Famous Players Lasky. No print of the film exists. However, in looking at extant articles from newspapers, it seems Fujiyama Feature Film Company's proprietors hoped the film would be an elevated form of entertainment since, as producers remarked for the papers, "the American public has grown tired of the very 'blaze' and trashy melodramas." Perhaps implicitly referring to *The Cheat*, the producers hoped to offer American audiences a "more beautiful story than Madame Butterfly." Moreover, they believed that their film was especially timely as the anti-Japanese movement surged in the United States and American filmic depictions of Japan reinforced negative portrayals of the race:

> In almost every edition of every American periodical, there is something regarding the Japanese question. The newspapers every day cry warnings to the American people to prepare for invasion from the Pacific. . . . The company has been besieged with Japanese people desiring to aid in some capacity in the production of *Nami-Ko* because it will show them in a position other than they have ever occupied. They have always been screened as evil doers, or servants, and the average citizen of other nations hardly knows that such a thing as the art of drama exists in Japan.[73]

Producers hoped that *Nami-Ko* would be a radical departure from such controversial films as *The Cheat*. They envisioned their film to not only eschew anti-Japanese sentiment but also contribute a positive representation to quell such agitation.

Whereas the Japanese American Film Company's *The Oath of the Sword* drew fairly directly from *Madame Butterfly*, the Fujiyama Feature Film Company distinguished itself from this filmmaking trajectory. Eschewing the Westernized stories and imaginings of Japan, Fujiyama Feature Film Company hoped to bring greater realism to audiences by turning to Japanese literature and drama for its source material. *Nami-Ko* was adapted from a classic novel written by the popular Japanese writer Kenjiro Tokutomi. The novel *Nami-Ko* portrayed the plight of a woman under the feudal family system in Japan. It was a sensation by the turn of the century in Japan and inspired poetry, adaptations to *shinpa*, and eventually the production of fifteen movies between 1908 and 1934.[74] Responding to the film's adaptation of the Japanese novel, contemporaneous reviewers described the film as "a realistic story of knighthood in Nippon."[75] Grace Kingsley wrote that, "the tale treats individuals of divorce according to the Japanese ideas." In further authenticating the film, Kingsley also noted that the "enterprise [Fujiyama Feature Film Company] has the endorsement of the resident Japanese and also of the Japanese Consul."[76]

This endorsement was perhaps necessary since the Fujiyama Feature Film Company was established and led by several non-Japanese individuals. The company also seemed to have closer ties to the American film industry. The company's board included the film actor and director Julius Frankenberg, W. E. Macarton as president, and an American woman named Mrs. E. L. Greer.[77] Whereas earlier film companies, such as Yamato Graph Motion Picture Company in Portland and the Japanese American Film Company in Los Angeles, were led exclusively by Japanese, the Fujiyama Feature Film Company was established by white American film producers and entrepreneurs who shared a similar vision in bringing Japanese subjects, story lines, and actors to the screen. Fujiyama's production of *Nami-Ko* was directed by the American filmmaker Frank A. Thorne, who had previously worked for American Film Company and directed *The Undertow* (1916). Other non-Japanese collaborators on *Nami-Ko* included William H. Bradshaw, whose company Trans-Pacific Films produced a travelogue called *A Trip through Japan* (1917). As a company operating under non-Japanese leadership, the Fujiyama Feature Film Company resembled other white-led race film companies like the Norman Film Company of Jacksonville and the Ebony Film Company of Chicago, both of which were led by white producers and filmmakers yet produced content with Black themes and acting casts.

Although the company leadership of Fujiyama was non-Japanese, Japanese individuals appeared both in front of and behind the camera. The actress Haru Fujita was a player with the company—and gained publicity for "being the first Japanese woman to make an ascent in an aeroplane." According to papers, this "New Woman" took to the skies in Venice and while wearing "her native costume."[78] The film crew for *Nami-Ko* partly consisted of several Japanese Americans, including George Y. Matsumoto, noted as "interpreting director," and Frank Takata, noted as "camera supervisor." In 1917, the film's crew and director traveled to Yokohama to shoot on location for several weeks. Newspapers noted that the production team left San Francisco and sailed through Honolulu before reaching the shores of Japan. The company further built on transpacific ties; not only was the film shot on location in Yokohama, but the company employed local Japanese extras and commissioned set designs from Japanese studios.[79]

THE EFFORTS IN FILM PRODUCTION by Japanese in the United States during the silent era were short-lived and limited in scope. Portland's Yamato Graph Motion Picture Company folded not long after it was first established. According to public records, the company lasted for a mere two years and dissolved in 1914.[80] The Japanese American Film Company in Los Angeles intended *The Oath of the Sword* to garner a broader audience market. Hoping to reach audiences across the United States, the company secured distribution services from Sawyer Film Corporation, an early independent film distribution company based in New York City and established by Arthur H. Sawyer. Promoted as the "World's Largest Film Mart," the company's network of distribution included direct rental to exhibitors and contracted with local firms for regional distribution. Newspaper advertisements seem to indicate that *The Oath of the Sword* was, in fact, released and circulated in various U.S. theaters, including in Oregon, Indiana, and Wisconsin (all states with comparably lower populations of Japanese), as well as in California.[81] However, the film's circulation was itself limited by its network of distribution when the Sawyer Film Corporation floundered. As Richard Ward notes, the company was essentially "a distributor without an actual distribution network" and collapsed a mere eight months after its incorporation.[82] Without an adequate system for distribution, reception for *The Oath of the Sword* was limited. Furthermore, there is no indication that the Japanese American Film Company made any other films after the production of *The Oath of the Sword*. Similarly lacking longevity, the Fujiyama Film Company produced only a singular film in *Nami-Ko*. It is unclear whether the film had a successful distribution run.

The one successful prolific Japanese-led film production company was Haworth Pictures Corporation. Established in 1918 by Sessue Hayakawa, the company produced at least nineteen feature-length films. The viability of Hayakawa's company was in part due to the Hollywood actor's fame and personal and industrial connection to the mainstream Hollywood production companies. Although Hayakawa envisioned producing films that were "authentic" and presented alternatives to the stereotypical representations of Japaneseness in the American film industry, many of these films reinforced idealized and formulaic representations of Japan. According to Daisuke Miyao, Hayakawa was too beholden to the tastes and expectations of American audiences as well as the idealized and nationalistic images of Japan.[83] Despite the significant output of production by Haworth Pictures Corporation, the company also had a relatively short life-span. Hayakawa lost control over his company a few years later and in 1922 filed a lawsuit against the film distributor Robertson-Cole for breach of contract. Like others frustrated with the racial barriers of the American film industry, Hayakawa left the United States shortly thereafter to pursue his career in Europe.

Film production by Japanese in the United States during the silent era was aspirational and ahead of its time. As independent filmmaking ventures, these companies unfortunately faltered and unraveled in the American and international marketplace. Stephen Gong has argued that early Asian American filmmaking failed largely because it lacked a reliable and coherent system of independent film distribution and circulation. The burgeoning vertical integration of the studio system foreclosed many avenues for exhibiting films made outside of Hollywood. The race film industry depended not only on independent studios and companies but also on an alternative network of film distribution and exhibition. These networks to reach Black audiences made early Black filmmaking possible.

Conversely, the films made by Japanese American production companies in this period never found a wide audience, neither a broad American mainstream audience nor a Japanese or Japanese American audience. However, Japanese Americans later did establish a multifaceted and dynamic system of film circulation and exhibition across the continental United States, but only in the years following the early production studios. This exhibition system took root in disparate localities and encompassed both theatrical and nontheatrical exhibition spaces. Moreover, this flourishing alternative system of film circulation and exhibition depended largely on films produced in Japan, which would have their heyday in the United States in the 1920s and 1930s. Rather than relying on films produced by Japanese in the United States, Japanese American audiences turned their sights to the films moving across the Pacific directly from Japan.

CHAPTER TWO

Moving Screens

Theatrical and Nontheatrical Film Exhibition by Japanese in the United States

> Everybody really went to the films in those days. All the parking places were chock full.
>
> —CLARENCE IWAO NISHIZU, on viewing Japanese films in an agricultural warehouse in Stanton, California

> An enthusiastic audience of approximately 1200 viewed the benefit program.
>
> —NICHIBEI SHINBUN, October 25, 1925, on viewing Japanese films in a Scottish Rites Temple in San Francisco, California

Films from Japan traveled along unexpected and circuitous routes in the United States in the years before World War II. Japanese silent films arrived at an agricultural warehouse in Stanton, California, around once or twice a month. Japanese proprietors rented a hall at the warehouse, ordinarily stocked full of a variety of chili peppers grown in the region. According to Clarence Iwao Nishizu, the films were mostly samurai films, exhibited with a benshi who "would stand in front on the side of the screen and while the picture was showing he would simulate the words spoken by the different characters in the movies." The Japanese films were typically shown in the warehouse to raise funds for organizations, especially the local Japanese schools. Given the rural setting, the Japanese film shows were a big draw for the Japanese community, and, as Nishizu recounted, "everybody really went."[1] Up north in San Francisco, audiences had the chance in 1925 to see Japanese films in a Scottish Rites Temple, which had been rented by the Kinmon Gakuen. While the Japanese school would later initiate a regular Japanese film exhibition program, this film screening was a special affair and attracted over twelve hundred attendees. Organizers set up the space like the grandest of picture palaces. "The boys and girls of the Kinmon Gakuen acted as ushers," according to the newspaper, "the girls wearing attractive black and white middy uniforms, which was the subject of comment from many." Arriving at the Scottish Rites Temple for an evening's entertainment, the large urban audience was purportedly "orderly and decorous . . . [maintaining] the decorum of the Japanese upon respectable grounds."[2]

Throughout the first half of the twentieth century, Japanese in the United States established an alternative system of film exhibition and circulation. Films were projected across a wide range of exhibition sites and venues and moved through an expansive geography of rural and urban regions in the United States. Japanese proprietors operated nickelodeons as early as 1903. Looking to work for themselves, Japanese in California and Washington joined the legions of immigrant proprietors who found running the motion picture enterprise to be a viable and accessible business. For many Japanese community leaders, entrepreneurship was a key aspect for uplifting and bolstering the community. Japanese film exhibitors not only provided entertainment to audiences but also contributed to a model of autonomy and self-sufficiency to the Japanese community.

Japanese in the United States also exhibited films in primarily nontheatrical venues. The exhibitors projected films across an extraordinary range of spaces, often makeshift and in arenas ordinarily used for other purposes. These included the agricultural warehouse and the Scottish Rites Temple mentioned above as well as churches, Buddhist temples, community centers, association halls, and school auditoriums. And sometimes film screenings took place in no space at all, projected outdoors under the wide-open sky. In writing about *nontheatrical cinema*, Gregory A. Waller notes, "The non-theatrical as a type of exhibition or more grandly, as a possibility of cinema, is less tied to the appearance of this specific term than to a particular awareness about the uses of cinema beyond commercial entertainment." Moreover, Waller notes that similarities between nontheatrical cinema and early twentieth-century magazine publishing in its corresponding focus on specialized readerships and viewerships. Moving against the logic of cinema as a homogenized and mass commercialized industry, the nontheatrical cinema presents modes for specialization, differentiation, and alternative forms of identification.[3]

For Japanese in the United States, the nontheatrical provided the terms for an alternative system of film exhibition and circulation. Bringing films to a range of spaces and for a range of purposes, Japanese film exhibitors reworked the cinema toward a *usefulness* for themselves and for their communities. This usefulness in cinema entails the kind of utility for organizations and institutions noted by Haidee Wasson and Charles Acland (as Japanese film shows were often given to support specific Japanese organizations or causes).[4] Yet it also entails an expansive set of viewing practices produced over and against a limiting and often exclusionary commercial system. In *Screening Race in Ameri-*

can Nontheatrical Film (2019), Allyson Nadia Fields and Marsha Gordon have argued that "if the big screens marginalized people of color, small screens often helped balance the scales." The wider range of spaces in nontheatrical cinema, and its less centralized means of production, distribution, and exhibition, provided varying possibilities not altogether circumscribed by the studio system in Hollywood or, I would add, the Japanese film industry.[5]

The nontheatrical provided the primary exhibition site for the circulation of Japanese films in the continental United States prior to World War II. Whereby audiences were able to view Japanese films in Los Angeles's Fuji Kan by the mid-1920s, it was in the many other spaces of film viewing that most audiences encountered films from Japan. The circulation of Japanese films was facilitated by such film exchange companies as Nichibei Kogyo Kaisha and, most importantly, by the benshi. Often moving from site to site transporting reels and film equipment, the benshi played a pivotal role in circulating and exhibiting Japanese films. In Japan, the benshi had been integral to the cinema. They gained the sort of notoriety reserved for movie stars as audiences came to admire their narrational and performative skills. Benshi in Japan appeared as a part of the first introduction of motion pictures to the country. The benshi initially provided background to the film story and also explained the mechanics of film technology to the audience at a time when the machinery was a novelty.[6] Known mostly as voice narrators for Japanese silent films, the benshi in the United States, perhaps even uniquely, took on the double duty of performer and film exhibitor. From Japan to the United States, and from the urban film theater to the rural show hall, Japanese films and the benshi were constantly on the move. Indeed, benshi were key in the formation of an alternative system of film exhibition and circulation in the United States.

Beginning in the 1920s, the benshi traversed across the United States to bring Japanese films to audiences near and far. Perhaps none moved more expansively nor had a broader all-encompassing reach than Takeshi Ban, a passionate minister, ardent racial uplift proponent, and a skilled lecturer and benshi. His personal papers chronicle an extraordinary career and the alternative filmgoing publics and practices he initiated while moving across almost every corner of the United States.

"An Air of Freedom": Japanese Operated Theaters in the Nickelodeon Era and Beyond

Japanese Americans entered the film theater business in the United States at the start of the nickelodeon era. As early as 1903, a Japanese named

Yamada operated at least two nickelodeons in Seattle, Washington.[7] Throughout the 1910s, motion picture theaters for Japanese American audiences were established in the major hubs of Japanese migration and settlement. Nickelodeons and more dedicated theaters emerged alongside the lodging houses, boarding rooms, pool halls, barber shops, grocers, and restaurants as part of thriving districts of commerce and social exchange. Similar to the formation of Chinatowns, many Japanese urban districts grew in relationship to escalating anti-Japanese hostilities and racial exclusions. The newly formed spaces of Little Tokyo offered a sense of greater possibility and, importantly, a respite from white racism. Commenting on the feeling of being in Seattle's Little Tokyo (now called the International District), one early resident noted, "There was an air of freedom."[8] The establishment of motion picture theaters in Japanese districts was a sign of these newfound possibilities.

Japanese theater proprietors found a receptive market in Los Angeles and other urban localities in California. Bankoku-za (International Theater) was opened on November 2, 1907, at 228 East First Street in Los Angeles. Its proprietors were George Bungaro Tani and Tadayoshi Isoyama. Tani was a prominent businessman who arrived in Los Angeles in 1899 from Wakayama Prefecture. He produced bamboo furniture at first and later became the vice president of Los Angeles's most successful prewar Japanese American business, a department store called Asia Company.[9] According to Ogihara, Bankoku-za endured for over a decade. It changed ownership in 1916 to Chuzo Takamori before shuttering its doors in 1918. During the same period, another Japanese-owned theater called Toyo-za (Oriental or Pearl Theater) opened nearby at 414 East First Street.[10]

In Northern California, the Nippon Theater (328 L Street) was first established in 1908 in Sacramento. The *Sacramento Union* reported, "The up-to-date Japanese have opened a moving picture called the Nippon. The theater is well ventilated, and the machine is at the side instead of the rear of the theater, thus ensuring better escape in case of fire."[11] The Nippon Theater had an enduring life in Sacramento and even reopened after internees returned following World War II. Sacramento city directories list the following individuals as proprietors of the Nippon Theater: S. Miyoshi (1910–1912), Y. Nishio (1913–1914), S. Shimada (1915–1917), and T. Horimoto (1918–?).[12] Soichi Nakatani resumed ownership of the Nippon Theater starting in 1930 until the war.

In nearby Fresno, the Iwata Opera House (909 F Street) was established in 1911. Advertisements describe it as the "most modern theatre in Fresno," fea-

The Bankoku-za (International Theatre) in Los Angeles, circa 1907. Courtesy of Seaver Center for Western History Research, Los Angeles County Museum of Natural History.

turing both motion pictures and vaudeville. According to Phillip Walker, the theater had a notable architectural feature as it was designed with a foot-lighted runway for Kabuki performances. "Although a conventional western-style orchestra pit was situated between this main stage and the first-row seats on the sloping auditorium floor," according to Walker, "the traditional accommodation for a Kabuki orchestra was also provided behind a lattice at stage-left." Moreover, "in the floor at stage-center was a small evolving disc, also for use in Kabuki performances." Over thirty-six actors and a six-piece

Photograph of Bungoro Tani, the owner of the Bankoku-za. Courtesy of Seaver Center for Western History Research, Los Angeles County Museum of Natural History.

orchestra with the Imperial Japanese Theatrical Company performed at the opening of the Iwata Opera House.[13] Newspapers described the Iwata Opera House as a theater "exclusively for the Japanese." The owner and namesake of the theater was H. Iwata, a prominent and successful businessman.[14]

In Seattle, Japanese proprietors took over previously established film theater operations. In 1919, newspapers reported that "ten of the smaller downtown theatres are now owned and operated by members of the Nippon race." These theaters were called Class A, Palace, Occidental, Bison, Jackson, Flag, High Class, Victory, and Electric.[15] Many of Seattle's film theaters had been shut down because of the influenza, or Spanish flu, that swept the country in 1918–1919. As Richard Koszarski notes, the pandemic forced many city officials to close down motion picture theaters alongside other urban businesses, causing some to declare the end of the film industry as they knew it.[16] Seizing on the opening in the market, Japanese proprietors in Seattle stepped in just as the outbreak ended, perhaps even initiating what we might consider as a bailout of a faltering industry.

IWATA OPERA HOUSE

Motion Pictures and Vaudeville

MOST MODERN THEATRE IN FRESNO

909 F St.   H. IWATA, Prop.

Advertisement for Iwata Opera House. Printed in *Fresno and Coalinga City and Fresno County Directory 1911* (Sacramento, CA: Polk-Husted Directory).

The grandest theater acquired by Japanese in Seattle was the Atlas Theater (412 Maynard Avenue). It was operated by two Japanese proprietors, one named Yamada and the other, Iwasuke Kaita. The theater held five hundred seats, housed a $4,500 Fotoplayer, and employed two skilled local musicians. "The interior," as the newspapers noted, "is simply but tastefully decorated." Moreover, reporters boasted that "there is a handsome marquee with a big electric sign over it . . . [and] the machines used are Power's 6-B and a Minusa Gold Fibre screen." The grand opening of the Atlas Theater in 1918 was an ostentatious affair. The epic historical drama *Cleopatra* (1917), starring "the Vamp" Theda Bara, was the premiere film on opening day. Prominent members of the Japanese community in Seattle were in attendance. Lining the walls of the Atlas Theater were "no less than fifteen large floral pieces," which were given by the major Japanese American businesses of the area.[17]

For Japanese throughout the United States, the nickelodeon era was a relatively opportune period to enter the film theater business. These new moving picture theaters, named after their cheap admission prices, surged in popularity during the first decades of the twentieth century. It is estimated that by 1907 there were eight thousand nickelodeons in the United States and over ten thousand by 1910. Whereas most opera houses and theatrical venues were operated by American-born and local elites, nickelodeons created opportunities for newcomers that were previously unavailable.[18] In New York, many proprietors of the nickelodeon were Jewish and Italian immigrants relatively new to the city.[19] Compared to the earlier phase of entertainment, there were fewer obstacles to entering film exhibition during and after the nickelodeon era. Many novice showmen could consult the abundant advice literature from the readily accessible film exhibitor's trade press.[20] Across the Pacific coast, Japanese proprietors established independently owned film businesses throughout the nickelodeon era and beyond. In the later period of grandiose and chain-operated picture palaces, Japanese proprietors continued to operate smaller neighborhood-style theaters, often retaining the space for live musical accompaniment or performance.

Entrepreneurship was relatively high in the Japanese American community. In Seattle, 40 percent of Japanese in 1920 earned their income from small businesses, a far greater percentage than in the United States as a whole. Outside observers and Japanese Americans themselves had long taken note of this feature among Japanese Americans. Writing for sociological study, Frank Miyamoto attributed this entrepreneurship to "individual enterprise and mutual responsibility."[21] In his 1973 history of the Issei, Kazuo Ito ascribed it to the "outstanding quality" of the Japanese in Seattle, especially the elites. "Japanese in this city were not mere floating laborers," Ito explained, "members of the intelligentsia who were skillful with tongue and pen, orators and aspiring politicians were in the forefront of the community."[22] Personal exceptionalism notwithstanding, many Japanese Americans faced limited opportunities in the American labor market due to racism and xenophobia. With constrained options in employment, entrepreneurship was also a viable means to owning one's own labor. Moreover, as Scott Kurashige notes, self-employment and entrepreneurship were actively promoted by many Japanese immigrant leaders in the 1920s and 1930s as an aspect of racial uplift and Japanese pride.[23]

To be sure, the ownership of moving picture theaters by Japanese and the patronage they would come to rely on was greatly shaped by pervasive and systemic racial segregation. As Cara Caddoo notes, the early film theater itself was "built into a landscape reconfigured by Jim Crow." When nickelodeons were first widely established across the United States, industry

handbooks discussed the "ideal location" for a motion picture house in racialized terms and according to already established logics of racially segregated neighborhoods and public schools. With the further support of Jim
Crow legislation in the South, according to Caddoo, "white theater owners
made the segregated motion picture theater an industry-wide standard."
Moreover, the uneven regional policies and practices of racial segregation
merely reinforced each other as white southerners could rest assured that
their northern counterparts also maintained the color line even without legal
mandate.[24] As Matthew Lassiter similarly notes, the assumption that de jure
segregation (legal segregation) was a unique feature of the South only meant
that other states remained largely insulated from civil rights litigation.[25]

Challenging the assumptions of segregation as an exclusively southern
phenomenon, Japanese confronted a color line across California and other
western states.[26] Some scholars have even argued that the western region of
the United States pioneered some of the first social and legal mechanisms
for race-based segregation.[27] In states with legal protections, racial segregation was indirect and subtle. Recalling his experience of Seattle in the 1920s
and 1930s, Frank Miyamoto commented, "It's difficult to know whether you
were excluded or not, you in a sense had to try it out."[28] Without a visible
sign or clearly designated boundaries, the color line was often not apparent
until it was crossed. Inside motion picture theaters, Japanese filmgoers faced
the kind of arbitrary and nonvisible color line that was commonplace outside of the South. Jun Kurumada remembered confronting racial restrictions
in the Capitol Theater in Salt Lake City, Utah, when an usher asked him to
leave his seat for the segregated balcony. "That's when I realized that the so-
called 'coloreds,'" Kurumada noted, "were directed upstairs."[29] Japanese
patrons in Seattle, like Heitaro Hikida, similarly recalled the second-class
treatment in mainstream movie theaters:

> They would never refuse us entry outright, but would simply never sell
> us a first class seat. Instead they gave us balcony seats. At stage shows,
> both box seats and reserved seats were high class, and at movie
> theaters the reserved seats were best. Knowing ahead of time that they
> would not sell us such tickets, I asked them to give me a seat where
> I would see well, such as the center of the main floor, near the high
> class seats, or the front seats in the balcony. Then they would say,
> "The seats are all sold out in the balcony." When I entered the balcony
> seats, there were many empty, and so I would try to go to an empty
> seat where I could see well, but the usherette would come and say,

"That's reserved", and would guide me to a seat where I couldn't see well.[30]

Within the moving picture theater, the color line could be enforced by partitioning the space of the theater, withholding certain tickets, or using ushers to move patrons to "lesser" seats and away from white audiences. In recounting his experiences, Sakigake Hideyoshi remarked, "Even when I bought the most expensive seat, I was taken to the so-called 'nigger heaven'—the highest and farthest back in the gallery."[31] In its practice in the South and directed toward African Americans, the segregated seating on the balcony of theaters came to be derisively known through a host of racist euphemisms, such as "buzzard roosts," "peanut galleries," and, most offensively, "nigger heaven."[32]

Japanese who operated film theaters provided patrons with an alternative to film viewing under Jim Crow. They cultivated a sector of the film theater business by seizing a segmented, if not captive, market. Proprietors devised varying strategies and exhibition practices for their film businesses. In 1911, a Japanese man named K. Kimura operated a cleverly named theater called the Fair Theatre in Fresno.[33] When the Atlas Theater opened in Seattle in 1918, according to newspapers, "a particular feature of the seating arrangement of this house is that there is no balcony, in spite of the fact that the theatre has 500 seats." While not entirely uncommon in this period, this architectural feature of the Atlas Theater made, at the least, balcony segregation a structural impossibility. Reporters also noted that "in establishing the policy of their house the managers [of Atlas Theater] are taking into consideration not only the large transient patronage which other theatres in this vicinity rely on, but also the family trade from the rooming houses and hotels in the immediate neighborhood and the nearby Japanese resident district. With this in view they made the rule that no smoking will be permitted."[34] In pursuing the "family trade," the Atlas Theater proprietors sought to appeal to Japanese American patrons by crafting an aura of cleanliness and respectability. Barring smoking, the theater managed the perceived offending sensibilities of male working-class culture, smells and all. One female patron even recalled, "In the old days, [when] all the single men would go to [the Atlas Theater,] there was a rope cordoning off the area . . . and a Japanese man would let the single women come in and sit in a section where there wouldn't be anyone else to bother them."[35]

Theater owners at the same time located their patronage in the working-class, immigrant men who relied on urban centers for their livelihoods. When the Nippon Theater in Sacramento was built in 1908, the owners planned the space as multipurpose with the "upper portion of the theater divided, one portion being used as a Japanese billiard and pool room, while the other a Japanese lodging house."[36] By the 1930s, Japanese proprietors cultivated non-Japanese patronage to support their theaters. As I explore in chapter 4, Filipino film patrons would become an important constituency for the Japanese-owned theater, especially after federal restrictions curtailed immigration from Japan. Not only would Filipinos supply Japanese theater owners with much needed revenue, but they would also shape the film culture itself as a number of these Japanese-owned theaters began screening films from the Philippines in addition to their regular programming.

However, the Japanese film theater proprietors were operating in an especially volatile time, and their theaters became a target for the growing anti-Japanese exclusion movement. Nativists and anti-Japanese proponents decried the theater operations as evidence of the larger problem of Japanese property ownership, casting the entrepreneurs as a yellow peril menace. In 1911, *Moving Picture World* reported: "On East First street, Los Angeles, the Japanese are already in control of three five cent theaters. Several times they have tried to buy leases in the business district, and also on the Strand at Long Beach, and other suburban cities. The Japanese, as every Westerner knows, are cooperative to extremes. They now control more than half of the pool halls in Los Angeles, and now they have entered the moving picture field and their appearance in this business has been viewed with alarm by local American exhibitors."[37]

Japanese property ownership in the United States was a major source of racial hysteria. The existence of a Japanese American merchant class exacerbated long-standing fears, undermining white supremacist notions of Japanese inferiority and degradation. These antagonisms ultimately led state legislatures to pass alien land laws, which restricted Japanese from owning and leasing agricultural land. In 1912, the Asiatic Exclusion League (which was formed in 1905 as the Japanese and Korean Exclusion League) convened in San Francisco to muster support for the alien land law. They discussed the alarming fact that "Asiatics produced nearly one-third of [California's] agricultural output." At their meeting, they singled out H. Iwata, the owner of the Iwata Opera House in Fresno. On account of his vast property holdings, Iwata was identified by the league as "the heaviest taxpayer on the land in Fresno city." Not long after, Iwata was arrested by immigration authorities for "harboring alien women" and threatened with deportation. Newspapers made specific mention that he was "the wealthiest Japanese of Fresno" and "said to be worth $200,000."[38]

As proprietors in contentious states like California and Washington, Japanese American film theater owners had to navigate a volatile political climate. City officials in 1911 visited the Nippon Theater in Sacramento to investigate "illicit gambling" and the possibility that "white women are permitted to visit." After several inspections, authorities concluded that no illegal activities were taking place at the theater.[39] When the so-called theater-buying movement by the Japanese in Seattle was met with, as a news article put it, "a feeling of alarm," the Japanese film proprietors responded by emphasizing their desire to conform to American norms. In 1919, E. Fujimoto, who managed seven of the ten theaters owned by the Japanese, spoke on record to the *Moving Picture World*:

> Japanese living in Seattle want to invest their money here but there are only three business lines open to them, truck farming, the hotel business, and the motion picture business. In entering the motion picture business we are not trying to take away from Americans as much money as possible and give nothing in return. We want our employees, who are invariably Americans, to have a square deal. We always co-operate with the unions, and our operators will be found to be as well if not better satisfied than those working in American-owned theatres. Neither are we trying to dominate prices of the film. We realize that the producers must be paid according to scale, if he is to continue to produce good pictures, and we are willing to pay our share.[40]

The stated desire to "pay our share" and offer a "square deal" was a direct appeal to the American standard of labor. In the twentieth century, Japanese American workers and businesses were perceived as undermining the American labor movement. As Dana Frank notes, the Seattle-based American Federation of Labor (AFL) excluded Japanese workers from union membership and promoted anti-Asian consumer campaigns to reinforce class solidarity and white identity. In the 1920s, a number of restaurant and craft unions in Seattle boycotted Japanese-owned businesses and labeled them "scab businesses." As such, both Japanese workers and Japanese-owned businesses were positioned as antithetical to the American standard of labor. "Not only was 'union' actively equated with 'white,'" according to Frank, "but the converse as well: 'nonwhite' functioned as an easily accessible code for 'non-union' . . . [and] a Japanese American-owned restaurant was by definition a 'scab' restaurant."[41]

In addition to defending their labor practices, the Japanese theater owners in Seattle exhibited pro-American and patriotic films. J. A. Koerpel, the manager of Seattle World Film Exchange, distributed "official war films" sponsored by the U.S. government. He reported that "the only Seattle exhibitors who have booked the official pictures, 'America's Answers,' and 'Under Four Flags,' are Japanese." Moreover, the film distributor noted, "[the Japanese] take the attitude of showing these pictures because the Government wants them to do it, not stopping to ask each time if the subjects will pay. Their experience with the war pictures justifies their business judgment, however, as well as showing their loyalty to the Government."[42]

Pacific Crossings: Japanese Films Travel to the United States

Most of the films exhibited in the Japanese-owned theaters during the nickelodeon years were American films. Films from Japan first made their way to American screens only infrequently and in a sporadic fashion. As Ogihara notes, the Bankoku-za in Los Angeles exhibited mostly American films yet occasionally presented films from Japan. In 1914, for instance, the theater exhibited the Japanese film *Nichiro senso horyo koi monogatari*. The film, however, did not have its own billing and was paired alongside the American film *The Perils of Pauline* (1914).[43] At Fresno's Iwata Opera House, one local mainstream newspaper sneered that "Japanese productions will not be given. The little brown men are such good patrons of the moving picture shows and delight so to see American soubrettes."[44] When the Atlas Theater opened in Seattle, its proprietors contracted for films from Paramount, Fox, Select, Vitagraph, Pathe, and Universal. However, the theater's co-owner Iwasuke Kaita did intend to import and distribute Japanese films. As the local newspaper reported, Kaita was "interested in a plan which he originated . . . of bringing over Japanese films, putting American titles on them, and distributing them in this country."[45] Plans to screen subtitled Japanese films, however, were not realized until the early 1920s when a film importer named S. Miyazaki secured Japanese films via contacts based in Hawaii. Miyazaki brought dozens of Japanese films to the Atlas Theater, including two films that the censors in 1923 identified as *The American Family* and *The Mother's Sin*, likely *Haha no tsumi* (1918). These films, according to the trade press, were barred by authorities because "he was unable to explain the plot to the satisfaction of the censors."[46]

The formation of Nichibei Kogyo Kaisha (Japanese Theater Association) bolstered the exhibition of Japanese films in the United States. The company was first incorporated in 1917 to import Japanese theatrical performances to the United States. It was headquartered in the heart of Los Angeles's Little Tokyo at 201 North San Pedro Street. The company was led by Yasusaburo

Fujimoto (1917–1926), Yoshiaki Yasuda (1926–1930), Hideichi Yamatoda (1930–1937), and Shunten Kumamoto (1937–1941). The film exchange began importing films from Japan for distribution in the United States in 1926 when it established a contract with Teikoku Kinema (also known as Teikine). It later contracted films with the major film studios of Japan.[47] This film company had varying ties to organized crime as several members were involved with the Tokyo Club (which facilitated gambling and prostitution). Yoshiaki Yasuda, who ran Nichibei Kogyo Kaisha along with serving as the head of the Tokyo Club, was murdered in 1930 by two gunmen in Los Angeles.[48] The film company's subsequent leader, Hideichi Yamatoda (who also led the Tokyo Club), was later involved in a kidnapping conspiracy.

Other companies involved in the distribution of Japanese films in the United States included the Mitsuba Trading Company (106 South San Pedro Street) in Los Angeles and the Star Film Distributing Company (1505 Geary Street) in San Francisco. Nichibei Kogyo Kaisha, however, had the strongest hold in distributing Japanese films in the United States. In 1926, the film exchange took over ownership of Fuji Kan, thereby ensuring an exhibition venue for its film distribution. Located centrally in Los Angeles's Little Tokyo, as described in the introduction, the Fuji Kan was a premiere motion picture theater and exhibited almost exclusively first-run films from Japan until its closure during World War II.

Due to theaters like Fuji Kan and film exchanges like Nichibei Kogyo Kaisha, Japanese films would have their first heyday in the United States starting in the mid-1920s. The production output by the Japanese film industry in this period was substantial. With the adoption of a central producer system, the major studios in Japan produced approximately six hundred to eight hundred films a year in the 1920s, far exceeding the annual output of Hollywood.[49] These high production numbers contributed to a steadier and more consistent stream of Japanese films coming to the United States. According to the U.S. Bureau of the Census, the import of Japanese films to the United States steadily increased throughout the late 1920s and 1930s. In 1928, 569,660 linear square feet of film positives and prints were imported from Japan, valued at $39,803. By 1938, the numbers rose to 1,497,150 linear square feet, valued at $120,358.[50] Moreover, these film circulations within and for the Japanese American community significantly predated the appearance of Japanese films in the art house circuit, often mistakenly credited as first "introducing" the Japanese cinema to the United States.[51]

Japanese American newspaper outlets played a significant role in publicizing and supporting the exhibition of Japanese films in the United States.

Photograph of Nichibei Kogyo Kaisha in Los Angeles. Pictured (left to right): Muneo Kimura (benshi and company partner), Hideichi Yamatoda (company president), Norio Maruyama, and Noboru Tsuda. Printed in *Nisei Year Book and Directory 1938–1939*. Courtesy of Japanese American National Museum (Gift of the Kosaku and Mitsuko Kiyohara Family, 95.250.1).

The newspapers not only printed advertisements for film showings, but they also generated a broad and dynamic field of film criticism and commentary. The newspaper *Rafu Shimpo*, based in Los Angeles, ran a column in the 1930s called News from the Film Colony, while the *Japanese American Courier*, based in Seattle, had a similar series called Kleig Lights. Critics like Larry Tajiri, James Hamada, and Steve Taniyoshi contributed commentary on popular films yet also kept abreast of Japanese American involvement in Hollywood.

The *Japanese American Courier* also had a column in the late 1920s called Across the Silver Sheet by a writer named Helen Swan (likely writing under a pseudonym), who offered a women-centered film commentary.[52] *Rafu Shimpo* ran regular announcements for Fuji Kan, and virtually every single Japanese American newspaper in circulation throughout the 1930s and 1940s published brief announcements advertising Japanese film screenings in the local community. Additionally, the newspapers offered readers lively criticism of incoming Japanese films. When the Japanese film *Kan tsubaki* (1921) debuted in San Francisco in 1925, a film critic from *Rafu Shimpo* offered the following assessment: "Like most of the Japanese drama the action was slow and the photography, except for a few flashes, was poor. Practically no close-ups were shown. However, the film contained much that had human appeal. . . . Unlike most of the Japanese productions this film contained elements of genuine humour. Happily it was free from sensationalism which mars even the best of the American productions."[53]

On the Road: Benshi and the Nontheatrical Film Exhibition

Alfred Miyagishima grew up in Scottsbluff, Nebraska. His family, like other Japanese families, settled in the region after working on the railroads. While small in size, the Japanese American community in Scottsbluff came together on certain occasions, including for the exhibition of a Japanese film show. As Miyagishima recounted, a Japanese man named Ban arrived in their small Nebraska town in a touring car loaded with films and a projector. His shows were publicized via word of mouth. "This man would portray all the characters in the movie, and a lot of those were tearjerkers. . . . Sometimes he would have a short *chambara* movie. . . . He used to look at the prompter and the words, and that was all in Japanese." Between the breaks, the benshi would head to the projector and rewind the reels. The Japanese film shows were a significant affair in their town and drew crowds of spectators. "Seeing a Japanese movie was quite an experience," according to Miyagishima, "so all the Japanese used to make time to get everything done, come into town and see the movies." When the film shows ended, Miyagishima recalled, "he used to load up and go to the next town."[54]

In the United States, the benshi played a pivotal role in the exhibition of Japanese films. Not only did a benshi provide narration, but he also performed the important role of itinerant film exhibitor. As the recollections of Miyagishima indicate, the benshi transported and exhibited the films by traveling from town to town in a touring car. The benshi arrived at each location with the Japanese films as well as all the equipment to screen the film. In the small Nebraska town, Ban was the film's narrator, projectionist, film and equipment supplier, and essentially the show's promoter and impresario. Equally significant, the benshi was largely responsible for enabling the circulation of Japanese films to the vast range of nontheatrical exhibition spaces that were the mainstay of Japanese film viewership in the United States. Indeed, Miyagishima and his fellow film patrons saw Japanese films not in a brick-and-mortar theater space but in an ad hoc film venue set up in a Buddhist temple. Like so many other benshi, Ban brought Japanese films to venues that were mostly provisional.

In some instances, these makeshift Japanese film viewing spaces resembled the earlier cinematic traditions at fairgrounds and open-air venues. In 1935, for example, Japanese film promoters in Florin, California, set up an informal, outdoor exhibition venue to screen the films *Sado jowa* (1929 or 1934) and *Ume miru koro*. The benshi Charley Hiyoshigawa Shugetsu provided narration and performance for this alfresco-style film screening.[55] The local resident George Uchida recalled that the Japanese church in Florin screened Japanese movies inside during the winter but then moved the screenings outdoors during the summer months. "They had a big blank wall at the end of the church hall, and they would put a big screen on the outside, on the wall."[56] Most often, though, Japanese films were exhibited in local and community venues used for other purposes by the Japanese community. When the benshi Muneo Kimura arrived in Fresno in 1925 to exhibit the Japanese films *Chijjo no seiza* and *Katauen tenmyo chin*, he did so at what the newspaper described as a "temporary 'theater' on the grounds of the Buddhist Church."[57]

Organizations, mutual aid societies, and religious institutions were all involved in the exhibition of Japanese films. Exhibited for purposes beyond entertainment, Japanese films were utilized to entice membership, raise funds, and to overall contribute to the benefit and betterment of the Japanese American community. For instance, the Young Men and Women's Buddhist Association (YMWBA) held a benefit movie program in 1936 at the Buddhist temple in Fresno. The films *Mabuta no haha* (1931), *Umi no uken*, and *Oka* (1929) were exhibited by Henry Miwa. In addition, the sponsored program included a stage show by members of the YMWBA and additional cartoon and comedy shorts. The funds for the show were used to "defray expenses for the coming Central California YMWBA conference."[58] Many of the various Japanese Associations across the country used Japanese film exhibitions to promote a myriad of causes and agendas, often pairing their programs with speaker programs and other related activities. In 1930, the Kaji

Yajima Union, a local Japanese chapter of the Women's Christian Temperance Union, hosted a movie program in a San Francisco hall for fundraising purposes. Charging fifty cents for admission, the union included a Japanese food buffet along with the film exhibition.[59]

The California Berry Exchange, Nojiri Fruit Company, and Northern California Berry Growers' Association, as another example, sponsored Japanese motion picture programs in 1937 to "celebrate the end of the berry season and to entertain the growers, their wives and children." Intended for neither commercial profit nor fundraising, the film shows were provided without cost.[60] By providing their workers with amusements, however, these companies did more than raise morale; they hoped to promote loyalty and worker efficiency. Writing about company towns and corporations of this era, Stephen Groening notes that company-made films as well as company-promoted film exhibitions facilitated Taylorist strategies of worker management. Often, many of these film shows also promulgated antiunion messaging.[61]

Japanese films were also exhibited in settings intended for a Nisei (second-generation) audience, to promote a sort of cultural immersion and education. In Long Beach, California, the local Japanese Presbyterian church exhibited a Japanese film they hoped would be "an excellent educational picture for second generation boys and girls." "The picture is so well produced," according to church leaders, "that those who do not understand or know the Japanese language will be able to understand this picture." To attract viewers to the featured Japanese film attraction, the church also offered several shorts, including a Mickey Mouse comedy and newsreels of the Sino-Japanese War.[62] In San Francisco, the Kinmon Gakuen (Golden Gate Institute), a Japanese-language school established in 1911 for Japanese American students facing racial segregation, featured a rotation of Japanese film exhibitions. In 1924, parents held a Japanese movie night and raised over $1,500 to fund school building projects. Japanese film exhibitions became regular features at the school throughout the 1930s and 1940s. Benshi like Muneo Kimura and Sensuke Mihara supplied Japanese films and performed at the school.[63]

Kinmon Gakuen also sought to attract younger audiences by hosting well-known actors and film stars. In 1926, the Hollywood actor Sojin Kamiyama came to the school and presented the evening's film program. He spoke of "movie acting as an art" and noted that "second generation young people, especially girls, should be encouraged to pursue this career." Over one thousand people were purportedly in attendance for Kamiyama's presentation.[64] In the following year, the Japanese actress Komako Sunada and director Frank Tokunaga also made guest appearances at the school.[65] By 1940, the Kinmon Gakuen

Japanese-American Film Exchange Inc.

Films For Rent

Phone WAlnut 7446
1701 Laguna Street
San Francisco   California

Main Office
135 N. San Pedro Street
Los Angeles, Calif.

Benshi:
Kenyu Hokutosai
Muneo Kimura
Shugetsu Hiyoshigawa
Namiyemon Tochuken
Taiyo Kawai

Advertisement for Nichibei Kogyo Kaisha (also called Japanese-American Film Exchange Inc.) featuring their cadre of benshi. *Pacific Citizen*, October 15, 1929.

auditorium, according to newspapers, was officially "converted into a movie theatre for a weekly program of the latest motion pictures from Nippon." Japanese films were furnished to the school by the Nichi-Bei Amusement Corporation, which by then was charging admission prices in the following manner: fifty-five cents for adults, thirty-five cents for Nisei, and fifteen cents for children.[66] Fuji Kan in Los Angeles also set up a similar kind of program targeting Nisei. In the late 1930s, the theater ran "Nisei Night Monday." Hoping to capture a younger viewership for Japanese films, the program featured, for instance, a double bill with one of the films starring the popular actress Hiroko Kawasaki, known as the "Shirley Temple of Nippon." In advertisements, the Fuji Kan featured a glossy celebrity photograph of the young actress.[67]

Benshi were key to transporting Japanese films from site to site in the continental United States. They moved alongside Japanese films, on the road and while projected on the screen. I have identified at least fifteen different benshi who worked throughout the continental United States in the period from the 1920s. Most of the benshi were men, but I did find one exception in which "a noted woman benshi from Japan" performed at a benefit held by

NICHIBEI KOGYO KAISHA, INC.

CABLE ADDRESS
"YAMAHIDE"
LOS ANGELES

TELEPHONES
MUTUAL 3523
MICHIGAN 8578

201 NORTH SAN PEDRO STREET
LOS ANGELES, CALIFORNIA

JAPAN BRANCH
TAKETA BUILDING
KOBIKI-CHO 2 CHOME
KYOBASHI-KU
TOKYO, JAPAN

BALANCE SHEET   Exhibit "A"
December 31, 1940

ASSETS

CURRENT		
Cash on hand	$ 61.60	
Cash in Theatre Box-office	175.00	
Cash in California Bank, Los Angeles	1,324.80	$ 1,561.40
Accounts receivable, film rentals		5,591.02
Unsecured loans and advances receivable		12,035.50
Film deposits:		
Cash in bank, Tokyo	$ 1,831.10	
Guarantees with producers–Japan	1,187.50	
Guarantees with producers–Los Angeles	3,000.00	6,018.60
Inventories:		
Films–depreciated valuation	$ 7,338.79	
Reels and cases	25.00	7,363.79
TOTAL CURRENT ASSETS		$ 32,570.31
FIXED ASSETS		
Theatre furniture & fixtures	$ 4,092.45	
Less–Reserve for depreciation	1,030.93	$ 3,061.52
Theatre picture and sound equip.	$ 3,038.10	
Less–Reserve for depreciation	892.68	2,145.42
Branch Picture & sound equip.	$ 4,187.85	
Less–Reserve for depreciation	382.51	3,805.34
Mobile picture & sound equip.	$ 1,776.44	
Less–Reserve for depreciation	626.47	1,149.97
Office furniture & fixtures	$ 159.64	
Less–Reserve for depreciation	7.98	151.66
Automobiles and trucks	$ 1,426.00	
Less–Reserve for depreciation	317.60	1,108.40 11,422.31
DEFERRED CHARGES		
Lease rent deposit–theatre building	$ 325.00	
Compensation insurance deposit	40.00	
Unexpired premiums–insurance	92.50	
Prepaid personal property taxes	183.69	
TOTAL		641.19
		$ 44,633.81

LIABILITIES

CURRENT		
Accounts payable	$ 4,165.49	
Note payable, California Bank–due 1-19-41	3,000.00	
Federal theatre admission taxes payable	639.63	
Social security taxes payable	254.52	
Federal income taxes payable–1940	703.25	
TOTAL CURRENT LIABILITIES		$ 8,762.89
CAPITAL AND SURPLUS		
COMMON STOCK ISSUED – 50 shares of $500.00	$ 25,000.00	
SURPLUS		
January 1, 1940, per previous audit report	$ 6,697.11	
Net income, year 1940, per Exhibit "B"	4,173.81	
TOTAL CAPITAL AND SURPLUS	10,870.92	35,870.92
TOTAL		$ 44,633.81

Invoice from Nichibei Kogyo Kaisha, Takeshi Ban Papers. Courtesy of Japanese American National Museum (Gift of the Ban Family, 97.5.200) the Japanese American Citizens League (JACL) in 1932.[68] Nichibei Kogyo Kaisha employed a cadre of benshi in Los Angeles, making the company a distributor of Japanese films, a theater owner, and a benshi retainer. The employment of benshi enabled Nichibei Kogyo Kaisha to reach far beyond Los Angeles, and indeed many of the benshi for the company fanned out across an expansive network of communities, providing Japanese films for all sorts of venues and for all sorts of purposes. Benshi were also part of the company's leadership. Muneo Kimura was a well-known benshi who performed regularly at the Fuji Kan and other venues. He later became a major shareholder and business associate. In the 1940s, he shifted his sights to Hawaii to run Nichibei Kinema, one of the main Japanese film exchanges responsible for reviving Japanese film culture in the region after the war.

Although benshi were initially voice narrators or explainers of the film, the art of the benshi in Japan changed alongside developing film technology. According to Hideaki Fujiki, the benshi's performance shifted to provide moment-by-moment narration as cinema developed and films became multiple reels. "The benshi's voice and word selection became more nuanced and sophisticated," according to Fujiki. "Intonation, volume, rhythm, and tempo all contributed to the aesthetics of speech, and the clarity, accuracy, fluency, poetic or humorous appropriation of words defined the performer's proficiency."[69] The benshi most often adapted narration to the film's genre, characters, scenes, and titles, although at times the benshi created performances "excessive" to the film text. In Japan, the benshi were eventually institutionalized by licensing systems and other bureaucracy. According to Aaron Gerow, these measures worked to contain the "excessive" performances by the benshi. By the late 1910s, the benshi typically adhered to the film text, becoming less autonomous in their performance.[70]

In the United States, one of the most popular benshi was Tochuken Namiemon, popularly known as *chonmage* because he wore his hair in the old samurai style. Born in Saga, Japan, in 1911, Namiemon first immigrated to Hawaii and then moved to California. According to Itakura Fumiaki, he studied *rōkyoku* (a traditional Japanese story singing, also known as *naniwa-bushi*) and brought this practice to the movies whereby he "sang" the story rather than just narrating them.[71] Namiemon had a prolific career as a benshi in California. When the Fuji Kan reopened in 1926, it was Namiemon who provided the narration for *Konjiki yasha*. Most significantly, he toured extensively throughout the 1920s and 1930s, bringing Japanese films to a wide range of venues and exhibition halls. He even brought Japanese films to a boxing auditorium in Sacramento in 1933.[72] Fumiko Kawai Nakajima and Noritake

Masuda fondly remembered Namiemon. They lived in Fresno, where a "Nippon Hall" exhibited Japanese films every other month in the late 1920s. When Namiemon came, his performances were particularly memorable because not only did he "mix in a little English," but he would conclude his performance by saying "no sabeta." Nakajima explained, "It's from 'no sabe,' which means 'I don't know' in Spanish, but in Central California, you used 'no sabe' when you didn't know or understand. So Namiemon said, 'No sabeta,' when a samurai is saying 'You don't know?' on the screen, and everybody laughed. Not at the core of the drama, but at his saying."[73] In some ways, Namiemon exemplifies the power of the benshi to recontextualize and redirect the audience's reception of a film. With Namiemon's narration, did the audience laugh when the film intended them to cry? In his usage of multilingual flourishes, it is also possible to appreciate the localization of the benshi's performance. Namiemon's referent is not only the film's narrative, but it is also based on audience and place. Within central California's complicated agricultural economy, is it also possible to imagine that Japanese and Mexican workers met each other not only in the lettuce fields but also in the Japanese movie hall?

Lecturer, Exhibitor, Preacher, Race Man: The Many Hats of the Benshi

Takeshi Ban traveled throughout the United States in the 1930s exhibiting Japanese films to eager and receptive audiences. Ban and his film shows were fondly remembered in oral history accounts. Tetsuo Ted Ishihara set up Japanese motion picture programs at a Buddhist temple in Ogden, Utah, for over a decade. He recalled that the itinerant showman exhibited the best of the films from Japan. "Mr. Ban's movies were good," Ishihara noted. "They were movies for education. The films had to do with religion. So good movies were usually brought."[74] It is estimated that Ban entertained tens of thousands of Japanese Americans in the 1930s with his film programs. He toured across the western states, including California, Arizona, Nevada, Utah, Colorado, and Oregon. His movies reached small towns and communities as far as Idaho and Wyoming and to such East Coast cities as New York City. Takeshi Ban was likely the benshi who arrived in Scottsbluff, Nebraska, in resident Alfred Miyagishima's recounting. Indeed, Ban's extraordinary career spanned a decade, and his reach was far and wide.

Ban was a man who wore many hats. He was, on the one hand, a Japanese film supplier, exhibitor, and promoter. He worked with Nichibei Kogyo Kaisha and the Fuji Kan, often retrieving his films from the company to take on the road. He brought Japanese American audiences the latest and most popular films from Japan's largest production studios. In the late 1930s, he also began showing industrial pictures and travelogues obtained from Nippon Trade Agency, an organization connected with the Japanese Ministry of Commerce. He often collaborated with fellow benshi Suimin Matsui. Ban was also importantly a performer. He was sometimes referred to as a benshi, but he also resembled an illustrated travel lecturer like the legendary American showman Lyman Howe. According to Charles Musser, early cinema's traveling exhibitor not only promoted the show but also transformed filmmaking with "post-production." The illustrated lecturer often selected and structured short films into a complex program enhanced by live sound accompaniment that included music, sound effects, and live narration. Showmen like Howe had a particular flair for organizing films along a variety of lines and for creating sustained narratives. He brought films to diverse social classes across the country and unified his audience using patriotism, enthusiasm, and a sense of national identity.[75] In many ways, Ban's work brought together these media practices, blending and mixing the traditions of the benshi with the illustrated travel lecturer.

Ban was a first-generation American, born in Japan's Kumamoto Prefecture. He had immigrated to Hawaii and been one of the first Japanese pastors in the Olaa/Keaau community. In 1912, he established the Olaa Japanese Christian Church and later graduated from the School of Divinity at Pasadena College. In 1931, Ban founded the Pacific Society of Religious Education to promote Japanese nationalism and Christianity and to educate Japanese Americans about the escalating Sino-Japanese War. Indeed, Ban's film programs were intended to bolster and support the gospel of the Pacific Society of Religious Education. When his film programs were advertised in local newspapers, he was often identified with his religious organization. Readers were informed that his Japanese film programs, sometimes given for no charge, were to be accompanied by "educational lectures." Often his credentials as a "doctor" or "reverend" were also acknowledged. Indeed, his film programs, as Eiichiro Azuma has noted, were intended to offer much more than mere entertainment. His company's motto was "education through motion pictures."[76] Ban believed his film shows would reinforce traditional Japanese morality and martial virtues as well as promote a vision of racial progress and uplift.

Ban was an exemplary promoter of Japanese film shows, and his shows drew significant numbers of Japanese filmgoers in the United States. His company business records track the breadth and pace of his show routes. Often staying for one or two nights, he rapidly moved from town to town with his touring film program. Ban exhibited films for residents in California's agricultural belt—Bakersfield, Cortez, Delano, Florin, Gardena, Chico, Visalia, and dozens of other small rural towns—showing a program of Japanese films.[77] According to Azuma, "Ban gave 257 lectures between March 1933 and September 1934. These shows entertained a cumulative total of 91,095 Issei and Nisei throughout the western states, nearly 70 percent of the 1930 total Japanese population."[78] His film programs appeared at almost every conceivable venue. He played at the Fuji Kan in Los Angeles and the Nippon Kan in Seattle as well as more ad hoc venues.[79] Remarkably, he also set up film exhibitions in some less likely spots, including farm settlements, lumber mills, fishing villages, and mining camps.[80]

Ban was a consummate showman and paid close attention to his audiences. He fashioned his film programs deliberately to harness and heighten effect. In his personal notes, he carefully documented countless film programs, making note when films were "well received" or when audiences seemed to "feel bored." When Ban screened a film depicting a "sad story of a woman who killed a mentally-ill younger sister," he made special note that the audience shed tears while watching the film. In other instances, he noted that a film had a *shitamachi* (old Japan) feeling and that it was "emotional." On several occasions, Ban made observations of the filmgoing responses of female audiences. He noted when "female fans of Shochiku Ofuna flocked together." He also keenly noticed and reported when films made his female audiences weep and cry.[81] Indeed, Ban's notes seem to indicate that the sentiments and reactions of audiences influenced his selection of films. Moreover, these cursory observations and reflections of audience reception suggest that heightened affect was the intended reaction of each of his film showings. For Ban, the audiences' display of emotions served as a bellwether for a successful program.

Looking to build on his audiences' emotional response, Ban paired each of his film exhibitions with an educational lecture. These lectures espoused the ideology of the Pacific Society of Religious Education, covering such topics as Japanese acculturation and national identity as well as "the problem of the color line" in the United States. In 1934, Ban set up a show in Hayward, California. Audiences were treated to *Shirayuri no hana* (1933). With over four hundred audience members in attendance, Ban gave a fiery lecture before the film screening on the politics of race and nationality. "It is vital necessity for the second generation to recognize the superiority of Japanese blood compared to any Occidental race," Ban exclaimed. "Discard your inferiority complex about being born yellow." His address was directed at the Nisei

```
                NICHIBEI KOGYO CHOKUZOKU
                   NIPPON EIGA RENMEI
```

PLACE	2 Nights	1 Night	Week-Day
(A)			
Alameda	------	75.00	------
Auburn	125.00	75.00	100.00
Armona	100.00	------	75.00
Arroyo Grande	80.00	50.00	
(B)			
Berkeley	125.00	------	100.00
Bakersfield	100.00		75.00
Brawley	110.00	75.00	100.00
Burbank		75.00	
Bangle	------	80.00	------
(C)			
Centerville	100.00	75.00	
Chico	75.00	50.00	
Colusa	75.00	50.00	
Compton	125.00	85.00	100.00
Concord	100.00	75.00	
Courtland	115.00	80.00	90.00
Cortez	75.00	50.00	
(D)			
Delano	150.00	85.00	
Del Rey	100.00	75.00	
Dinuba	100.00		75.00
(E)			
Elk Grove	100.00		
El Centro	135.00		
El Monte		100.00	
(F)			
Florin	100.00		
French Camp		50.00	
Fresno	200.00	------	-------
Fowler	100.00	------	75.00
(G)			
Gaudalupe	150.00 ~~175.00~~	100.00	
Gilroy	75.00	50.00	
Gardena	150.00		

Schedule showing Takeshi Ban's extensive show routes, Takeshi Ban Papers.
Courtesy of Japanese American National Museum (Gift of the Ban Family, 97.5.200).

(second generation). "Recognize the important mission that is lying before their path," he implored, "and make an extensive study of Japanese culture [to] contribute [your] learnings to the American people."[82] Ban typically gave his lectures before each film screening, thereby ensuring an audience among patrons who came for film entertainment, not preaching. Like other Japanese feature-length film exhibitions in the United States, Ban concluded the show in Hayward with a program of short films depicting the "beautiful scene of Modern Japan."[83] While nurturing sentimental and idyllic ties to Japan, these short films also presented a form of cultural and political education for the Nisei.

Ban also developed an English-language lecture series titled "Japanese Racial Culture." The lectures were led by Ban and other educators, clergy, and community leaders. The program of eighteen lectures was given in Los Angeles from 1937 to 1938 and included such titles as "The Vital Programs of the Peace between the United States and Japan" and "The True American Spirit and Americanization of Japanese in America." In addition, a number of the lectures addressed the growing racial divide in the United States and the place of Japanese in American race relations. Ban gave lectures entitled "The Study of Discriminations and Racial Problems in America," "The Japanese Race in America after the Second Generation," and, notably, a talk called "The Study of Negro Problems in America."[84]

Like other Japanese men of his generation, Ban was an ardent proponent of racial uplift. While his work was inextricably tied to Japanese imperialism and nationalism, it also intersected with the projects of racial progress led by African Americans. In 1936, Ban sent a letter to W. E. B. Du Bois, who was the nation's leading voice for African American rights and social advancement and a professor at Atlanta University at the time. Ban wrote to Du Bois to request a copy of his book *Black Reconstruction*, a 750-page book that revised the historiography of Reconstruction by highlighting the agency of freedmen.[85] In his letters, Ban also invited Du Bois to meet him in Los Angeles. He asked Du Bois to consider attending the "Japanese Racial Culture" lectures and to discuss "the present situation of the Japanese race in America."[86]

While Du Bois was ultimately unable to make the trip, the exchange of letters is illuminating. The connection between Ban and Du Bois continued a much longer history of Afro-Asian connection and of Du Bois's relationship to Japanese Americans and Japan. The scholar famously wrote of Japan as a "champion of the colored race" after Japan's defeat of Russia in 1908, yet he also, according to Yuichiro Onishi and Toru Shinoda, looked to Japan's modernization and imperialist ascendance in a set of later writings on Black internationalism and self-determination.[87] Furthermore, the exchange of letters

THE FOURTH LECTURE

OF THE

JAPANESE RACIAL CULTURE

JULY 1937 — JUNE 1938

Sponsored by the

PACIFIC SOCIETY OF RELIGIOUS EDUCATION

505 S. CUMMINGS ST.
LOS ANGELES, CALIFORNIA
TELEPHONE ANGELUS 17508
Cable Address "BANTAKESHI"

FACULTY

Professor Takeshi Ban, A.B., B.D., D.D., Dean
Professor Jiro Nagura, Former Professor of the
Yamaguchi Higher Commercial College
Professor Takeshi Matsumoto, English Literaturer
Professor Shinichiro Hasegawa, M.A.
Professor Hozen Seki, M.A.
Professor K. Suzuki, Principal of the Golden Gate
Japanese School, San Francisco, Calif.
Professor K. Shimano, Principal of the First L. A.
Japanese School, Los Angeles, Calif.
Rev. Hisanori Kano, B.S. (Imperial University, Tokyo,
Japan), North Platte, Nebraska
Rev. S. Hata, A.B., B.D., D.D., Salt Lake City, Utah
Rev. Otoe So, Pastor, Japanese M. E. Church,
Tacoma, Wash.
Professor Katsuya Koshitani, L.L.B.
Assistant, Helen R. Ban, A.B., Secretary

SUBJECT OF LECTURES

1. The Problem in the Relations of International Cultures, and Japanese Culture.
2. The Fundamental Spirit of America and Her Civilization.
3. The Study of Discriminations and Racial Problems in America.
4. The Vital Problems of the Peace between the United States and Japan.
5. Birth Control and the Economical Life at Present in America.
6. The Japanese Race in America after the Second Generation.
7. The Japanese Language in the American Public Schools.
8. Who Are Ineligibles in the Constitution of United States of America. (A Man Without a Country).
9. An Educational Rescription of Meiji Emperor and the Fundamental American Spirit of Abraham Lincoln.
10. The True American Spirit and Americanization of Japanese in America.
11. At the Bunker Hill.
12. The Vocational Problems of the Nisei and Their Farming.
13. The Study of the Negro Problems in America.
14. The Inter-marriage Problems of After Dai Nisei.
15. The Japanese Language Schools and the New Establishment of Higher Institutions of Japanese Literature.
16. The Females of Nippon.
17. Romaji and Furiganatsuki—Chinese character of the Japanese Language.
18. The Modern Japanese Literature and Its Tendency.

"Japanese Racial Culture," Takeshi Ban Papers. Courtesy of Japanese American National Museum (Gift of the Ban Family, 97.5.200).

REV. TAKESHI BAN, D.D.
PRESIDENT

CABLE ADDRESS
"BANTAKESHI"

PHONE ANGELUS 17508

Request for inf 1937

THE PACIFIC SOCIETY OF RELIGIOUS EDUCATION

505 SO. CUMMINGS STREET
LOS ANGELES, CALIFORNIA

June 30, 1937

Dr. W. E. Burghardt Du Bois
Atlanta University
Atlanta, Georgia

Dear Sir:

The Fourth Lecture Series from July 1937 to
June 1938 has begun since the establishment of
our institution, The Pacific Society of Religious
Education, Inc.

Friends, you are cordially invited to participate with us in our program of lectures for they
are extended to both Japanese and American audiences
and we urge your untimely consideration for them.
The questions for discussion deal with the present
situation of the Japanese race in America.

These lectures are being led by the leaders of
our organization who have dealt with the many social
problems confronting the Japanese people in this
country.

Our underlying principles is to create a true
understanding between Japan and America and to
promote an eternal friendship. Hence, we ask if
institution might provide at sometime a timely
visit with us and share a few moments in discussion of the welfares of our people and our country.

We shall cooperate in every way to extend our
appreciation for your sincerity. We remain,

Respectfully yours,

Takeshi Ban

Pacific Society of Religious Education, Inc

Letter from Takeshi Ban to W. E. B. Du Bois, June 30, 1937. Courtesy of the
Department of Special Collections and University Archives, W. E. B. Du Bois
Library, University of Massachusetts Amherst.

between the two men demonstrates Ban's ambitions for his film program. In his bid for "education through the movies," Ban wanted his moving picture shows to offer more than diversion or amusement. With a roving film projector in one hand and a copy of *Black Reconstruction* in the other, Ban sought to entrance his audience to lift their sights and to reenvision a collective future.

THE ROUTES OF JAPANESE FILMS onto screens across the United States were multiple and crossed a plentitude of borders. Theater owners, itinerant film exhibitors, entrepreneurial benshi, and film companies based in the United States all played roles in bringing Japanese cinema to the United States. According to Kerry Segrave, the U.S. market for foreign films dramatically fell after World War I. Hollywood would come to dominate not only the international market but the domestic screen as well. U.S. distributors and exhibitors, as well as government officials, enacted strict controls over the foreign film market by using block booking and imposing a tariff on foreign film imports. Exhibition groups like the American Educational Motion Picture Association ran campaigns in 1920 to curtail foreign film exhibition. Their slogan was "American Films for American Theatres." European film producers sought to push their way into the American market by setting up their own exhibition companies based in the United States but were largely unsuccessful. By the 1930s, Segrave counted only forty theaters in the United States playing foreign films exclusively and from the following cinemas: German, Russian, Spanish, French, Yiddish, Italian, and Swedish.[88]

During a period when options to view films made outside of the United States were severely limited, Japanese American film exhibitors established a viable alternative circuit for Japanese cinema. This network of film circulation and exhibition was untethered to the commercial film industry and routed across a wide range of nontheatrical venues. Japanese film exhibitors not only relocated the viewing spaces for films, but they also redirected the cinema toward their own means. Using the cinema to promote their own community-based organizations and varying agendas, many Japanese film exhibitors hoped to locate a usefulness for cinema beyond mere entertainment and profit. In establishing these alternative modes of viewing, the benshi was key; not only did the benshi provide narration alongside the screen, but he or she often also served as the traveling itinerant film exhibitor who brought the films on the road and set up the whole film show. In the United States, the benshi would have an enduring and long-standing presence, unthwarted even as the coming of synchronized sound technology began transforming the entirety of cinema.

CHAPTER THREE

Audible Divides

Japanese Americans and Cinema's Sound Transition

Sojin Kamiyama began his career in Hollywood at the height of the silent era. His work in silent American films was extensive, most notable for his portrayal of the Prince of the Mongrels, alongside Anna May Wong and Douglas Fairbanks, in the classic silent-era film *The Thief of Baghdad* (1924). He was also one of the few Asian actors to portray the fictional detective Charlie Chan, a role he played in *The Chinese Parrot* (1927). When the American industry began converting to sound, Kamiyama experienced the changes up close. Indeed, the coming of synchronized sound in cinema transformed many aspects of the film industry. Silent films had never been without sound (with live musical accompaniment in the theater), but the advent of sound technology enabled sound to be synchronized on a soundtrack. Early sound films were often referred to as "talkies" as it was the audibility of dialogue that defined the synchronized sound film. Working in Hollywood during this transformative period was volatile and chaotic. While the art of the silent screen did not always translate well in the new medium, the actor with a "foreign accent" was, as one newspaper put it, "an impossibility."[1]

The transition to sound took place relatively swiftly in the United States. By the 1930–1931 season, all the major studios moved completely to full sound feature production. It took less than a year for the major studios to plan and construct new sound stages, an exorbitant cost in construction and technological infrastructure. Hollywood even expanded their studio system at this time beyond Los Angeles by reopening offices in New York and moving overseas to work on multiple-language film production. The major film studios in the United States responded to the technological change by further consolidating the industry and monopolizing the market.[2] The sound era, as Ross Melnick notes, was the birth of media convergence as the new radio and sound technologies converted the U.S. film industry into the vast and expansive modern entertainment industry.[3] Consolidated across industries, the U.S. film industry would come to dominate the channels of distribution, both nationally and internationally, such that the industry would emerge as the dominant global industry with the transition to sound.[4]

During this transformative period, Kamiyama would find himself moving within and between the film industries of the United States and Japan.

His career in sound-era Hollywood took unexpected turns as he found himself working on early American sound films, including films intended for multiple-language global film markets. But like other international silent-era actors, such as the German-born Emil Jannings and Hungarian actress Maria Corda, Kamiyama also returned to his home country during the sound transition to work in the domestic film industry. In Japan, Kamiyama found a film industry transitioning to sound at a differing scale and pace. The film industry in Japan moved slower in the conversion to sound compared to the United States. The major film studios in Japan were producing silent films well after the advent of sound. Over 80 percent of films produced in Japan in 1933 were still silent. In 1938, nearly a third of all films remained silent productions.[5] According to Kenji Iwamoto, the Japanese film industry faced considerable technological challenges with the new medium and confronted the problem of establishing an entirely new means of expression since "the popularity of Japanese cinema was due more to its aural aspect (the benshi) than to its visual aspect."[6] The benshi continued to exert considerable influence through their connection to exhibition even as production studios began to shift to sound technology. Theaters in Japan were also reluctant to install costly sound systems when their films had never been silent in the first place.

This chapter follows the routes of people like Kamiyama to explore the sound transition as it took place within and between the film industries of the United States and Japan. Across a rapidly changing industry, Japanese in Hollywood found themselves incorporated into the efforts of the major studios as they sought to recapture global audiences. The emergence of sound technology introduced the problem of Hollywood's nationalization— as film became audible not only of sound but also of national languages. Hollywood looked to Japanese working in the industry to engage the development of the new medium as translators, interpreters, foreign-language actors, and writers. Yet these changes in the film industry also reinforced and fortified the system of racialized casting and production practices. In the transition to sound, early Hollywood sound films reengaged the screen Orientalism of the silent era, animating and making audible a new field of racialized speech sounds and sonic effects.

Moving between the dominant film industries on both sides of the Pacific, Kamiyama also ventured into independent production, hoping to establish an independent film company to pioneer the production of new sound films. His efforts were not singular, but like many others, they were unsuccessful. Tracing the circulation within and between the major film studios and the sphere of independent film production, this chapter also uncovers unseen and unmade independent films and production companies during the early sound era. Affected by the rapid changes in the U.S. film industry, James Wong Howe found his own successful silent-era career sidelined by the era's transformation. While most well known as a cinematographer in Hollywood, the sound era propelled Howe to take a detour into producing the first (and perhaps only) independent Japanese-language film made in the sound transition in the United States. In addition to Wong's films, a handful of Japanese American filmmakers also made films in the 1930s, largely influenced by a growing trend in amateur filmmaking. While produced in the more readily accessible 16 mm format, these films were produced exclusively in the silent medium. Moreover, these films circulated within the exhibition networks established for Japanese silent films, making their way to Japanese American audiences in a wide range of nontheatrical exhibition venues.

These residual practices of the silent era continued across multiple aspects of Japanese American film culture within the era of sound cinema and beyond. Due to their continual production in the Japanese film industry, Japanese silent films remained in circulation in the United States well after the advent of sound and the conversion of theaters to sound film exhibition. Japanese American audiences consequently continued to view silent Japanese films and even indicated preferences for silent-film-era practices. While a critical figure in the silent cinema, the benshi also remained a presence within the sound era. The benshi not only endured the sound transition in the United States, but their work seemed to even gain momentum and greater relevancy, especially with the outbreak of war in the Asian Pacific and as Japanese war and propaganda films began their circulation in the United States.

The coming of synchronized sound transformed the cinema, but in its wake, it left thwarted film careers, failed film production companies, and unwilling participants who continued to make, circulate, and view silent films. The technological transformation pulled together and consolidated the major film industries, but such developments were never totalizing. Between national contexts and across the sphere of production and exhibition, together these discordant aspects of the sound transition mark the era's audible divides.

Hollywood and the Transition to Synchronized Sound

Many Japanese in Los Angeles were initially optimistic about Hollywood's sound transition. Japanese American newspapers reported extensively on cinema's sound transition and the possibilities it held for Japanese participation in the film industry. Writing about Fox Studio's Japanese-language dubbing of *The Man Who Came Back* (1931), one writer optimistically opined, "Should the production of the Japanese version turn out to be a success it will revolutionize the talkie industry of the world, on which occasion Japanese actors and actresses will find a profitable profession in Hollywood as 'interpreters' behind the talkies."[7] Another critic speculated that "should other film companies follow the lead taken by Fox, it is believed that it would open an altogether new field in the film industry creating a demand for more Japanese in Hollywood."[8] *Rafu Shimpo* reported in 1932 that Warner Brothers would produce an astounding forty Japanese-version films. Although the studio never made so many films, such anticipation indicated the hope and desire in the potential opportunities for Japanese Americans as the industry began to undergo this major transformation.[9]

What the sound transition propelled the industry to confront was its relationship to the multiplicity of its audiences. Sound technology encouraged the universalizing vernacular of silent-era cinema to give way to the audibility of national languages. If limited linguistically, sound-era Hollywood faced the possibilities of losing its global reach. According to Natasa Durovicová, these transformations "would be costly and endanger American cinema's world markets, which by 1929 generated between 30 to 40 percent of a major studio's profits."[10] Film industries outside of the United States, in turn, saw the introduction of sound as an opportunity to recapture their own domestic markets and strengthen national cinemas against the worldwide dominance of Hollywood. As Abe Markus Nornes notes, these dynamics set the stage for a short period of volatility and experimentation in film industries across the globe.[11] Within the Hollywood film industry, producers began working on various ways to reinternationalize a cinema now audible of national languages. They employed a range of methods—including the production of non-English-language films and on adapting the newly audible English-language sound films for multiple-language audiences. Multiple-language-version films (also known as direct versions) were typically shot simultaneously in different languages and may have changed directors with each version or used varying casts.[12] In the early sound era, Hollywood adapted films for Japanese-language markets and produced several Japanese-version films.

In 1931, Fox Film Corporation enlisted Ken Nakazawa to join the Scenario Writers Department and work on translation for the dubbing of *The Man Who Came Back*. Nakazawa was Issei and a professor at the University of Southern California. He had little experience in the film industry and turned to

MAYO IKEDA

One of the versatile Oriental actors who is making headway these days is Mayo Ikeda. He recently appeared on the Metropolitan lot in Harold Lloyd's new production "Feet First." Speaking about "versatile," Mayo speaks English fluently as well as his native tongue, Japanese. With his natural dramatic ability Mayo expects to keep quite busy during the balance of the 1930 season.

Mayo Ikeda

Asian American actors sought to enter the sound film industry by promoting their multiple language skills. *Hollywood Filmography*, June 7, 1930.

local residents and nonactors from Los Angeles's Little Tokyo to provide vocalization for Japanese-language dubbing. Working in this new medium, Nakazawa expressed considerable frustration at the challenges of dubbing and synchronizing vocals. According to reports from Japan, audiences of the dubbed film were aghast at the sound of the immigrants' particular Hiroshima dialect—so much so that Nornes argues that audiences' disdain in hearing the immigrants' nonstandard Japanese may have even contributed to the wholesale abandonment of dubbing, instead offering subtitles in Japanese-version films.[13] Fox Studios not only utilized local Japanese to provide vocalization and translation, but they also tapped Japanese Americans from Los Angeles's Little Tokyo to preview and gauge the marketability of the film, suggesting the viability of the city's immigrant population as a resource for the film industry as it made the transition to sound.[14]

Paramount Studios led the effort in trying to secure a global market for American sound films. Not only did this major studio heavily invest in multiple-language film production, but it also established a satellite of foreign-language production studios, most notably Joinville in Paris, France.[15] Paramount Studios also undertook a smaller-scale effort to establish personnel and departments for producing and distributing films for Japanese-language markets. In 1930, its New York offices began producing short-subject talkies, including in Japanese, by "obtaining from the ranks of New York's many races the personalities to appear before the microphone."[16] According to newspapers, Paramount Studios had employed Japanese on both coasts to aid in the sound transition. "Besides the four Japanese translators employed in the Paramount of New York office," according to a Japanese American newspaper, "there are twenty Japanese workers in the Paramount Hollywood studios, one of them in the camera department and the other workers in various departments."[17]

Paramount Studio's grandest effort in penetrating the Japanese market was its production of a Japanese version of *Paramount on Parade* (1930). Its producers enlisted Tokyo's most well-known benshi Suisei Matsui, the "benshi-in-chief" at the city's premiere Shibazonokan Theatre. Paramount Studios also produced numerous other foreign-language versions of the film, including in Spanish, Scandinavian, French, Polish, German, Dutch, Hungarian, Romanian, Serbian, and Italian. Except for the Spanish version, all these foreign versions of *Paramount on Parade* maintained the musical sequences in the original English while using onscreen "hosts" to introduce the film and perform in segments interspersed in the film. The use of extradiegetic narrators, or a "master of ceremonies" as they were often promoted as, was a strategy commonly deployed in early sound films. These techniques required minimal alteration to the original, which producers initially preferred given the high production cost of reshooting and recasting a film in a different language.

As a popular figure in Japanese cinema, Matsui garnered significant attention upon his arrival to work in Hollywood. *Rafu Shimpo* promptly announced that "Suisei Matsui, one of the leading movie 'Benshi' [sic] of Japan arrived here last week to be the first man to test the feasibility of the Paramount experiment."[18] Japanese American newspapers ran human-interest stories on the benshi's background, biography, and stardom. Referring to him as the "Oriental Horatio Alger," one article noted "in adolescent years he worked a factory night shift, attending school during the day to study Occidental languages and customs. He now speaks English, Spanish, French and German."[19] Other articles described him as "a handsome, not tall, man with a pleasing personality whose thirty years on this universe has made him a man of the world," while another story covered a beach party held in his honor in Los Angeles.[20] Matsui even received coverage in mainstream newspapers, including a feature-length article in the *New York Times*: "If one contemplates a trip to Tokyo in the near future, Mr. Matsui is very likely to be met there, if not in person then on the talking screen, for he has made what is technically known as a Japanese version of 'Paramount on Parade,' the revue in which most of the Paramount group of satellites appear."[21]

Photograph of Suisei Matsui in Hollywood. Courtesy of Nippu Jiji Photo Archives, the Hawaii Photo Archives Foundation, and Densho: The Japanese American Legacy Project.

SHOWMANSHIP

MERCHANDISING PARAMOUNT PICTURES IN EVERY CORNER OF THE GLOBE

BYRD "SOUVENIRS" IN WINDOW DISPLAY!
Our Tokyo exploiters made good use of the Byrd "souvenirs" sent them from Home Office. Above is a window display of clothes worn by members of the expedition that was featured by the big Matsuzakaya department store of Tokyo.

DE LUXE DISPLAY!
This atmospheric display on the Byrd film occupied the biggest show window in the largest department store in Tokyo.

scenes made in Hollywood with the Japanese master of ceremonies, Benshi Matsui, who also made brief personal appearances before each showing of the film in the Hogaku Za and Musashino Kan theatres.

Again Paramount pictures plus Paramount showmanship have scored a notable triumph!

We heartily congratulate Mr. Cochrane's great gang, whose latest exploit is but added evidence of their initiative and spirit and resourcefulness.

"BYRD-PARAMOUNT ON PARADE" PROGRAM A RECORD-WRECKER IN THREE DAY AND DATE TOKYO THEATRES

PRECEDED by one of the most spectacular and comprehensive exploitation campaigns in the history of Japan, the double-barreled program of "With Byrd at the South Pole" and "Paramount on Parade" opened on September 11 for a triple simultaneous showing in the three theatres operated by Paramount in Tokyo—the Hogaku Za, Musashino Kan and Denki Kan.

All records for receipts and attendance were smashed to smithereens right from the start and new peak grosses were confidently expected by Mr. Cochrane who reported that

A JAPANESE "FIRST NIGHT"
Upper portion of the photo shows the marquee of the Denki Kan Theatre, Tokyo, with its stunning Antarctic display flanking the trademark. Lower part reveals the capacity crowd inside the theatre on the opening night of the Byrd film.

PARAMOUNT SHOWMEN!
Left to right, Messrs. Takeyama, publicity manager; Matsui, master of ceremonies in Japanese version of "Paramount on Parade"; Ouchi, manager of the Hogaku Za theatre Paramount operates; and Tom Cochrane, our representative in the Orient.

the pictures would run until September 30. That both attractions have captured the imagination of Tokyo picturegoers is evidenced by the applause which greets the end of each showing — an almost unheard of thing in Japanese houses.

Quite apart from the money the pictures will bring in is the added factor of good will and prestige. All Japan is Paramount-conscious as never before. The Byrd film, backed by unprecedented publicity, has aroused nation-wide interest. And "Paramount on Parade" has benefited enormously through the

A HERALD OF GREAT ENTERTAINMENT!
This is a reproduction of the back and front pages of the large size four-page Japanese rotogravure herald on "Paramount on Parade." A similar herald was issued on "With Byrd at the South Pole." Both heralds are chock-full of selling appeal.

"PROSPERITY WEEK" AN UNQUALIFIED SUCCESS

AS we write this, reports are flowing into Home Office testifying to the overwhelming success throughout the United States of Paramount's monster Prosperity Drive from Oct. 5th to 11th. Not only did this drive give added impetus to box office grosses, but there is ample evidence to show that it had a profound effect on business in general. In many instances, city officials cooperated in making the Paramount campaign the basis for a big civic celebration.

We shall be very much interested to hear of the results achieved by our Argentine division, which took the initiative in staging a Prosperity Week celebration simultaneously with the domestic drive.

TELLING THE U. S. A.!
This is the cover that graced the September 30th issue of the GREATER NEW SHOW WORLD, house organ of our domestic distribution department.

Publicity spread for Japanese version of *Paramount on Parade* (1930). Printed in the trade publication *Paramount around the World* (1930), Media History Digital Library.

Paramount Studios heavily promoted the release of *Paramount on Parade* in Japan. The film's advertising and publicity campaigns prominently featured Matsui as if he was the main attraction, and not the newly audible sound film itself. A photograph of Matsui, as well as his highly recognizable name, was emblazoned on the film's promotional materials for the Japan release. In so doing, Paramount Studios borrowed from, and indeed reproduced, the template of the silent era, whereby the benshi was so prominently featured, at times outshining the film's star actors. At the film's premiere at the Denki Kan Theatre in Tokyo, moreover, it is Matsui, not the film's roster of celebrity film stars, making a live appearance.[22] With Matsui at the center of its promotional campaign, *Paramount on Parade* had unprecedented runs in Japan's multiple show houses, with capacity crowds. As one source noted, the film was exhibited for three consecutive weeks at all the downtown Paramount theaters "with a total of five thousand seats packed at every showing." In Japan's other theaters wired for sound, "the picture showed for several times the normal length of the run."[23]

Significantly, Matsui's vocal performance on *Paramount on Parade*'s soundtrack, as well as his live appearance at the premiere, made him, in effect, a participant in his craft's ultimate demise. Synchronized sound not only transformed the medium but also threatened to eliminate the exhibition-oriented attraction of silent-era cinema. Chika Kinoshita has argued that Matsui's vocalizations for Kenji Mizoguchi's *The Downfall of Osen* (1935) "inscribed onto the soundtrack under the supervision of filmmakers, underscores the benshi's historical erasure by sound cinema. The benshi's elimination constitutes an integral part—perhaps one of the last chapters—of the world film-historical process in which the locus of control was transferred from the sphere of exhibition to that of production throughout the silent period."[24] Matsui's earlier vocalization in *Paramount on Parade*, performed five years before Mizoguchi's film, can be understood similarly. By synchronizing the benshi on the soundtrack, *Paramount on Parade* subsumed and integrated the live and performative dimensions of the silent era into the mode of production. Matsui's vocalization and role as "host" in the Hollywood film both anticipated and contributed to the eventual downfall of the benshi and the exhibition-oriented cinema of the silent era.

Hollywood's major studios produced several additional Japanese-version films. Universal Studios established a foreign-language department and produced nine foreign-language versions of *King of Jazz* (1930). They tapped the Japanese American actor Tetsu Komai to "host" the Japanese-version film and provide translation. David Pierce and James Layton note that most of the cast and production crew for all the foreign-language versions of *King of Jazz* were immigrants from the Los Angeles area, anecdotally recounting a story from casting about all the immigrant and "foreign" actors who suddenly showed up on the studio lots for employment in these multiple-language Hollywood films. Even the film's producer was himself an immigrant from the Czech Republic.[25] Interviewed by a Japanese film magazine, Komai recounted his work on the Japanese-version film, complaining of the difficulty in translating a Hollywood script as well as of working under harsh technicolor lighting and according to an ad hoc production schedule with minimal rehearsal time.[26]

While Hollywood devised varying strategies to surmount the challenges posed by the audibility of national languages in the shift from the silent to the sound medium, it also converted other aspects of screen representation. The sound era transformed the representation of race from a primarily visual marker to a sonically oriented and audible one. As Jennifer Lynn Stoever notes, the emergence of sound technology in the cinema transformed the representational power of cinema's "looking and to be looked at" to a mode of racialized sounds, or, what she calls, the sonic color line.[27] In the context of Japanese Americans and Hollywood, early sound films reengaged the screen Orientalism of the silent era, to animate and make audible a new field of racialized speech sounds and sonic effects. Astoundingly, these sonic film practices, of translation and incorporating multiple national languages and that of racialized speech, were being performed by the same individuals. While Japanese and Japanese American benshi, actors, and translators like Suisei Matsui and Tetsu Komai performed in Japanese-version films, they can also be seen in early Hollywood sound films using pidgin English and mock Asian accents and dialogue. That is to say, they also appeared in numerous early Hollywood sound films performing what Hye Seung Chung calls "yellowvoice," the cinematic use of dialogue and speech effects to mark racial and national alterity.[28] The coming of sound, it would seem, also synchronized the sonic side of screen Orientalism.

Like Matsui and Komai, Sojin Kamiyama served as "host" and translator for the Fox Studios' Japanese version of *Happy Days* (1929).[29] But his most prolific work in early sound-era Hollywood was in a slew of minor roles, some of which were uncredited. Between 1929 and 1930, he appeared in at least eleven Hollywood films, including *Seven Footprints to Satan* (1929), *Careers* (1929), *The Unholy Night* (1929), *Show of Shows* (1929), *Golden Dawn* (1930), *The Dude Wrangler* (1930), and *Way for a Sailor* (1930). Kamiyama himself was highly aware of this turn in Hollywood and the market for yellowvoice performance. When a Japanese American newspaper asked him about whether he was worried about the end of his Hollywood career due to the advent of sound, he sarcastically remarked, "In view of the fact that [mine] was a purely Oriental role and that broken English would be better suited to this role, [my] original worries are over. . . . [I have] even abandoned drinking to devote [my] best effort to [my] art."[30]

In the film *Painted Faces* (1929), Kamiyama offers a prototypical performance of yellowvoice. The film was an early talkie revolving around the notion of the foreigner, and Kamiyama appears only briefly in a scene set in a Chinese restaurant. The film's main character, a heavily accented Scandinavian actor/clown named Beppo, refused to concede to cojurors and convict an alleged murderer on trial. In the Chinese restaurant scene, Beppo enters with two American companions and is greeted by the unnamed Kamiyama kowtowing and cloaked in traditional Chinese garb. Unacknowledged even in the film's credits, Kamiyama's character in the short sequence is derisively referred to as "Chang," "Chung," "John," "Charley," and "Joe," the interchangeable naming of the archetypal "John Chinaman." Kamiyama speaks in varying scenes using broken English and a faux, unintelligible Asian language. The scene is played comically, pivoting on racial gags and the abjection of Chinese food. As the accented Beppo continues to insist on "ham and eggs," his American companion opens the restaurant's menu to read off the names of Chinese dishes using a mock Asian accent. Yellowvoice, in this instance, is performed by both Kamiyama and the American character. The scene ends with Beppo calling Kamiyama "stupid" for his seeming incomprehensibility, a gesture made comical by the narrative development of Beppo himself as a naive (white) foreigner. Reminiscent of *The Jazz Singer* (1927), the accented Scandinavian "becomes American," or something closer to it, through his racial distance from Kamiyama.

Similarly moving from his role as translator and host of the Japanese version of *King of Jazz*, Komai performed yellowvoice in several early American talkies. In films like *Welcome Danger* (1929) and the part-talkie *Chinatown Nights* (1929), Komai donned exaggerated accents and varying voice effects that denoted Asian otherness and abjection. His vocal soundings in the films melded into other sonic effects like clanging gongs and musical instruments. Many of these racialized sounds were surplus to narrative dialogue, functioning to animate the film's atmosphere and mise-en-scène.

With cinema's sound transition, varying forms of speech and an actor's voice, style, and tenor of speaking emerged as essential components of character and narrative development. In a 1930 article from *Picture Play Magazine*, Caroline Bell describes the new importance of voices in the sound-era cinema. The author uses the term "vocal make-up" to address the ways that voices become central, if not the primary, means for crafting characterization and even the personalities of stars: "There are no vocal duplicates. Each voice has a distinctive coloration for acute ears, shall we in time elect our favorites by their voice personalities? Whose tones are natural? And how does an actor 'makeup' his voice? Certain voices soar with a lark-like poignancy, or sustain a vibrant depth, marking them immediately as soloists. . . . There is in Kay Johnson's voice a subtle refinement [while] Julia Frye reminds me of a Fourth of July celebration."[31] Speech or a style of speaking herein inflects individuality, the development and depth of character, and registers not only in casting but also across the star system. As Mary Beltran has noted, what emerges with the talkies is "a speaking style associated with middle class status and lack of identifiable ethnicity [that] came to be associated with desirable notions of American whiteness."[32] In other words, speech and characterization work in tandem, marking what is considered normal and desirable, standard and American.

In the same article, Bell offers particularly illuminating insight into the workings of yellowvoice:

> Voice make-up is part of preparatory work in characterization — lining, slanting, shadowing the voice, learning dialogue. Coaching is sometimes necessary in a foreign tongue, or instruction in accent. . . . The ability to capture and translate into English the weird fascinations of Oriental tongues flashed Myrna Loy from the decorative ensemble into the spot. Her method is to hear the language spoken, and note certain peculiarities; these characteristics she translates into the English dialogue, trimming her speeches with that piercing scream she has evolved. The result is a voice of mobile timbre, impressing a malignant, opalescence, weaving a fibrous, verbal spell. Analyzed, it follows a pattern, screeching a scheduled acceleration.[33]

Yellowvoice herein is a learned practice, made available to the white actress Myrna Loy by instruction. It is also a practice divorced from actual language. Yellowvoice is an artifice indexing neither realism nor authenticity. Even though Sojin Kamiyama and Tetsu Komai were Japanese, their roles as Chinese characters was a non sequitur. As Bell further explains, "Though Chinese is the most difficult language to learn, a single word being given dozens of different meanings by inflection, emphasis merely for drama being negligible, it is the easiest to simulate for the talkies. One merely chants pidgin jargon and singsong monotony."[34] Whereas the voice in sound-era cinema is keynote for character and subjectivity even beyond the screen, yellowvoice is not a voice at all. Within the racializing logic of the sonic color line, yellowvoice is essentially what Stoever describes as "noise," a constellation of unintelligible and incomprehensible sounds marking Otherness.[35]

Additionally, yellowvoice, as "easiest to simulate for the talkies," functions as a trick for the new medium. Alice Maurice has noted that early talkies used Black voices and performance to offset the early sound cinema's technological vulnerability and limitations. Early sound films essentially harkened back to the precinema days of vaudeville and minstrel shows and the use of low-level cinematic trickery, to mesmerize the viewer and obfuscate the cinema's fakery (made more obvious by the clunky technology of the newly sound-synchronized cinema).[36] Yellowvoice performs a similar function, offering a low-level cinematic trick taking us back to the racial spectacle of the silent era's screen Orientalism.

In making voices audible, the sound transition transformed the American film industry's casting and star system. Actors who had fared well in the silent era faced new racialized barriers in the new medium. In the silent era, Anna May Wong and Sessue Hayakawa were the most prominent of Asian stars in the American industry, embodying the visual markers of screen Orientalism. Yet, in sound era Hollywood, Wong and Hayakawa found that American film producers were less interested in casting them in early sound films, and their careers never reached the heights of their silent-era success. Hollywood's bid for a global and multilingual market in the sound era did not yield more complex on-screen representations for Asian actors. Indeed, they found their screen roles continuing to be delimited, if not even further marginalized by the new sonic field. As the film critic Larry Tajiri astutely observed, "The lack of stories precludes any possibility that a Japanese actor will rise to prominence on the sound stages of movieland."[37]

Before returning to Japan, the benshi Suisei Matsui, who had appeared in the Japanese version of *Paramount on Parade*, was enlisted to appear in the Hollywood film *Hell and High Water* (1933), which was also released under the title *Captain Jericho*. To write dialogue for the benshi's character, Joe Satsanuki, Paramount Studios hired Frank Watanabe as the "Japanese characterization writer." Watanabe was the name of a character in a popular radio program called *Frank Watanabe and the Honorable Archie*. On air from 1932 to 1939, the radio program riffed on the format of the *Amos 'n' Andy* show on air from 1928. The radio character Frank Watanabe was played by the white voice actor Eddie Holden, who performed the character as a stereotypical Japanese American houseboy by using broken English and a faux

Publicity photograph for Eddie Holden (a.k.a. Frank Watanabe) signed in pidgin English, "Sweet thinks at you please." Courtesy of John Schneider.

Asian accent. Holden not only popularized yellowvoice on the radio airwaves, but he also "advised Japanese actors [on] how to talk pigeon-English" in early sound films. For *Hell and High Water*, Paramount Studios hired Holden to not only write the benshi Matsui's dialogue but also, as one paper reported, teach him to sing and perform in the style of Frank Watanabe.[38]

Yellowvoice, in this instance, reverberated across the radio airwaves to the sound stages of Hollywood. The cinema in the sound transition drew on already established conventions, as yellowvoice traveled across one medium to another. With the white voice actor Holden's performance of yellowvoice on the radio, the referent was never far, even when not visible. On the cinematic screen and in the body of the benshi Matsui, yellowvoice was reattached to its signifying body.

Matsui was arguably one of the most well-known and distinguished benshi of the time. His pathways into Hollywood, as host for *Paramount on Parade* and then as yellowvoice performer in *Hell and High Water*, followed a well-traveled route in the sound era, as the similar trajectories of Sojin Kamiyama and Tetsu Komai attest. Hollywood's technological transformation relied on the racialized labor and vocal performances of Japanese actors and performers. Indeed, the transition was as much about amplifying national and racial difference as it was in making cinema audible.

Beyond the Studios: Independent Film Production and the Sound Transition

Japanese film production in the United States persisted into the transition to sound but also faced considerable challenges. Some Japanese film producers sought to adapt to the industry's rapid transformation by forming new production companies and charting a new course for Japanese-language filmmaking. Suisei Matsui and Sojin Kamiyama, as well as Sessue Hayakawa, made concerted efforts in Japanese sound film production. None did so successfully. Following his industry peers, the Chinese American cinematographer James Wong Howe also left the Hollywood studios to find a place in the new era of sound cinema. Unlike his contemporaries, however, Howe successfully produced a Japanese-language sound film. Made in 1930, *Chijiku o mawasuru chikara* was an independent film and likely the first Japanese American sound production in this era. The film is not only noteworthy because of its Japanese-language soundtrack but also because it was able to be screened for Japanese American audiences. Unlike the earlier era of Japanese filmmaking in the United States, *Chijiku o mawasuru chikara* found its way to Japanese American audiences. The film did so by tapping into the circuit of nontheatrical film exhibition set up for Japanese silent films. Buoyed by a burgeoning arts community in Los Angeles's Little Tokyo, as well as developing trends in amateur filmmaking, a new cinema began to emerge in the 1930s. With an expanded reception within Japanese American communities, Howe's film, along with the handful of Japanese American films produced in the 1930s, came closer to providing a cinema "by, for, and about" Asian Americans.

After working on *Hell and High Water*, the benshi Matsui shifted his sights to film production. His longtime involvement in the Japanese film industry, as well as his newly acquired experience as an actor in Hollywood, may have provided him with greater insight into the future of the film industry in both countries as filmmaking began to move toward synchronized sound. Toward that end, he purportedly set out to establish a "Japanese-American production unit . . . [for] producing pictures in Hollywood for American and Nippon audiences."[39] In this period of transition to sound, Kamiyama also planned to form his own company. After a short stint in Japan for work on a Shochiku production, Kamiyama intended to "return to America and then form an international talkie producing company in co-operation with American producers."[40]

Both Matsui and Kamiyama sought to fill a gap resulting from Hollywood studio's very modest interest in Japanese-language film productions. *Paramount on Parade*, *King of Jazz*, and *Happy Days* were some of the few Japanese-version films made by the major studios in the 1930s. Broadly, the American industry never made multilanguage-version films for the Japanese-language film market at the scale they did for the Spanish-language film market. Spanish-language film production became especially important for Hollywood when European countries began to enact protective legislation against American imports, making Hollywood films less competitive. Films made in the United States constituted anywhere from 80 to 95 percent of films screened in all Latin American nations. Hollywood, consequently, heavily invested in Spanish-language film productions in the 1930s, although the efforts were abandoned when these films failed to generate the kind of earnings necessary to justify the extra expense.[41] In contrast, Hollywood had never gained a significant foothold in Japan. As Hiroshi Kitomi notes, a reorganized Japanese film industry and star system contested Hollywoodization. Propelled by a "pure film" movement, Japanese with work experiences in Hollywood returned to Japan to adapt the industry according to Hollywood-style techniques and practices. The sound transition further diminished the American film industry's influence. "In prewar Japan," as Kitomi explains, "Hollywood was at best a prominent minority."[42]

Joining Matsui and Kamiyama in the search for an entryway into sound film production was Sessue Hayakawa. Having gained his success and stardom in the silent era, Hayakawa found himself marginalized with the industry's transition to sound. As one critic caustically wrote, "In all his years of stay in America, [Hayakawa] never learned to handle the language with any degree of proficiency."[43] After a seven-year sojourn in the United States, Hayakawa in 1929 returned to Japan. Shoring up his star power, industry connections, and Hollywood-earned capital, Hayakawa set out to establish a new film company that would specialize in the production of sound films. Calling it "Japan's new Hollywood," his intended company, a studio called Sessue Hayakawa Kokusai Eiga Kabushiki Kaisha, was to be built not in the United States but in Takarazuka, a city in Japan's Hyogo Prefecture. The studio was purportedly capitalized with 1,000,000 yen, with "50 prominent Japanese theatrical, literary and businessmen being stockholders in the corporation."[44] Hayakawa also intended to bring to Japan "a troupe of American actors, actresses and scenario writers, numbering about twenty, to begin preparations for production."[45]

Addressing inquiries into his plans, Hayakawa described his venture as "Hollywood in name only." While he intended "half [of the pictures] to be shot in Japan and the other half in America," his studio would tailor to the perceived moral concerns of Japanese audiences and "not include the sensations, the morals and the theme-songs of the Cinema Capital."[46] Assessing opportunities resulting from the Japanese film industry's more gradual sound transition, Hayakawa envisioned a modern studio adapted to technological transformation. "I return to my beloved Japan to interpret into motion pictures of the most modern type," Hayakawa stated, "including sound, technicolor, and the new fourth dimensional depths the traditional spirit of Japan."[47] Indeed, Hayakawa had ambitious plans to reaffirm and possibly to revive Japan's national cinema.

Despite his star power and transpacific capital, Hayakawa's planned production company did not materialize. News of Hayakawa's return to Japan set off protests. Newspapers reported that Kyokuto Remmei Kyokai, a nationalist labor organization based in Osaka, organized efforts to "keep [Hayakawa] from Japan . . . and [from establishing] a moving picture producing corporation for the production of talking films."[48] Abandoning his plans, Hayakawa instead signed a contract with Shochiku and then later returned to Hollywood to work alongside Anna May Wong in *Daughter of the Dragon* (1931).[49] Neither Hayakawa or the benshi Matsui or the actor Kamiyama were able to realize their aspirations for sound film production. Even with capitalization and industry connections, their would-be companies never materialized.

Looking to also bridge the sonic divide was James Wong Howe. Like Hayakawa, his successful career in silent-era filmmaking was abruptly halted by the sound transition. Howe left for China in 1929, and when he returned to Hollywood, he found that he could no longer obtain employment. The major studios wanted to hire cinematographers experienced with photographing sound pictures. Howe recounted in several interviews the many challenges of working during this volatile period of transformation. Technically, the boom microphones used with the early talkies often interfered with the key lighting, forcing him to adjust the lights as the sound equipment moved around and produced shadows. Though he understood these aspects of the camera, producers were, as Howe recalled, unwilling to hire him.[50] To be sure, cinematography as a profession was undergoing significant changes with the sound transition. According to Ronny Regev, the use of sound-on-disc technology between 1929 and 1931, by which action and sound were recorded simultaneously, required new production practices, in particular filming with multiple cameras. With the need for multicamera work, the size of camera crews increased and became subdivided. These changes eventually led to the professionalization of cinematography as "the director of photography" emerged as a managerial position distinguished from the mechanical work of camera operator and on par with the creative work of director and writer.[51] Howe would play a central role in professionalizing the field of cinematography; however, at the start of the sound era, he was working for the studios on a contract and freelance basis.

While temporarily thwarted in sound era Hollywood, Howe looked to prospects elsewhere and outside of the studio system. Trade papers note that in 1930 he joined efforts with a producer named Tom White to "make a series of Japanese talkers, using native actors from local and Frisco theatres."[52] White was formerly at Paramount Studios but left to set up his own film company in Monrovia, California. Hoping to seize a segment of the sound film market, his company was set up for producing "foreign language films for the foreign colonies of the United States—the Germans and Scandinavians of the Northeast, the Japanese of the Pacific Coast and the Mexicans and Spanish along the southern border."[53] Howe himself envisioned producing Chinese-language sound films in the United States, although it does not seem as though he was ever able to do so.[54]

These desires of Howe to produce and direct his own films, to work on independent features, and to use Asian languages in the sound medium may have been inspired by his trip to China in the late 1920s. According to Curtis Marez, Howe shot film while in China and intended to make a feature about working-class Chinese who lived in sampans. As a result of this work, Howe was named the chief technical adviser to the Nanjing government in its efforts to use film to unify China's diverse population. Marez argues that Howe's unmaterialized filmmaking aspirations and later Howe's approach to cinematographic techniques like deep-focus photography reflected his engagement with revolutionary Chinese nationalisms and the leftist and Popular Front politics of the 1930s Hollywood film industry.[55] This was also the period when Howe met (and later married) Sonora Babb, a radical writer and member of the Communist Party.[56] Other scholars like Gordon H. Chang and Mary Ting Yi Lui have illuminated Howe's largely unknown film production and directing efforts in the postwar era, revealing a career trajectory that expanded well beyond cinematography.[57]

In 1930, Howe, Tom White, and Teruo Mayeda collaborated to produce a ten-reel independent feature-length Japanese American sound film called *Chijiku o mawasuru chikara*. The film was produced under Mayeda's independent film company based in Los Angeles, Hollywood Nippon Talkie Company (also known as Japanese Talking Picture Company).[58] While it is unclear where and how the Chinese American cinematographer met Mayeda and formed this partnership, working behind the scenes in the film industry placed Howe in connection with a wide range of people and projects. His connections to international film work in China and the interracial and leftist networks of the film industry in the United States may have shaped Howe's working relationship between Hollywood and independent film production. In addition, Howe developed connections to the local arts scene in Los Angeles's Little Tokyo. According to Karin Higa, Howe was a frequent visitor to Toyo Miyatake's photography studio (233 1/3 East First Street), which became a hub in the 1920s for painters, poets, and photographers working in the fine arts. Like Sessue Hayakawa and the artist Takehisa Yumeji, Howe would "stop by and hang around."[59] Howe and Miyatake were also close associates and collaborators in a shared photographic practice. Moreover, Miyatake's studio was one site in a broader arts movement that included art associations like Shaku-so-sha and photography clubs like the Japanese Camera Pictorialists of California. These clubs and associations helped to foster a transpacific presence in "salon photography." Partly influenced by the nearby film industry, Miyatake and other Japanese American photographers of this period, according to Dennis Reed, cultivated a "modernist style" in photography.[60]

While no print of *Chijiku o mawasuru chikara* exists, the production credits list Howe as director, Thomas Joseph Hayashi as associate director, Wakaba Matsumoto as writer, and Helen Warwick as scenarist. The film featured a cast of relatively inexperienced Nisei actors, including Taruyo "Jack" Matsumoto and Ruth Washizu, the daughter of a prominent California agriculturalist and newspaper editor. The producer Mayeda even gave himself a bit role in the film. The film employed over a hundred actors, many from the local Japanese community.[61] According to trade papers, Howe deliberately cast nonactors because he preferred "the method of the great Russian directors in choosing types, to that of the Americans, who cast pictures almost wholly around some personality or star."[62]

Set in modern Japan, the film's plot revolves around a father's sacrifice and relationship to his son. Returning to Japan from studying abroad, the lead character Mitsuru Yoshii is betrayed by his wife and left to care for their son. Leaving his own career as a doctor behind, he takes a menial job as a janitor to support his son's aspirations. As the son prospers and experiences romance and success, the father "trudges along the road of life, tired, sick, yet proud and happy in his son's glories."[63] Sources note that *Chijiku o mawasuru chikara* resembled the plot of *Sorrell and Son* (1927), which Howe had previously worked on.[64] Intending to appeal to Japanese-language audiences, producers boasted that the film "surpasses the best in Japan in the matter of photography and continuity."[65] Howe himself described a scrupulous attention to the exterior and interior sets. While unable to shoot in Japan, Howe utilized the transpacific ethos present in Southern California, filming on location in the Japanese gardens of Los Angeles and Pasadena. In addition, he sought the so-called expertise of the Japanese American cast to "arrange each minute detail of the interior sets to conform to the best taste and tradition of their people."[66]

Scholars have noted that early sound films were often limited by the new apparatus of sound technology; many early talkies, for instance, were shot with a stationary camera and in long static takes to accommodate microphones and clunky recording equipment. In filming *Chijiku o mawasuru chikara*, Howe seems to have established a more dynamic visual field. Drawing on his experience and creativity as a silent-era cinematographer, Howe's outdoor shooting locations and elaborately designed sets may have signaled a cinematography unusual among sound films of the era. Indeed, several contemporaneous critics of *Chijiku o mawasuru chikara* make note of these features. "James Wong Howe's photographic ingenuity should not be overlooked," wrote one critic, "for much of the beauty of the [film] depends on his skill."[67]

The film's producers also took considerable measures to ensure the audibility of *Chijiku o mawasuru chikara*. The film's Japanese American associate director, Thomas Hayashi, was specifically tasked with "superintending the synchronization of Japanese dialogue." While several critics commended the film's "careful accuracy" in sound synchronization, still the accents of the Nisei actors and their nonstandard Japanese disrupted the film's attempted verisimilitude. Critics described the Japanese-language dialogue in *Chijiku o mawasuru chikara* as "garbled" and "drawing more laughs than the plot outline would indicate."[68] According to Fumiaki Itakura, the reception of *Chijiku o mawasuru chikara* was shaped by the imperial context of Japan and the association of regional dialects and nonstandard varieties of Japanese language as occupying lower status close to the "improper" Japanese spoken by non-Japanese imperial subjects in the colonies. Itakura notes that the commentary about the film's lack of "standard Japanese" situates the language environment of the immigrant community, and the Nisei in particular, as similarly lower in status.[69]

The film was further limited by its modest financing and inadequate production facilities. Mayeda capitalized Hollywood Nippon Talking Pictures with relatively minimal funds; the company's other planned film, *Annoying Age*, never materialized. Without adequate funds for *Chijiku o mawasuru chikara*'s budget, Howe used his own money to supplement the production costs. As a relatively new enterprise, the production facilities at the Monrovia lot lacked the extensive infrastructure and resources of the major Hollywood sound stages and studios. Newspapers described White's facility as a "hastily converted orange packing warehouse" and reported that "the members of the cast were often discouraged on account of the many obstacles that they had to face while the picture was being taken at the Monrovia Studio."[70]

With a first run in the United States, the film was released under a plethora of confusing English language titles: *The Strength to Turn the Globe*, *Turning the Earth's Axis*, *The Tragedy of Life*, *Eternal Passion*, and *The Inevitable Urge*. The film's circulation in the United States was hindered by inadequate equipment and limited venues capable of exhibiting sound films. *Chijiku o mawasuru chikara* initially debuted in spaces not exclusively catering to Japanese Americans, despite the producers' intention to release the film in "various cities of the Pacific Coast which have large Japanese populations."[71] The film had a prescreening at the "George Eastman company offices," where "several prominent Japanese members of filmland and members and families of the cast attended the showing."[72] Following this initial screening, the film booked short runs in Los Angeles at the Fox Brooklyn Theatre and the California Theatre (also known as Teatro Californio), which would become an epicenter for Mexican film culture and the exhibition of Spanish-language films in the 1930s.

Months after the release of this film, Japanese American community leaders were able to equip the Nishi Hongwanji (a Buddhist temple and community hall in Los Angeles) for exhibiting sound films. Demand by local Japanese for viewing *Chijiku o mawasuru chikara* had prompted organizers to "secure a portable talkie apparatus" from New York.[73] "Through the installation of this instrument," the *Rafu Shimpo* reported, "it will be possible to show any talkie film at the Hongwanji hall in the future. Because no Japanese hall had this machine, it was impossible to show this first Hollywood-made Japanese talkie in the local community. . . . Now that the talkie machine is in the community, the film can be shown exclusively to the Japanese."[74]

With the use of the new portable sound equipment, *Chijiku o mawasuru chikara* was able to follow along the nontheatrical exhibition circuit previously utilized to screen Japanese silent films in the United States. The film was picked up and distributed by Nichibei Kogyo Kaisha in Los Angeles. Organizers debuted the film in the "Guadalupe, California farming district" and intended to move the film along the same circuits of Japanese film exhibition, through "42 halls from San Diego to Vancouver." The film also purportedly had a circulation in Hawaii. Producers arrived in the islands in the 1930s with "five prints and two portable sound sets."[75] Moving further across the Pacific, *Chijiku o mawasuru chikara* then reached audiences in Japan when producer Tom White arrived with the film's leading player Jack Matsumoto, sixteen prints of the film, and four portable sound machines. Matsumoto was scheduled to make personal appearances at the film's exhibitions.[76] Another source noted that *Chijiku o mawasuru chikara* was exhibited at Paramount's Korakuza Theater in Osaka, Japan.[77]

Despite *Chijiku o mawasuru chikara*'s success in utilizing various networks of Japanese film circulation in the United States and abroad, Howe and others considered the film an abysmal failure. Critics in Japanese American newspapers said the "dialogue left much to be desired."[78] Playing off the film's English-language title *The Tragedy of Life*, Larry Tajiri described the film itself as a "distinct tragedy."[79] Thirty years later, Jack Jacobs made note of *Chijiku o mawasuru chikara* in an article about Howe in *Films in Review* but noted that Howe himself could not even remember the name of the film.[80] Even in today's published filmographies, *Chijiku o mawasuru chikara* is seldom acknowledged.

Nevertheless, *Chijiku o mawasuru chikara* holds a place as the earliest Japanese-language feature-length sound production made in the United States. The film also serves as a touchstone for a short wave of filmmaking that emerged later in the 1930s. Like Howe's film, these films were made for a Japanese American audience and thematized the concerns of the second generation, or American-born generation (thereby differing from the earlier period of filmmaking described in chapter 1). Significantly, this filmmaking was influenced not only by the local arts scene in Little Tokyo, of which Howe was a part, but also a growing trend in amateur filmmaking. According to Charles Tepperman, the 1930s was the heyday for nonprofessional filmmaking and amateur film production. Movie clubs, filmmaking contests, and trade magazines encouraged amateur film culture and a participatory filmmaking as an alternative to the commercial Hollywood film industry.[81]

Starting in the 1930s, Japanese Americans established and participated in amateur filmmaking and cinema clubs. Japanese working in Hollywood established the Fifty-Fifty Club in 1931 in Los Angeles for "the purpose of getting together once a month to share each others' knowledge of the motion picture industry." Hosting talks by "studio technicians," the Fifty-Fifty Club was purportedly "a club for *everybody* who is interested in the motion picture art." Harry A. Mimura, who worked in the camera department of United Artists, led the group, which included the actor Tetsu Komai as well as several Japanese who worked behind the scenes in Hollywood, Edie Imazu (Metro-Goldwyn-Mayer), K. Y. Ohara (Fox Studios), and K. Takamura (RKO Studios). Kazuo Takimura, from Japan's Nikkatsu Studio, also participated.[82] Other filmmaking clubs emerged in the later 1930s. In San Francisco, a rather remarkable amateur filmmaking club was established as a part of the San Francisco Japanese Camera Club. The Movie Club, as it was called, was created in 1938 and boasted of "organizing more than 1000 Japanese owners of 16-millimeter movie cameras." The amateur film club was headed by Bill Nakahara and Victor Yamakawa.[83] Other Japanese who were also a part of photography or camera clubs, like John Hirohata and George Miyao of the Sierra Camera Club of Sacramento, entered and competed in amateur filmmaking contests.[84]

In 1934, brothers Ikuo and Seuo Serisawa produced an amateur film called *Nisei Parade* (1934). The film was shot on 16 mm film, and unlike Howe's film, it was made without sound synchronization. With a meager budget, the film was produced in a makeshift studio located in Los Angeles's Little Tokyo. With production lasting for three months, the brothers purportedly had a "home-made dolly fashioned from pans . . . [and] a cutting room layout set up in their hotel room."[85] The film was five reels in length and included English and Japanese subtitles. The film's plot, according to one source, "centered on Jiro, one of the three Nisei who is employed in one of the many huge produce markets in Southern California, and who is torn between the choice of a career as a photographer necessitating years of study and his love for Sumi, the girl."[86]

Nisei Parade was the Serisawa brothers' only film. Seuo Serisawa was among a group of artists producing and showing work in the arts scene supported by associations like Shaku-so-sha. Like other working artists of this era, he had formal training, having attended the Otis Art Institute (founded as an adjunct to the Los Angeles Museum). He later became a successful painter. Ikuo Serisawa, who wrote the script, had experience working as a cameraman with Fox Moviefone in Tokyo. The brothers were the sons of the well-known artist Yoichi Serisawa.[87] Critics praised *Nisei Parade* for its cinematography. The film received an honorable mention from the *American Cinematographer*'s amateur filmmaking contest in 1935.[88] Despite its shoe-string budget, the film had substantial support in circulation and exhibition. Following the routes of Japanese films, *Nisei Parade* found an audience in churches and community halls and through sponsorship by organizations like the YMCA and local community groups.[89]

In the 1930s, independent producers established a company called Hollywood Japanese Picture Association. The studio was based in Los Angeles and produced at least five films, all of which were silent productions.[90] In 1933, they released *Taichi ni shitashimu* (1933), a film about the second generation aspiring to leave the farm for the city yet eventually experiencing regret and longing to return.[91] The screenplay was written by Jack Matsumoto, who worked on Howe's *Chijiku o mawasuru chikara* and who also produced or directed the company's other productions. *Iminchi no haha* (1936) was a film about the hardships of a typical Issei farmer and a Japanese picture bride. *Nobiyuku Nisei* (1936) was a film about a young Nisei who revolted from a dominating father by leaving the farm and pursuing a love affair with an American girl. All of Hollywood Japanese Picture Association's films revolved around rural and farming communities and thematized the "back-to-the-farm" movement that leaders in the community hoped might inspire the second generation.[92]

Similar to *Nisei Parade*, all of the productions from Hollywood Japanese Picture Association were shot on 16 mm gauge film. As Gregory Waller notes, the introduction of the 16 mm film format (along with the emergence of film schools) propelled the movement in amateur filmmaking. The film gauge was readily available as a moderately priced technology for recording and displaying motion pictures. Marketed as multipurpose, 16 mm film was often used for filmmaking for classroom use; its portable projectors made it easy to transport to varying locations. Waller also notes that the 1930s saw a "marked increase in the United States of 'foreign' and 'foreign language' films on 16mm."[93]

All of Hollywood Japanese Picture Association's films were 16 mm silent productions utilizing English and Japanese subtitles. Most of the casts featured novice actors, mostly from the local community. Because the film was produced without sound and audible dialogue, the casting call for *Nobiyuku Nisei* in 1934 specifically noted that no knowledge of the Japanese language was required.[94] At a preview screening of *Iminchi no haha* at the Los Angeles residence of the consul Tomokazu Hiro, the film's director, Jack Matsumoto, even stepped out to act as the benshi, likely an exceptional moment as most of the films' exhibition runs did not feature a benshi.[95] While both the silent medium and silent film practices remained in play during the transition period, critics did take note of the inaudibility of these independent Japanese American films. Observing *Nobiyuku Nisei*'s moralizing plot and overuse of subtitles, one reviewer exclaimed, "When are we going to see a Nisei talkie?"[96]

Whither Benshi?

Silent-era practices persisted not only in the film production by Japanese in the United States but also in the context of film exhibition. In 1941, when a Japanese film was exhibited at a Buddhist temple in Reedley, California, as a benefit show intended to raise funds for the Young Men and Women's Buddhist Association, it was the name of the benshi, not the film's title, that was highlighted in the local newspaper.[97] The lingering presence of the benshi into the early 1940s suggests that silent film exhibition practices also endured well after the development of synchronized sound. While most American theaters were wired for sound by the late 1920s, Los Angeles's Fuji Kan did not exhibit sound films until 1935 when proprietors installed a Western Electric sound system.[98] The film historian William M. Drew even speculated that the Fuji Kan was one of the last venues in Los Angeles for silent film exhibition.[99] Indeed, silent-era viewing practices persisted within the context of Japanese film exhibition in the United States. The sound transition did not eradicate the silent-era practices; nor did it represent a swift and all-encompassing transformation of the medium. Instead, Japanese filmgoers in Los Angeles met the coming of sound with considerable disinterest, misapprehension, and even outright refusal.

Across the United States and elsewhere, the synchronization of sound displaced the live musical and performative components of the silent-era cinema and facilitated the demise of the neighborhood theater.[100] These developments, however, were not unchallenged. As James P. Kraft notes, the advent of synchronized sound in the United States was especially devastating for theater musicians and orchestras as it coincided with the start of the Great Depression. In response, film theater musicians who were organized under the American Federation of Musicians (AFM) waged a multipronged campaign to resist the sound transition and protect workers. Union organizers for the most part deployed trade union tactics, such as strikes and boycotts.[101] In addition to the challenges by musicians, audiences were not uniformly enthusiastic about the new so-called talkies. As Henry Jenkins notes, signs of regional resistance to early sound films came from small town audiences. While the major studios sought to overcome the early technical challenges of the sound medium by using well-established Broadway performers like Eddie Cantor (the star of *The Jazz Singer*), some audiences, particularly outside of the northeastern United States, were often unfamiliar with stage performers and resented the displacement of their favorite silent film stars. Such sentiments were further exacerbated by rising nativism.[102]

In Japan, the benshi continued to exert their considerable influence on Japanese film exhibition. Like the theater musicians in the United States, some of the benshi were unionized and organized campaigns against the encroachment of sound technology and its impact on their employment and livelihoods. When the American musical short *Marching On* arrived at the Musashino-kan in 1929, the musicians and later the benshi from other leading theaters went on strike. In 1932, benshi at the major studio Nikkatsu also organized a strike after learning about the possible start of sound film production. The strike "hit the company so hard that its studios were closed down and foreign films were booked to fill out its distribution commitments." With the strong influence of the benshi, theaters in Japan were slow to the conversion as they could utilize "the less expensive all-talkies in the form of the benshi."[103] In conjunction with the uneven development of theaters wired for sound, the Japanese film industry continued to produce silent films well after the advent of sound technology. Silent films were made by Japanese film studios until the late 1930s, and together these developments prolonged Japan's sound transition.

Due to their continual production in the Japanese film industry, Japanese silent films remained in circulation in the United States throughout the 1930s. For example, the silent film *Konoko no michi* (1933) had a first-run exhibition at the Fuji Kan in the same year it was released by Nikkatsu. A benshi named K. Kunimoto was scheduled to perform, according to newspapers, "the 'talkie' end of the feature."[104] Furthermore, the early Japanese sound films that did make their way to the United States often received a less than enthusiastic reception. *Furusato* (1930) was one of Japan's earliest sound films, produced in 1930 by Nikkatsu and directed by the famed Kenji Mizoguchi. The film was perhaps more accurately a "part talkie" rather than a fully synchronized sound film. Like *The Jazz Singer*, *Furusato* featured a limited use of synchronized sound, focused primarily on music, not dialogue. As Iwamoto notes, the producers of both films cast well-known singers whom they hoped would detract audiences' attention away from the technological limitations of the new medium. Both films similarly were melodramas featuring a singer impresario and retained silent-era elements like intertitle cards and pantomime acting. In the case of *Furusato*, according to Iwamoto, "voices sounded unnatural as a result of such factors as poor microphone reception and the necessity for actors to continuously modulate the loudness of their voices in accordance with their distance from the microphone."[105]

Furusato debuted in the United States in 1931 in Los Angeles's California Theatre (or Teatro Californio).[106] Larry Tajiri attended the film's premiere and wistfully recalled "the exactly 32 persons in the theater."[107] Steve Taniyoshi, another local Japanese American critic, also made note of the film's failure to gain a Western audience, citing "the language barrier and the slow tempo . . . [as] stumbling blocks for the Nipponese producer in his bid for the occidental market."[108] The underwhelming reception for the early Japanese sound film was also reported by *Motion Picture Herald*, which calculated an annual gross of $1,000.[109] Japanese American audiences had a chance to see the film in Hawaii a few years later, although no comment was recorded about the audience reception.[110]

The arrival of early Japanese sound films in the United States was met with skepticism and, at times, harsh opprobrium. When *Hanayome no negoto* (1933) screened in Hawaii, one critic wrote, "It doesn't compare in mechanical perfection. . . . The Japanese have a long way to go yet before they can reach the degree of perfection of Hollywood products." Moreover, "none of the players give any outstanding performance," continued the critic. "Even Miss Tanaka is below par. She's far better as a silent artiste. Her voice is sometimes squeaky."[111] In 1935, Fuji Kan exhibited another early sound film, *Uramachi no kokyogaku* (1935). "The production is without doubt a considerable improvement over the ordinary run of the talking pictures of Nippon that are being shown here recently from the point of sound technique," wrote the critic in attendance, "and the departure from the slow tempo that has been one of the faults of Japanese films." Moreover, the most compelling aspects of the film were the Nisei actress, Fumi Kawabata, and the "tap and toe dances taken during [an] actual performance in the Hibiya Park auditorium," which brought the film "on par with the popular musical stage revue films or Hollywood."[112]

James Hamada reviewed *Bukinaki hitobito* (1936) and noted that while the actor Noburu Kiritachi had "a pleasant voice," the film was ultimately an "old fashioned melodrama of the silent pictures vintage."[113] Hamada delivered even harsher criticism for *Tsuma yo bara no yo ni* (1935), which was released in the United States under the title *Kimiko*. The film debuted in the

United States with positive praise and recognition from art house critics.[114] Hamada, however, believed "it would have been funnier had she [Sachiko Chiba] copied Claudette Colbert and showed her leg instead, but that would have been too much for the Japanese censors. That 'thumbing' incident is absolutely unnecessary, for the players were waiting for a taxi, not trying to get a lift. It was undoubtedly put in because producers wanted to show American style, and to tell the cock-eyed world that they had seen 'It Happened One Night.'" Hamada also made note of the film's technical challenges, particularly a scene with a "dialogue mix-up." "The producers were probably drunk when they made those scenes," Hamada caustically wrote, "for I hate to think that they would seriously indulge in such stupidity."[115]

The financial cost of the sound transition placed a significant burden on Japanese film exhibitors in the United States. Even if audiences were receptive to the new medium, benshi remained a vital aspect of film performance to many filmgoers. Exhibitors managed the transition to sound by continuing some aspects of the silent film era's sonic environment while exhibiting sound pictures. In 1932, for instance, the Fuji Kan exhibited a film called *Komori uta* (1930), a sound film produced by the Japanese film studio Teikine using Eastphone technology. The advertisement for the sound film's exhibition at Fuji Kan listed Suimin Matsui as the accompanying benshi.[116] In other words, this early Japanese sound film was exhibited in the mode of a silent film accompanied by live performance and narration by a benshi. Presenting early talkies with a benshi was also evident in nontheatrical venues. In the summer of 1935, a local church group in San Francisco screened the sound films *Sado jowa* (1934) and *Ume miru koro*, not in a theater but "in the open air," as the papers put it. The papers noted the accompanying benshi by name, Charley Hiyoshigawa Shugetsu, explicitly announcing his performance alongside the sound films.[117] At a community hall in Dinuba, California, the local papers also reported that "Suimin Matsui will act as benshi . . . for pictures that will be vitaphones," a reference to early sound technology using sound on disc.[118]

The exhibition of early Japanese sound films accompanied by a benshi carried on the silent-era format. Despite the novelty of sound technology, critics and audiences continued to appreciate the contribution of the benshi, making benshi narration indispensable through the 1930s. Rather than disappear with the arrival of sound technology, as might have been predicted, the benshi continued to stage their acts to enhance the new features. The benshi not only endured but also creatively adapted their performances in the new era of synchronized sound.

The pairing of benshi with sound films in the United States is not entirely surprising given their endurance in Japan. As Abe Markus Nornes notes, the first sound films exhibited in Japan were American productions in the English language. The benshi maintained their roles alongside the screen, often serving not only as lecturers and narrators but also as translators. This practice continued into the early years of the sound transition in Japan. In performing alongside early sound pictures, the benshi would often reserve their commentary for the moments of silence on the soundtrack. Some benshi used what came to be called *kirisetsu*, or "cut-in explanations," in which the projectionists would be cued to cut off the sound to make space for the benshi's interjection. Some prominent benshi retained their own control of the volume at their podiums or used microphones to "put themselves on even ground with the electronic amplification of the sound tracks."[119] However, in contrast to the Japanese settings where benshi translated English-language American productions, the benshi in the United States performed alongside early Japanese sound films featuring Japanese-language dialogue. The appeal and endurance of the benshi in the American context cannot be reduced to acts of translation.

Throughout the 1930s and leading up to the outbreak of the Pacific wars (the Sino-Japanese War and, eventually, World War II), the benshi not only persisted but also gained greater popularity. Indeed, the benshi's role seemed reenergized to accompany propaganda films and newsreels about Japan's war efforts that made their way to the United States. The benshi Namiemon (mentioned in chapter 2) gained a considerable reputation for his presentations of Japanese war films. In 1938, Namiemon brought Tomotako Tasaka's famous war film *Gonin no sekkohei* (1938) to audiences throughout California. Considered to be one of Japan's most significant war films, *Gonin no sekkohei* was filmed in Manchuria and portrayed the struggles of Japanese soldiers during the Sino-Japanese War. The film follows five scouts who embark on a search mission for enemy soldiers in the harsh terrain of northern China. While the film features spectacular and rousing battle scenes, critics have also characterized the film as more humanistic than other propaganda films of the era, acknowledging its realism and portrayal of the mundane aspects of soldiers' lives.[120]

Namiemon took *Gonin no sekkohei* on the road in California throughout the late 1930s. Traveling up and down the coast, the benshi set up exhibitions of the film all over the Golden State, including in Visalia, Dinuba, Parlier, Monterey, San Jose, Oakland, Lodi, Suisun, Newcastle, and San Juan.[121] The film also had a run at a theater in Honolulu in February 1938.[122] The film was promoted in local advertisements as "award-winning" and "approved by Imperial

Headquarters." As a sound film, Namiemon's role was as a promoter and exhibitor, although one advertisement for a screening in Monterey explicitly noted, "The benshi will be Namiemon," suggesting that he may have also provided interpretation.[123] Throughout the 1930s, Namiemon was responsible for exhibiting countless Japanese war films, including *Aa Nakamura taii* (1931), an early war film about the martyred Japanese colonel Nakamura Shintaro, which Namiemon brought to audiences in Gilroy and Salinas, California, in 1932.[124]

Filmmaking in support of Japan's imperial ambitions and war efforts was an important part of Japan's cinema. With the escalation of the Sino-Japanese War, the Japanese government established greater controls over the production of film for purposes of propaganda. Earlier wartime films that contained humanistic elements like *Gonin no sekkohei* gave way to ultranationalistic and militaristic films encouraged by the state. In 1939, the Japanese government established stringent film production codes, following the model of Nazi Germany. Officials promoted and later mandated the production of films to promote "national policy." In addition, Japan's wartime filmmaking migrated overseas to establish propaganda film production in the occupied territories of Manchuria, Korea, China, Taiwan, Thailand, Indonesia, and the Philippines.[125]

In the United States, Namiemon's enthusiasm and support of Japan's wartime ambitions and allies were unbridled. However, just a few months before the attack on Pearl Harbor, Namiemon was apprehended by the police in Bellingham, Washington. After fellow Japanese reported their activities to the authorities, Namiemon and his assistant Kazuo Kato were detained for exhibiting "a German war film accompanied by commentaries in the Japanese language." The police eventually released Namiemon and Kato, but they confiscated the Nazi film. The film had been exhibited several times in Seattle by Namiemon before reaching Bellingham.[126]

Other benshi were also instrumental in introducing Japanese war films to audiences in the United States. Muneo Kimura was involved in exhibiting *Nishizumi senshachoden* (1940), another of Japan's most well-regarded and popular war films. The film was featured in a two-day program in San Jose, California, in which, according to papers, "a large crowd [was] expected on both nights with circulars and tickets given a wide distribution."[127] Suimin Matsui traveled to a local hall in Woodland, California, to present *Bakuon* (1939), a propaganda film that depicted the story of a Japanese village supporting military airplanes. Interestingly, the exhibition was held as a fund-raiser to support "Woodland draftees now serving in the various army camps of the United States, including Illinois, Texas, Missouri, Alaska and California."[128]

Namiemon takes his war films on the road to Gilroy, Watsonville, Salinas, Isleton, Walnut Grove, and Sacramento, California. The advertisement also states, "Come and shed tears of earnest patriotism and solidarity with your fellow countrymen!" *Japanese-American News*, March 2, 1932.

Throughout the late 1930s, Japanese war propaganda newsreels and shorts were also in wide circulation in the United States, often billed alongside feature-length narrative films. With the Japanese invasion of Manchuria, filmmakers with Japan's news media organizations began to film on location. Major film studios such as Shochiku and Nikkatsu soon followed and set up units for producing newsreels. By the late 1930s, several companies merged to form the Nihon News Film Company. As Peter High notes, most news filmmakers kept in tune with government policy. With Japan's entry into World War II, the Japanese government exerted even greater influence in the country's media and film industry.[129] Newsreels and documentary footage of the 1937 Battle of Shanghai garnered extensive circulation in the United States, including in Salinas and Turlock, California.[130] In the small town of French Camp, California, the newsreel footage of the Shanghai bombings was exhibited with no admission charge at the local Japanese grammar school with a benshi named Matsumoto providing interpretation.[131]

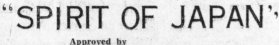

Namiemon Presents

GONNIN NO SEKKOHEI

A DYNAMIC WAR PICTURE

A NIKKATSU PRODUCTION

Awarded Highest Honor In
Italy by the International
Film Council in Italy

The Outstanding Japanese Film
Hit of the Decade Depicting

"SPIRIT OF JAPAN"

Approved by
Imperial Headquarters
Home Ministry
Educational Ministry

July 26 — Newcastle	July 30 —San Jose
July 28 —San Juan	July 31-Aug. 1—Visalia
July 29 —Monterey	Aug. 2 —Dinuba
Aug 3-4—Parlier	

Advertisement for
Gonnin no sekkohei.
New World Sun,
June 26, 1938.

The arrival of synchronized sound neither eliminated nor drastically abated the work of the benshi. In the context of Japan's wartime mobilization, their roles as exhibitors and explainers gained renewed urgency as an eager public in the United States yearned for the stories and images of wars that remained—at least for the time being—far away.

THE PERSISTENCE OF SILENT-ERA PRACTICES marks a disjuncture in cinema's shift to synchronized sound. The practices and publics that had for so long shaped the filmgoing experience did not just immediately disappear. It is often described that the sound era further consolidated the film industry, concentrating power from the top to the bottom. Studio conglomerates further integrated the film industry, taking control not only of production but also of the sphere of distribution and exhibition. From this vantage, Japanese Americans were out of sync with sound cinema's transition. Film exhibition by Japanese remained dispersed, not consolidated; it was catered to the audience, not the shareholder. And so long as audiences yearned to see them, the benshi and the show would go on.

CHAPTER FOUR

Filipinos Always Welcome

Japanese-Owned Theaters and
Working-Class Migrant Culture

In 1948 Shigeaki Hayashino found himself in front of the California Supreme Court in a case that sought to challenge his lease of several movie theaters under the Alien Land Laws.[1] Significantly, the attorney for Emil Palermo, the litigant who had brought the suit against the Japanese entrepreneur, was particularly interested in who the actual patrons of the theaters were. "You know, do you not," the attorney queried, "that a very large portion of the business of your Star Theater has always been the Filipino people, has it not?" To this question, the usually straightforward Hayashino responded evasively, neither admitting nor denying the large-scale Filipino patronage of his theaters. He simply said, "We have many, many kind of trade in that theater."[2] Hayashino's reticent response belied the vigor and enthusiasm with which he and other Japanese proprietors courted Filipino patronage in the decades leading up to World War II. Located in the heart of Little Manila in Stockton, California, the Japanese proprietor's theaters were an integral part of Filipino public life in the 1930s. Japanese-owned theaters defied the color line, not only eschewing the logic of "Positively No Filipinos Allowed" but also in cohering an all-Filipino-film viewing public. Indeed, it was in the Japanese-owned theaters where audiences in California had their first viewings of Filipino films. Throughout the 1930s, the Japanese-owned theater emerged as a site for the circulation of films from the Philippines and, in particular, sound films in Tagalog.

This chapter explores Japanese film culture in the United States at its edges. Japanese-operated moving-picture theaters and venues in the United States had a patronage that extended well beyond a Japanese immigrant audience. In his 1933 study, the sociologist Edward K. Strong noted that, while most Japanese businesses in Walnut Grove, California, depended on the patronage of their fellow countrymen, the Japanese-owned moving-picture theater was "patronized by all the races."[3] Indeed, film theaters operated by Japanese proprietors increasingly relied on a working-class, multiracial, and heterogeneous filmgoing public. What do the non-Japanese working-class film audiences in Japanese-owned theaters tell us about the broad appeal of

Japanese-supported film culture? How do these cinematic exchanges entangle nation-oriented assumptions of diasporic cinema? With their population dramatically rising after 1924, Filipino workers represented a significant group of consumers for Japanese businesses writ large and film theaters in particular. Japanese and Filipinos grew increasingly interconnected in the intervening years as immigration laws and demographic changes transformed both communities. These interrelations were shaped by uneven and unequal relationships to capital as well as the colonial relationship between Japan and the Philippines. Throughout the 1930s, Filipino participation in the public culture of the region was shaped by the earlier arrival of Japanese and their economic presence. Eiichiro Azuma argues that the class antagonisms between Japanese proprietors and farm owners and Filipino workers presaged a growing nationalism among Japanese communities in the United States in the 1930s: "Issei nationalism had another dimension beyond identification with the Japanese state, that of constructing a localized concept of 'race' . . . rooted in their experience of living in a racial hierarchy in the delta."[4] Hayashino's reticence about his theater's large Filipino audience was in part a response to these mutually constitutive relations of class, race, and nationality.

Not only did Japanese own or operate many of the theaters patronized by Filipinos, but they also played a role in exhibiting films produced in the Philippines for U.S.-based audiences. Filipino filmgoers in California and Washington (and similarly in Hawaii) had some of their first encounters with viewing Filipino films abroad at the Japanese-owned moving-picture theater. This chapter resituates the Japanese-owned theater as a site for the multidirectional movement of films across and between the Asia Pacific. In moving across national borders, Filipino films circulated extensively and made their way to audiences via alternative film circuits and independently owned theaters. These film-viewing sites served as a focal point for the formation of a Filipino public culture at a pivotal time in the United States. Throughout the region, a new politics began to materialize as Filipino laborers and civic leaders sought to politicize their purchasing power and transform their public identities. Film exhibitions linked these cultural politics in the United States to a public discourse on national cinema that was emerging in the Philippines. With the arrival of sound technology, Filipino films contributed to an "imagined community" that brought together a diverse constituency in the Philippines and beyond.[5] The multilayered circulation routes of Filipino films via Japanese-operated film networks in the United States offers a complex picture of transpacific film culture. It is a view of the cinema moving across borders yet also reproducing the national at the scales of both the local and the regional. Thus, it is rethinking national cinemas that also need not tell a singular story of reimagining national identities and communities.

A Theater for "All the Races"

Following the pathways of labor and immigration, Japanese theater proprietors not only established film venues in major cities but also turned their sights to the growing towns around the region's agricultural and industrial development, or what Carey McWilliams called "the factories in the fields."[6] Theaters operated by Japanese not only provided entertainment but also emerged as multifaceted institutions serving the varying needs of immigrant and working-class patrons. As mentioned in earlier chapters, Japanese-owned theaters like the Nippon Theatre in Sacramento served a clientele of migrant workers returning to the city after the cycles of seasonal employment. Even in its original 1908 architectural construction, the theater was built to enable the partitioning of the space for film viewing, recreational activities, and for lodging. By the 1930s, the Nippon Theatre was operated by Soichi Nakatani and began catering to Filipinos, a population that had become a significant work force in the region's agricultural sector. To promote the Nippon Theatre, Nakatani ran regular advertisements in the *Philippine Examiner* and the *Filipino Pioneer*, two newspapers that circulated extensively in California. Promising double features and daily program changes, his advertisement for Nippon Theatre explicitly informed Filipinos of their open doors by plainly stating in a print headline, "Filipinos Always Welcome."[7]

The courting of Filipino patronage by Nakatani and other Japanese theater owners presented Filipinos with an avenue to circumvent, at least nominally, racial restriction and segregation elsewhere in the city. Throughout the Pacific coast, Filipinos, like other racialized groups, were subjected to the color line. Faced with "Positively No Filipinos Allowed" pronouncements in housing, work, and public accommodations, Filipinos were very familiar with the region's de jure and de facto racial exclusion. As colonial subjects of the United States, Filipinos were legally designated "noncitizen U.S. nationals" under the Treaty of Paris (1900). This juridical construction situated all persons from the Philippines in a liminal status between alien and citizen. On the one hand, this status differentiated Filipinos from "aliens ineligible for citizenship" and from all persons subjected to immigration restrictions passed by the federal government in 1924. On the other hand, Filipinos were also subject to exclusion from naturalization citizenship based on racial ineligibility. Until the 1946 amendment to the Nationality Act of 1940, U.S. courts ruled against granting naturalized citizenship to Filipinos on racial grounds.[8] These acts of racial exclusion were exacerbated in a series of anti-Filipino riots in Washington and California starting from 1926 and reaching a climax at the height of the Depression and with the death of a Filipino farm worker, Fermin Tobera, in Watsonville, California.[9]

In the colonial context, the subjection to U.S. racial exclusion contradicted the expectations for social equality held by many Filipinos who were educated in U.S. colonial institutions in the Philippines. Among those who left during the American colonial period was Mariano Angeles, an Ilocano from the coastal region of Luzon, who came to the United States shortly after completing high school. In the Philippines, his family had hosted American missionaries in their home, and the majority of his schoolteachers were American women from the Midwest. In recounting his education in the Philippines, he recalled, "Democracy and equality, justice and freedom you know, those are the American teachings there."[10] American policies and institutions of "benevolent assimilation" passed on significant lessons to Angeles. Moreover, these colonial lessons informed the perceptions that many Filipinos held prior to their arrival in the United States. When Filipino workers unionized in the 1930s, for example, they did so under the aegis of equal wages, individual rights, and the desire to emulate American wage standards. These expectations for social equality were also experienced in the public cultures that Filipinos encountered in the United States.

By welcoming Filipinos, Japanese theater owners countered the racialized logic of exclusion by seizing on the equalizing promises of consumerism. Businesses in cities like Stockton actively sought Filipino patronage within a racially segmented marketplace. As Mina Roces notes, it was commonplace practice for many businesses to explicitly tailor their appeal to Filipino patronage and a sense of equal treatment. Businesses advertised their services in Filipino spaces and responded specifically to Filipino desires for consumer goods, recreational and other marketplace commodities. Businesses also did more than offer alternative sites to access consumption; in some instances, they explicitly denoted the racial discrimination experienced by Filipino consumers by promising them in their advertisements "courteous treatment."[11]

While these forms of consumer inclusion created opportunities for Filipinos to participate more broadly in the public culture, attracting Filipino dollars was also highly profitable and advantageous for proprietors. As consumers, Filipinos represented a captive market as they were not only barred from many white-owned establishments but also had lower rates of their own entrepreneurship in comparison to Chinese and Japanese immigrants, whom had arrived decades earlier and ascended the agricultural ladder. As the late historian Dawn Mabalon notes in *Little Manila Is in the Heart: The Making of the Filipina/o Community in Stockton, California* (2013), Japanese and Chinese residents had an almost total monopoly on neighborhood businesses in Little Manila. Stockton's Japanese managed more than fifty-four single-residency occupancy-style walk-up hotels and also ran most of the drugstores, restaurants, dentist offices, midwife businesses, beauty shops, florists, barbershops, soda fountains, and, importantly, motion-picture theaters.[12]

For Japanese, Filipinos were an especially important consumer and worker base for their commercial businesses and farms. With immigration from Japan halted, the arrival of Filipinos to the United States revitalized many Japanese immigrant communities and economies. Exempt from immigration exclusion because of the Philippines' status as a U.S. colonial territory, Filipino immigration surged after 1924. Census figures note the Filipino population in 1930 rose to 45,208 in the continental United States and 63,052 in Hawaii. Approximately 85 percent were under the age of thirty while 93 percent were male and 77 percent were single.[13] The 1924 Immigration Act, which established a quota system based on national origins, essentially nullified the prior Gentleman's Agreement. The immigration law not only barred the entry of merchants, teachers, and students from Japan but also ended the ability of Japanese already in the United States to send for their wives, children, or parents. Japanese immigration to the United States, consequently, dwindled to a negligible 3,503 between the years 1931 and 1950. Thus, while Filipino immigration to the United States dramatically rose after 1924, immigration from Japan had virtually ended.[14]

Throughout the 1930s, Japanese and Filipinos grew increasingly interconnected as their livelihoods became bound together by labor and commerce. While these interconnections represented some level of cooperation, they also entailed significant conflicts. These dynamics came to a head when Filipinos began boycotting and organizing against Japanese-owned businesses. In 1930, Filipinos led a three-month-long boycott of Japanese businesses in Stockton in response to outrage within the Japanese community over an interracial marriage between a young Nisei woman and a Filipino man.[15] The boycott was followed by a labor strike targeting Japanese celery growers and their white landlords in 1936. When Japanese farm owners moved to break a strike led by the Filipino Agricultural Laborers' Association (FALA), Filipinos retaliated again by boycotting Japanese businesses. According to Eiichiro Azuma, Filipino organizers carried anti-Japanese placards into town and

LINCOLN
THEATER

Phone 724

28 S. EL DORADO ST.
STOCKTON CALIF.

S. Hayashino, Mgr.

and

NIPPON
THEATRE

328 L STREET
SACRAMENTO, CALIF.

S. Nakatani, Mgr.

Flipinos Always
Welcome

Program Change
Every Day
With

BEST DOUBLE
FEATURES
and
Selected Short
Subjects

Soichi Nakatani's Nippon Theatre and
Shigeaki Hayashino's Lincoln Theatre
advertising "Filipinos Always Welcome."
Filipino Pioneer, July 30, 1938.

On the occasion of the Seventh Anniversary of the Philippine Examiner, allow me to take this opportunity of extending my most cordial Greetings to the Filipino people.

May your organ have its continued success as in the past, and thanking you for your continued patronage.

Star & Lincoln

Theatres

H. S. HAYASHINO, Manager

STOCKTON   CALIFORNIA

Hayashino providing the touch of a neighborhood ethnic theater. *Philippine Examiner*, October 15, 1938.

"forcibly dragged Filipino customers out of Japanese stores and talked others out of patronizing them." Azuma argues that the conflict with Filipinos redirected white hostility and heightened a growing nationalism among Japanese in the United States in the 1930s. Particularly in California, Japanese elites and leaders used the construction of Filipino degeneracy and "sexual menace" to articulate their own moral superiority and undermine the growing labor militancy of Filipino workers.[16] Filipinos, in turn, responded by drawing together their purchasing power and labor organizing.

Shigeaki Hayashino operated several theaters in California catering to Filipino patrons. Hayashino immigrated to the United States in 1907 from Nara, Japan, settling first in Seattle and earning a living as a domestic servant while putting himself through school. Relocating to Stockton after 1926, Hayashino was able to pursue a pathway toward upward mobility as a motion-picture theater entrepreneur. Like many Japanese businessmen, he was an upstanding member of the community, participating actively in the Japanese Association and later becoming an officer in the Military Virtue Society of

North America. Like other Japanese-owned businesses, his theaters would later become sites of Filipino boycotting during the war years.

Located in the hub of Stockton's Little Manila, Hayashino operated the Star Theatre (26 E. Market Street), Lincoln Theatre (28 S. El Dorado Street), and Imperial Theatre (19 S. El Dorado Street).[17] Listed in city municipal directories and Japanese immigrant business directories, Hayashino ran these theaters throughout the 1930s with a group of Japanese business associates under the name Stockton Theatres, Incorporated.[18] In a court filing, one observer described the Japanese proprietor's theaters as frequently packed with Filipino audiences who "see the same film three or four times."[19]

Like Nippon Theatre's Soichi Nakatani (who was also a close associate of Hayashino's), Hayashino advertised his theaters extensively in Filipino American newspapers. His advertisements targeted a Filipino audience by brandishing monikers like "A Favorite of Filipinos."[20] In one printed advertisement, the Japanese proprietor directed a personal address to Filipino filmgoers, indicating his larger support for both the newspaper and the community: "On the occasion of the Seventh Anniversary of the *Philippine Examiner*, allow me to take this opportunity of extending my most cordial Greetings to the Filipino people. May your organ have its continued success as in the past, and thanking you for your continued patronage."[21] The advertisement, which promoted both the Star Theatre and the Lincoln Theatre, provided the personal touch of a neighborhood theater attuned to the local specificity of audiences and the community's consumer politics. Further endearing these sentiments was the inclusion of the Japanese proprietor's own signature, "H.S. Hayashino, Manager."[22]

Film theaters operated by Japanese were an ambivalent site, exemplifying class antagonisms yet also facilitating a public culture for many Filipinos in the 1930s. Peter Jamero in his 2004 memoir, *Growing Up Brown*, remembered his experiences at Hayashino's theaters in particular. From the time of their arrival from the Philippines, Jamero's family migrated frequently until they finally settled in the Yamato Colony, the farming settlements established by Japanese farmer-colonists (and also the subject of early Japanese filmmaking as described in chapter 1). Peter's father was a labor contractor, and in exchange for supplying Japanese farmers with Filipino workers, the Jamero family was provided rent-free housing in the Yamato Colony. Traveling fifty miles across the agricultural beltway from Livingston to Stockton, Jamero's father recruited workers for the Japanese-owned farming settlements. At other times, they headed to Stockton to experience the city life. As Jamero recalled, "We usually accompanied Papa to Stockton on the Fourth of July since he also recruited workers on this day. Stockton was an exciting place in the 1930s and 1940s. Our uncles were generous with their recently earned asparagus money and eager to treat us to Chinese food at the Gan Chy restaurant or take us to a movie at the Star or Lincoln Theater, both fleapits. We never ventured to theaters on Main Street, since Filipinos were not allowed in that part of town at the time." Stockton was not only a place where Jamero felt welcomed, but it was also where he felt rejuvenated in livelihood and belonging. "El Dorado Street was," Jamero longingly reminisced, "the closest thing to the Philippines I could imagine."[23]

Coming to Theaters Near You: Films from the Philippines

Throughout the 1930s, Japanese-owned theaters were among the circuit of neighborhood and small-town theaters in the United States showcasing films from the Philippines. In 1938, a spectacular lineup of Filipino films, enthusiastically dubbed the "Filipino Show Parade in California," made their way to theaters in Stockton, Sacramento, Los Angeles, Oakland, and San Francisco. The showcase featured Tagalog talkies from the industry's major film studios and included titles like *Sa tawag ng dio* (1934), starring the widely popular actress Rosa Del Rosario. The Japanese-owned Imperial Theatre in Stockton and the Nippon Theatre in Sacramento exhibited and heavily promoted the Filipino film showcase. George Potamianos argues that theaters like those owned by the Japanese proprietors benefitted from the standardization of film distribution and, in particular, their access to productions from the major studios in Hollywood. In studying the business records of the Nippon Theatre, Potamianos notes that Nakatani used block booking to create a regular stream of diverse films each week and ensure repeat patronage. Such a system sustained small theaters like the Nippon, as "it would have been impossible for the theater manager to negotiate on a film by film basis each week."[24] While offering a steady stream of Hollywood productions, however, Japanese proprietors, including Nakatani and Hayashino, also sustained their enterprises on the secondary market and via alternative film circuits. Significantly, Japanese proprietors bolstered their patronage and sustained their theaters by exhibiting films from the Philippines. At least once, Hayashino's theater also exhibited "Mexican films," which were promoted in the Filipino press and likely understood by Filipino audiences through Spanish loan words in Tagalog. Like the aforementioned benshi Namiemon using Spanish words in his performance, the exhibition of both Filipino and Spanish-language films in the same Japanese-owned theater in Stockton signals the

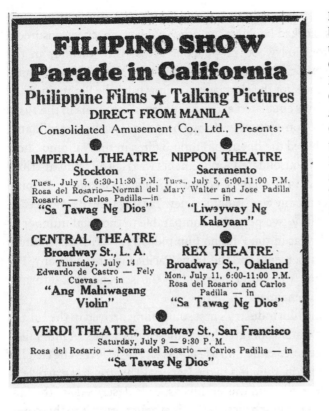

FILIPINO SHOW
Parade in California
Philippine Films ★ Talking Pictures
DIRECT FROM MANILA
Consolidated Amusement Co., Ltd., Presents:

IMPERIAL THEATRE
Stockton
Tues., July 5, 6:30-11:30 P.M.
Rosa del Rosario—Normal del
Rosario — Carlos Padilla—in
"Sa Tawag Ng Dios"

NIPPON THEATRE
Sacramento
Tues., July 5, 6:00-11:00 P.M.
Mary Walter and Jose Padilla
— in —
"Liwayway Ng Kalayaan"

CENTRAL THEATRE
Broadway St., L. A.
Thursday, July 14
Edwardo de Castro — Fely Cuevas — in
"Ang Mahiwagang Violin"

REX THEATRE
Broadway St., Oakland
Mon., July 11, 6:00-11:00 P.M.
Rosa del Rosario and Carlos Padilla — in
"Sa Tawag Ng Dios"

VERDI THEATRE, Broadway St., San Francisco
Saturday, July 9 — 9:30 P. M.
Rosa del Rosario — Norma del Rosario — Carlos Padilla — in
"Sa Tawag Ng Dios"

Filipino sound films brought to theaters throughout California by Hawaii's Consolidated Amusement Company, including the Japanese-owned Imperial Theatre and Nippon Theatre. *Filipino Pioneer*, July 1, 1938.

Welcome Friends!
IMPERIAL THEATRE
From Monday to Saturday
MEXICAN PICTURES!
Sundays – Extra, American Pictures!
ALWAYS GOOD PICTURES!
19 S. El Dorado St.   Stockton

Films from Mexico at the Imperial Theatre. *Philippine Examiner*, March 31, 1945.

shared histories and spaces of immigrant working-class communities. Furthermore, whereas blocked booking and other industry practices ensured a virtual monopoly for Hollywood productions across U.S. theaters in the 1930s, the Japanese proprietor's theaters emerged as an alternative exhibition site and, in this instance, for the circulation of films from the Philippines.

Indeed, Filipino films circulated extensively across California in the 1930s and early 1940s. A motion-picture exchange based in Hawaii, Consolidated Amusements, distributed the lineup of Filipino films in the "Filipino Show Parade in California." Consolidated Amusements was Hawaii's film distribution monopoly and in 1934 established a division specializing in Filipino films. By 1939, the company was bringing a new Tagalog title to Hawaii each week—a staggering fifty-two per year, comparable to the total number of films produced each year in the Filipino film industry.[25] With distributors like Consolidated Amusements and the Trans-Pacific Picture Company, Filipino films made their way "after market" to the screens of California, Washington, and other mainland localities.

Some of the Filipino film industry's first sound films arrived in the United States, including in theaters operated by Japanese proprietors. A film billed as *Ang kasakiman*, likely the same film as *Pag-iimbot* (1934) given the cast list and the billing description, debuted in the Imperial Theatre. In an article in the *Philippine Examiner*, the film was enthusiastically described as "the first and only Filipino mystery talking picture that is ever imported into this country. It was produced in the Philippines directed acted and written by Filipino brains [*sic*]." The film featured the actress Norma del Rosario in the lead as well as actors Eduardo de Castro, Faustino Maurat, and Fermin Barva. Featuring dialogue in Tagalog, the film was, according to the article, "enriched with the country and city sceneries and true Philippine atmosphere." Produced earlier in 1934, the film was screened in Stockton in the Japanese proprietor's theater for two consecutive days in 1937.[26]

Hayashino's Imperial Theatre also has the distinction of being one of the few venues that exhibited what is possibly the earliest Filipino film produced in the United States. In 1932, Festo G. Asprer established a film production company in San Francisco called Manila Pictures Company, which was billed, according to advertisements for the Imperial Theatre, as "Exclusive Producers of Filipino Feature-Length Talking Pictures Owned, Operated, Managed, and Controlled by Filipinos." Shot on location in California, the company's only known production was called *The Rose of Manila* and featured an all-Filipino cast. No print of the film exists, and little is known of the film or the company.[27]

IMPERIAL THEATRE

STOCKTON · PHONE 5496

Manila Pictures Company, Inc.
Exclusive Producers of Filipino Feature-Length Talking Pictures
Owned, Operated, Managed, and Controlled by Filipinos

PRESENTS

"THE ROSE OF MANILA"
The First Feature-Length Talking Picture in English

PORTRAYING
NATIVE ROMANCE — NATIVE MUSIC
NATIVE COSTUMES — NATIVE DANCES

THE CAST

ROSITA LAMONT   ROSITA LAMONT
RAMON CARINO   RAMON VALENCIA
DR. CALDERON alias
    DR. R. ZAMORA   LEON LONTOK

"THE ROSE OF MANILA" Will Play 3 Days Only
Thursday - Friday - Saturday
October 17, 18 and 19
DO NOT MISS IT! — LET'S ALL FOLLOW THE CROWD!

Advertisement for *The Rose of Manila*, a Filipino film made in San Francisco by a company called Manila Pictures Company. *Philippine Examiner*, October 15, 1935.

The Rose of Manila had an exhibition in Mountain View, California, on October 24, 1933.[28] Given this early release date, the film is not only noteworthy as a film produced in the United States but also as possibly one of the earliest Filipino sound films ever produced. Jose Nepomuceno's *Punyal na ginto* (1933) is credited by most film historians as the first all-talking Filipino picture (in Tagalog). The film was released in Manila on March 9, 1933. While *The Rose of Manila*'s exact production date and earliest exhibition date are unknown, its appearance in a California theater in the year 1933 presents possibilities for reconsidering the historiography of the Philippine cinema and the sound transition. Moreover, given *The Rose of Manila*'s production in San Francisco, this historiographical reconsideration extends beyond the scope of national cinema and the film industry based in the Philippine archipelago.

In 1934, *The Rose of Manila* was exhibited at a midnight screening in Santa Maria, California. The film was presented alongside a live stage show in which the film's star Rosita Lamont performed. Aspre, the Manila Pictures Company's founder, was also on hand to perform, as he was an accomplished violinist and composer.[29] These live and performative aspects accompanying the exhibition of *The Rose of Manila* continued film practices popularized in the silent film era. Were Lamont's and Aspre's live performances similar to the work of the benshi? Was the audience as engaged by them as they were of the film? How did their musical or vocal accompaniment, if that was what was performed, line up with the film's soundtrack? The following year, the film made its way to Hayashino's Imperial Theatre in Stockton. Anticipating great interest, the Japanese proprietor exhibited the film for three consecutive days over the weekend on October 17, 18, and 19, 1935. It remains unclear whether *The Rose of Manila* circulated in the Philippines; however, the company's vice president Vicente G. Guerrero purportedly absconded for Manila with a print in 1934.[30]

The sound transition was an especially important turning point for the production and circulation of films from the Philippines. While the industry in the Philippines, like other national film industries, struggled with the sound transition's technological challenges, the era provided an unexpected boost and ushered in a new studio era in the Philippines with the emergence of companies like Parlatone-Hispano Filipino, Sanpaguita Pictures, LVN, Excelsior Pictures, and X-Otic Pictures. Cinema's audibility of language propelled a greater domestic interest in a national cinema in the Philippines.[31] As Vicente Rafael notes, the transition to and development of sound in the Filipino film industry coincided with the adoption of Tagalog as the official national language by the commonwealth government. Timely in their production, Tagalog sound films were in no small measure responsible for the circulation and spread of Tagalog throughout the Philippines. By reaching audiences throughout the ethnically and linguistically diverse regions of the Philippine archipelago, Filipino sound films in the 1930s facilitated the dispersion of Tagalog and consolidated a mass audience across the Philippines.[32] Native filmmakers were highly conscious of this new role of the cinema. Vincente Salumbides, for example, utilized this development to lobby the local government for reduced taxation, reasoning that the dissemination of Tagalog made the cinema a crucial tool in nation building.[33]

During the 1930s and early 1940s, Filipino audiences in the United States experienced an almost exclusively Tagalog cinema. Japanese theater proprietors exhibited Tagalog films like *Sakay* (1939) and *Buenavista* (1940) in the early 1940s, while other productions like *Paki-usap* (1938), *Paro parong bukid* (1938), and *Ikaw rin* (1940) circulated in the postwar years. One exception to Tagalog, a "Visayan talkie," made its way to audiences in Hawaii's King Theatre in 1939.[34] Nevertheless, the predominance of Tagalog cinema abroad further shaped the lingua franca of the Philippines, given that a large majority of Filipino laborers in the United States in this period (who were the audience of the Japanese proprietor's theaters) were also Visayan and Ilocano, not Tagalog.

Recognized as the Filipino film industry's first production for international distribution, *Zamboanga* (1937) had an extensive run in the United States.

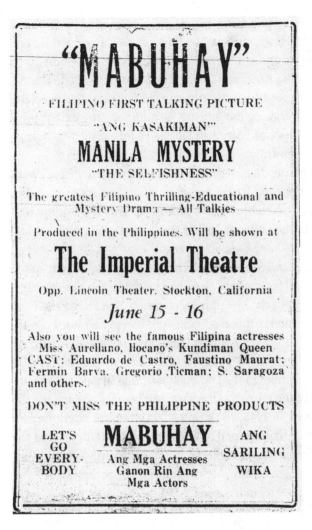

"MABUHAY"

FILIPINO FIRST TALKING PICTURE

"ANG KASAKIMAN"

MANILA MYSTERY

"THE SELFISHNESS"

The greatest Filipino Thrilling-Educational and Mystery Drama — All Talkies

Produced in the Philippines. Will be shown at

The Imperial Theatre

Opp. Lincoln Theater. Stockton, California

June 15 - 16

Also you will see the famous Filipina actresses Miss Aurellano, Ilocano's Kundiman Queen. CAST: Eduardo de Castro, Faustino Maurat; Fermin Barva, Gregorio Ticman; S. Saragoza and others.

DON'T MISS THE PHILIPPINE PRODUCTS

LET'S GO EVERY-BODY   **MABUHAY**   Ang Mga Actresses Ganon Rin Ang Mga Actors   ANG SARILING WIKA

Tagalog sound films featured at the Imperial Theatre. *Philippine Examiner*, June 15, 1937.

A print of the film was discovered in 2003 by Nick Deocampo and has become the source of important discussions over film restoration, archival preservation, and the historiography of the national cinema in the Philippines.[35] It remains only one of five surviving films made in the prewar era. Two Americans, Eddie Tait and George Harris, established Filipino Film Productions in 1933 and produced the film. With greater capitalization than earlier established studios, the Americans' film studio in the Philippines was, according to Nick Deocampo, "the first professional film studio in the country fully equipped to meet Hollywood quality in filmmaking."[36] *Zamboanga* was intended specifically for international and global distribution, as the producers aimed to, for the first time, bring a Filipino production into the world film market. The film was directed by Eduardo de Castro, whose real name was Marvin Gardner and whose father was an American soldier who had fought in the Philippine-American War and married Ceferina de Castro, from whom Gardner adapted his screen name. Significantly, *Zamboanga* featured dialogue not in Tagalog but Tausug. In addition, the extant print included subtitles in English and Swedish (as the 16 mm print was discovered by a collector in Finland).

Nick Deocampo has produced the most comprehensive and well-researched account of the production and circulation history of the film. According to Deocampo, much of the film utilizes the tropical settings and genre conventions established by such earlier Hollywood productions as *Moana* (1926), *Chang* (1927), *White Shadows in the South Seas* (1928), *Tabu* (1931), and *Goana-Goana* (1932). *Zamboanga* received unprecedented publicity in the United States and garnered favorable reviews by renowned film directors like Frank Capra and Ernst Lubitsch. The film premiered in San Diego and New York City. Marketed for international screens, producers had not even intended for the film to reach audiences in the Philippines, although it did have a screening in Manila in 1937.[37] In my own research, I found that *Zamboanga* also reached Filipino audiences in the United States, due in part to the publicity the film received in the Filipino American newspapers. Reviewing the film for the *Filipino Pioneer* in 1938, the writer P. C. Morantte rated the film "true to stories of adventure patterned after Hollywood" and described the film's "photography of underwater subjects . . . [as] not only veritably authentic but also exquisitely handled."[38] In considering the reception of *Zamboanga* in the United States, moreover, I found that the film had an exhibition history well beyond its premiere, as the film was screened after the war in 1945 in Stockton.[39]

Midnight Ramble

Within the continental United States, Filipino films were most often screened at the midnight hour. These shows were "after hours," taking place when theaters concluded their "regular" standard programming. When the Manila Picture Company's *The Rose of Manila* debuted in Santa Maria, California, in 1934, it did so at midnight. *Sakay* (1940) and *Buenavista* (1939) were billed at the Sierra Theatre in 1940 as "special midnight shows." Throughout California and Washington, theaters held their Filipino film exhibitions in these nonstandard time slots. Filipino films like *Panibugho* (1941), *Mariposa* (1941),

Panambitan (1941), *Ang gulong ng buhay* (1935), *Bituing marikit* (1937), *Ikaw rin* (1941), and *Paki-usap* (1938) all came to audiences in Stockton, Sacramento, Fresno, and Delano as late-night or midnight screenings. *Zamboanga*, the most popular and extensively publicized of the films, was also screened in Stockton's Rialto Theatre in 1945 at the midnight hour. Moreover, film exhibition venues like the Sierra Theatre in Stockton and the Japanese-owned Atlas Theatre in Seattle were regularly open all night long and served a large clientele of Filipino patrons.

The exhibition of films during off hours or after "regular" first-run showtimes were euphemistically called "midnight rambles." These practices were part of a myriad of strategies deployed to racially segregate motion-picture theaters during the heyday of Jim Crow. Movie theaters in the South were regulated by the same statutes legally separating races at playhouses and vaudeville theaters. In the absence of all-Black theaters, white theater owners in the South often maintained the color line by operating split-week policies for white and Black audiences to view films on different days of the week; partitioning the theater or relegating Black audiences to less desirable seating, often on the balcony; or utilizing separate entryways, staircases, concession stands, and ticket windows. In conjunction with the midnight ramble, these film exhibition practices in southern states reinforced the mandate of de jure segregation.[40] Midnight rambles, however, were not exclusive to the South; midnight film exhibitions for Black audiences were conducted in northern and western states as well. When the all-Black cast film *Hallelujah* (1929) debuted at the Embassy and Lafayette Theaters in New York City, it did so as midnight shows. Other midnight film exhibitions for Black audiences were held in Oklahoma, Missouri, and Arkansas. According to *Variety*, at one midnight ramble featuring a "Negro show" in Texas, "one-third of the audience was white, with a good sprinkling of the elite."[41]

Similarly, the midnight and after-hours film exhibition of Filipino films also reproduced segregation and the color line in the United States. These practices adjoined varying racialized exclusions experienced by Filipinos when they went to the movies in white-owned establishments. In recalling his experience of visiting a picture palace operated by the corporate chain Fox West Coast in Stockton, Johnny Latosa confronted a sign at the entrance that read, "No Filipinos Allowed."[42] Stockton's Rialto Theatre similarly relegated Filipino audiences to second-class seating. "Here the minorities were segregated," a Filipino patron recalled. "We were always led to sit on the right side of the theatre."[43] Beyond California, Felix Zamora in Oregon recounted, "They segregate the Filipinos, Japanese, Chinese, colored people and they

Midnight exhibition of "Philippine Pictures" at Star Theatre. *Philippine Examiner,*
June 30, 1947.

stay on the balcony and all the white on the first floor."[44] Roque de la Ysla
similarly recalled his experience at the cinema in Utah when the usher
prohibited him from sitting on the lower floor and instead escorted his
party to the segregated balcony. De La Ysla even brought a legal suit against
the theater in a case that reached Utah Supreme Court in 1933.[45]

Even as the midnight ramble reinforced racial segregation and white supremacy, these after-hours spaces for Filipino filmgoing also emerged as
important spaces for Filipino sociability and alternative film spectatorship. In
1945, a program of Filipino films billed as "Pre-Invasion Philippine Made Pictures" traveled across California, reaching audiences at the midnight hour in
Stockton, Delano, and Fresno. The lineup of films were all productions from
the period before Japan's occupation of the Philippines, which lasted from
1942 to 1945. During this period, film production in the Philippines was sus-
pended and supplanted by Japanese film propaganda. The billing of films as
"pre-invasion," however, marks more than a production date. Promotional
materials embellished the film lineup with description like "The Story of a
Courageous People/A Living Monument of Our People's Triumph in the Field
of Art, Music and the Drama." Each film showing was intended to "Remind
You of the Beautiful Philippines." All the program's films were Tagalog sound
films and featured "kundiman songs" and "folk dances in colorful native costumes."[46]

Writing in the context of British period films, Andrew Higson uses the
term "heritage films" to describe a genre "retreating from the social, political, and economic crises of the present . . . to recapture an image of national
identity as pure, untainted, complete, and in place."[47] In many ways, the

lineup of "Pre-Invasion Philippine Made Pictures" was presented to audiences in postwar California as a similar retrenchment, a reminder of a "Beautiful Philippines" replete with sentimental ballads and precolonial fantasy. This nostalgic return proffered in the extrafilmic discourse also returns us to the production history of the Filipino film industry. Such returns rearticulate the moment of self-determination and the full-fledged emergence of a national cinema for the Philippines, even as that history has always been complicated by the omnipresence of colonialism and American filmmaking, as Deocampo has argued. The circulation of Filipino films in the United States as "pre-invasion," nevertheless, serves as its own form of curation, both marking and commemorating a forlorn past, or a way to "Remind You of the Beautiful Philippines."

Filipinos in the United States largely experienced the cinema as consumers and filmgoers and rarely as owners of production or exhibition. In returning audiences to imagined pre-invasion pasts, the film program more specifically recuperated a Filipino filmgoing public so often dependent on venues owned and operated by non-Filipino proprietors. Segregated to the midnight hour, these Filipino film exhibitions were remade as a separate cinema for specifically Filipino audiences. Whereas Filipino laborers were owners of neither the mode of production nor the means of film exhibition, I would suggest that the midnight ramble presented these filmgoers with a provisional autonomy in the formation of an all-Filipino viewing public.

Hayashino's Star Theatre and Lincoln Theatre were located in the hub of Stockton's Filipino district on the El Dorado Street so vividly recounted in the renowned writer Carlos Bulosan's *America Is in the Heart* (1943). El Dorado Street was a cornerstone for the livelihood of many Filipinos in the 1930s and 1940s, drawing together a community dispersed across vast stretches of the region's agricultural beltway. As Linda Maram notes, the city itself was a crucial geographic site of return for Filipino workers on the move. As they traveled from one seasonal employment site to another, the city and places like El Dorado Street were a respite from work as well as an important arena for congregation. This was where, as Maram puts it, a "portable community . . . [on the constant move] called itself into being wherever it was."[48] In their patronage of the Japanese-owned theaters, viewership of films from the Philippines, and in the formation of El Dorado Street writ large, Filipinos remade their place in Stockton, reterritorializing the space into meaningful forms of collectivization and belonging.

In their participation in film culture, Filipinos transformed the space of the theater itself. Relegated to the latest of hours, Filipino filmgoers

Zamboanga exhibited as a part of the midnight show program. *Philippine Examiner,* May 31, 1945.

repurposed the spaces and times of their film viewing. Willy Torin recalled that after the taxi dance hall closed, in Seattle, Filipinos would all head to the Japanese-owned Atlas Theatre, which stayed open throughout the night showing films.[49] Seattle's Atlas Theatre epitomized the kinds of Japanese-owned theater spaces catering to racialized, working-class audiences.[50] Commenting on the Japanese-owned Atlas Theatre, Chris Mensalves noted the importance of the show hall's use as a place of provisional lodging for Filipinos, especially at the height of the Depression. "A lot of us who got no rooms especially the single guys you don't got no room you have to go to all night movies," remembered Mensalves, "so you stay there all night. You get out there in the mornings." Serving as forms of provisional housing and sustenance, the Japanese-operated moving-picture theater was especially important to Filipinos during the Depression as their exclusion from citizenship made it impossible to access federal provisions accorded by the Emergency Relief Appropriations Act.[51]

BEFORE THE CALIFORNIA SUPREME COURT in 1948, Shigeaki Hayashino chose to omit mention of the presence of Filipino audiences. His theaters had served the film-viewing desires of Filipinos for over a decade, yet he remained silent on the stand. Emil Palermo, the white litigant mounting a case against Hayashino, sought to take advantage of Hayashino's wartime misfortune as he and his entire family were incarcerated at the Rohwer Relocation Center in Arkansas. Unable to manage their theaters or company while detained, Hayashino and his associates were advised to sell their theaters. Rather than relinquish their theaters at a profit loss, however, they placed the management of the company and theaters in the hands of two white associates: T. W. Thomas and Mr. Lippert, both of whom received large percentages of the net profit. Lippert alone received $1,500 per month in management fees, an unprecedented amount for the Stockton Theatres company, which paid Hayashino, prior to evacuation, only $150 per month. The fees dealt to the white overseers of the Japanese theaters exceeded the profits of the entire company in the years of internment.[52]

With limited options, Hayashino made cursory arrangements for his theaters with white associates eager to take advantage of his vulnerabilities. Lawyers and other consultants advised many evacuees with valuable property holdings to give power of attorney to agents or white friends. Hayashino, however, quickly realized his mistake and contacted the Federal Reserve Bank in 1944 to report the mishandling of his businesses by T. W. Thomas, who had failed to account for the income received while operating Hayashino's theaters.[53] In the handling of evacuee assets, the Wartime Civil Control Authority designated the Federal Reserve Bank (FRB) and created the Evacuee Property Department (EPD) to purportedly protect the assets of Japanese internees from profiteers and minimize financial loss. However, as Sandra C. Taylor argues, the FRB and the EPD were ineffectual and largely concerned with expediting the disposal of evacuee property and aiding in the war effort.[54]

Eager to overtake and gain control of his businesses, Thomas guided (and most likely convinced) Emil Palermo to bring legal suit against Hayashino's corporation. Palermo sought a declaratory judgment against the lease of the Stockton theaters on the grounds of violation of the California Alien Land Law. Emil Palermo had inherited the leased property from his father, Angelo, who passed away in 1941. He was thirty-one years of age when he

Ink portrait of Shigeaki Hayashino (on left) by George Hoshida at Lordsburg Justice Department Camp, New Mexico. Written in black ink below left image: "2004 S. San Joaquin St. / Stockton Calif. Age 52 / Oct 1. 1942." Written in black ink to left of left image (in Japanese and English): "Hayashino Shigeaki / Motion Picture Theatre Circuit OWNER." Courtesy of George Hoshida Collection, Japanese American National Museum (Gift of June Hoshida Honma, Sandra Hoshida, and Carole Hoshida Kanada, 97.106.2DA).

brought the lawsuit against Hayashino. For over a decade, he had worked for the theaters as a doorman and ticket attendant; at the time of the lawsuit, he was unemployed.

In the local newspaper, Palermo stated that he had filed the lawsuit because he strove to uphold much more than the California Alien Land Law. He believed that the "stigma of the Japanese owned theater would eventually deteriorate the value of the property."[55] Should the court rule in his favor, Palermo was poised to gain financially. Yet, when the EPD representative Edgar Bernhardt, investigating on behalf of Hayashino, met with Palermo, he concluded, "It isn't a matter of money with him at all. He just wants to get rid of the Japs—and there is considerable pressure on him from friends and others."[56]

Significantly, among the supporters of the lawsuit, according to Bernhardt, were some Filipino residents who allegedly shared in the racism against the Japanese entrepreneur. The return of internees to Stockton, according to Thomas, was a "real danger particularly on account of the Philipinos [sic], some of whom had already indicated how they felt by saying, 'that is good to have the Japs coming back—good shooting.'"[57] For Filipinos, World War II and the imprisonment of 120,000 Japanese Americans in concentration camps brought more than a decade of contentious relations with Japanese immigrant communities to a head. Japan's invasion of the Philippines and China galvanized many Filipinos and Chinese in the United States to rally behind the American war effort and to decry Japan's occupation of their own countries. American perceptions shifted to identify the Japanese as the "enemies within" and the Filipinos and Chinese as the "good Asians in the good war."[58]

In the end, the California Supreme Court ruled against Emil Palermo and in favor of Hayashino, allowing the Japanese proprietor to resume operation of his movie theaters in Stockton.[59] The court concluded that a 1911 treaty that allowed Japanese nationals to lease commercial property in California sufficiently protected Hayashino's righ to lease and operate the theater, without ruling on the constitutionality of the Alien Land Laws.[60] California courts would not decide that the state's Alien Land Laws were unconstitutional until 1956 in the landmark ruling *Sei Fujii v. California*.[61] Nevertheless, the World War II reversed many of the fortunes for Japanese and Filipino communities and irrevocably transformed the entirety of the prewar era's Japanese film culture in the United States.

Epilogue

Several months before Executive Order 9066 was issued by U.S. president Franklin D. Roosevelt, federal authorities arrested the founder of the Yamato Graph Motion Picture Company. Toyoji Abe was apprehended on December 7, 1941, in San Francisco. After his initial foray into filmmaking in 1912, Abe redirected his efforts to a career in print journalism. Having led several Japanese American newspapers in Oregon, he took over the *New World Sun* based in San Francisco in 1935. This newspaper was one of the major news outlets for Japanese Americans in Northern California. Compared to its rival *Japanese-American News*, Abe's *New World Sun* was far less assimilationist and more aligned with the Buddhist segments of the community. Abe was among the early roundup of Japanese Americans by federal authorities immediately following the bombing of Pearl Harbor. As early as the 1920s, the U.S. federal government began taking note of leaders in the Japanese American community as well as the cultural politics they presumed would reinforce allegiances to the Japanese imperial state. In the period before the United States' entry into the war, the counterintelligence agencies of the Office of Naval Intelligence (ONI), the Bureau of Investigation (which later became the FBI under J. Edgar Hoover), and the Military Intelligence Division (MID) were in nascent stages of development. The surveillance of domestic communities represented a major forum for the agencies to organize themselves.[1] Furthermore, Japan's occupation of China in 1931 undermined the U.S. governmental ambitions for the Open Door policy, which granted the United States equal access to trade in China. As the State Department began to perceive a greater possibility for war, federal authorities heightened their surveillance of Japanese Americans. The domestic spying on Japanese in the United States contributed to the pre-1942 detention and incarceration of Japanese Americans into sixteen imprisonment camps operated by the Immigration and Naturalization Service (INS). The roundup of these individuals, as Bob Kumamoto argues, deprived Japanese Americans of their community's social organization and leadership.[2]

Federal authorities classified Toyoji Abe as a "dangerous enemy alien" and imprisoned him in the Department of Justice internment camps at Fort Missoula, Montana, and later Crystal City, Texas. During the war, persons identified as enemy aliens were not allowed to own contraband articles, such as weapons, signal devices, and cameras. They were also required to always carry certificates of identification. From the perspective of federal authorities, Abe's newspaper reflected pro-Japan viewpoints that made him especially suspect. Officials made a special note in their files about his 1940 visit to Japan in which he led a delegation to celebrate the 2,600th anniversary of the imperial Japanese government. This anniversary was a grandiose nationalist celebration by the imperial Japanese government to establish its own legitimacy in a so-called unbroken imperial line.[3] Not only did federal authorities identify Abe's participation in these nationalistic celebrations, but they also made note of his alleged fund-raising efforts in support of the Japanese Navy Department. Even though Abe's own son served in the U.S. Army, and he displayed favorable conduct while in the camps, his multiple requests for release were rejected. He remained incarcerated until 1946. Like so many, he did not return to rebuild his community nor his enterprises after the war. Instead, he passed away shortly after his release from the camps.[4]

Key members of Nichibei Kogyo Kaisha were also identified and apprehended by federal authorities. The film exchange was itself singled out by the Office of Naval Intelligence. In 1941, officials filed a report identifying the organization as a syndicate of the Tokyo Club, a notorious gambling and organized crime enterprise. They made note of the troubled history of Hideichi Yamatoda, the former head of both Nichibei Kogyo Kaisha and the Tokyo Club. Most significantly, officers reported that the film exchange was distributing highly nationalist Japanese films, which "portray[ed] Japanese expansion in Asia and the might of the Japanese Army." They also noted that Nichibei Kogyo Kaisha "booked lectures which praised Japanese customs as being superior to America."[5]

Federal authorities had long taken note of Japanese film propaganda in the United States. As early as 1935, a government informant attended a gathering of 250 Japanese in Los Angeles to view a moving-picture program presented by the Japanese Association in honor of the arrival of an imperial vessel from Japan. Celebrations of the Japanese imperial navy grew increasingly common with the escalation of the Sino-Japanese War. These celebrations were at times bolstered by the exhibition of Japanese films in support of the war effort (as mentioned in chapter 3). In the report, the informant made note that "except for explanatory interjections, [the benshi] did not extend his remarks beyond the scope of the subtitles." However, the program did include, according to the government report, a comical scenario placing Emperor Meiji in contrast to the interchangeable leaders of other nations. Images of the vaudeville performer El Brendel donning various hats and making silly facial expressions were presented to illustrate the ineffective and always changing leaders of nations controlled by national assembly or popular ballot. Furthermore, the report pointedly noted the exhibition of naval training films and pictures of industries, locomotives, steamships, and railways in Japan.[6]

The benshi were among the federal government's designated "suspect class." Takeshi Ban was classified as a "class A" suspect. In the rating system established by the United States government, persons classified A were considered the most dangerous. Federal authorities described Ban as "exceedingly active as a propagandist." Officials noted that he served as an imperial army officer during the Russo-Japanese War and won the Seventh Order of the Rising Sun. They noted that his film company not only distributed nationalist Japanese films, but it also received subsidies from the Japanese Trade Promotion Bureau of the Ministry of Commerce. In their report, federal authorities even named specific Japanese films exhibited by Ban, like *Nishizumi senshachoden*, as well as newsreels and films produced by the Army Ministry. Compared to Abe, however, Ban was granted earlier release in 1943 because "the Board found subject to be a Christian."[7]

Classified by the United States government as B suspect class, Muneo Kimura was apprehended in Honolulu. Although Hawaii did not fall under the military evacuation orders proscribed by Executive Order 9066, the federal government did round up several thousand individuals in Hawaii after the bombing of Pearl Harbor, detaining many of them in internment camps established on the islands. In a hearing on December 19, 1941, Kimura defended his film exhibition activities, citing that "they were not any bad films." He contended that his films came from the large commercial studios in Japan, namely, Toho, Shochiku, and Shinko. He stated that his films had "nothing to do with military things or battle or war" and that the films he exhibited all passed the censors. FBI reports extensively chronicled Kimura's extraordinary career as a benshi, making note of his sprawling film exhibition network reaching across California, Oregon, Washington, and Hawaii. Ultimately, the government found in the case of Kimura, "there was a general statement that he rented films which were of a historical and general nature. That under certain circumstances certain parts has been cut out by request of the censor or upon the initiative of people here who exhibited them but there was nothing definite as to whether that was propaganda. However, it is believed that the tendency of historical films was for the purpose of keeping before them the ancient history of Japan, and at least to continue their loyalty to Japan, and not to imbue any loyalty to the United States."[8]

Photograph of Japanese acting troupe posing with Nichibei Kinema banner.
Courtesy of Nippu Jiji Photo Archives, the Hawaii Photo Archives Foundation,
and Densho: The Japanese American Legacy Project.

In the aftermath of World War II and the mass incarceration of Japanese
Americans, little remained as it did before the war. Much of the prewar film
culture and its viewing publics dissolved, but some remnants continued to
find expression in a variety of forms. According to Chie Gondo, Muneo
Kimura and his company resurrected themselves in the years after the war
with a company called Nichibei Kinema. In 1946, they held a screening of
Japanese films that had been confiscated by federal authorities. Kamesuke
Nakahama, a popular benshi from Hawaii, performed alongside the cache
of silent-era Japanese films. As Nakahama recalled, "When they brought me
back, the lines were unbelievable to see the benshi again . . . and local Japanese after the war stood eagerly to buy doubly-priced tickets."[9] As Gondo
notes, Kimura and Nichibei Kinema were responsible for reviving Japanese
film culture in Hawaii after the war. They operated the Kokusai Theatre, the
largest venue for Japanese film exhibition in Hawaii, until 1964. The company
established a vibrant network of film exchange between Hawaii and Japan.
Furthermore, the revival of Japanese film exhibition in the postwar years
helped to establish Hawaii as a film shooting location for major studios.[10]

In the continental United States, a Buddhist temple in New York sponsored a Japanese film program in 1946 with a benshi. "The first Japanese movies to be offered in New York since evacuation," according to newspapers, "will be presented by the popular [benshi] Tayo Kawai."[11] Like in the prewar era, the postwar film program, which included the films *Ai no shinpan* (1932) and *Michi wa hitotsu*, was presented as a part of a community benefit and in a nontheatrical exhibition venue. With the massive bureaucracy of the war still lingering, prewar Japanese films were also presented in 1947 by the Military Intelligence Service Language Program, which employed many Nisei during the war as translators, interrogators, and interpreters. As the newspapers noted, the Japanese film program "attracted more than a filled SRO hall of two thousand persons. It is true that many persons have already seen the picture during the pre-war days, but it has been some time since Japanese pictures were shown to the public during the pre-war days, and there is a great demand for even the so-called old pictures as *Shina no yoru* (1940)."[12] As former internees resettled in localities other than the prewar hubs on the Pacific coast (a strategy of dispersal encouraged by federal authorities), some Japanese film exhibitions would find their audiences wherever they now took root. In Utah, Japanese films made their way into church halls and community centers across Ogden, Salt Lake City, Bowles, and Syracuse.[13] Even the Chicago Resettlers Committee turned to Japanese films to continue their community work and efforts to support resettlement.[14]

Coda

Hollywood today is yet again debating the diversity problem within the industry. NBC announced it will no longer air the Golden Globes after protests, which included Tom Cruise handing back three of his awards, over unethical practices and the news that not a single member of the Hollywood Foreign Press Association is Black. Just months earlier, the Academy of Motion Picture Arts and Sciences announced their new inclusion standards for films seeking a Best Picture nomination at the Academy Awards. Voted in by a board in the wake of George Floyd's murder, these measures were intended to respond to campaigns such as #OscarSoWhite, a hashtag created in 2015 by April Reign after the academy awarded all twenty acting nominations to white actors for the first of two consecutive years. Yet these new inclusion criteria (which will be implemented in 2024), as Maggie Hennefeld notes, are so flimsy and vague that many of the racist films made in the past could easily fit within this category, including *The Birth of a Nation* (1915).[1]

Various Asian American media campaigns have adjoined the calls for inclusion and diversity in Hollywood. Trending hashtags like #StarringJohnCho or #ExpressiveAsians have been utilized to foreground the marginalization of Asian American actors and industry practices like whitewashing (when white actors are cast in nonwhite roles). Studies like the recently published USC Annenberg Inclusion Initiative underscore the acute problems of Asian American underrepresentation. In a survey of the representations of Asian and Pacific Islanders (API) across the one hundred top-grossing films during 2007–2019, researchers found that 39 percent had no API speaking characters at all and only 3.4 percent featured an API lead or colead—and a sizable proportion of this percentage comes from a single actor, Dwayne Johnson, a.k.a. The Rock.[2] Within this context, Asian American media campaigns have tended to focus on these representational concerns. Bolstered by hashtags such as #GoldOpen and #AsianAugust and theater buyout campaigns, the box office success of films like *Crazy Rich Asians* (2018), *Searching* (2018), and *To All the Boys I Loved Before* (2018) were widely celebrated as milestones for Asian American representation. As Lori Kido Lopez notes, Asian American media campaigns contributed to the success of these films by creating a sense of "must-see Asianness" and tapping into a desire for mainstream visibility within audiences who have remained largely devalued by the media industry.[3] *Minari* (2020) and the Oscar winning filmmaker Chloé Zhao for *Nomadland* (2020) have been similarly celebrated and acclaimed within the rubric of diversity.

Whether these campaigns for inclusion will yield any substantial or meaningful changes remains to be seen. Moreover, it is important to ask, what is left unaddressed in these diversity efforts? To write the history of the cinema is to think about what is valued and what is remembered. Girish Shambu notes that film evaluation itself requires a fundamental rethinking. It has long privileged the auteur and centered its praise and attention on the formal and aesthetic qualities of film. "Auteurist criticism customarily searches films for evidence of the worldview of the filmmaker," writes Shambu, "but why stop at the boundaries of the film text and the world on the screen?"[4] Filmmaking has never been a solitary act, so why value it as such? Moreover, what *are* the metrics for calculating the uneven forms of access and institutional power in the history of the cinema?

Throughout much of its history, Hollywood has not just incidentally neglected the film work of people of color. As Cara Caddoo reminds us, the industry has a long and defining history of actively working to undermine the work of nonwhite filmmakers and producers. As one example, the demise of the early independent race film industry was in part a result of Hollywood's business tactics and their ability to form a monopoly and control the market. The early film industry had never been willing to invest in Black films, but they locked out any competition for audiences by forcing independent theaters into block booking, which required licensing films as a unit from the major studios. Hollywood's control over the channels of distribution was highly detrimental to independent filmmakers. While the Supreme Court eventually ruled against these monopolistic practices, it was not before hundreds of race film companies faltered and permanently closed. Hollywood also undermined the early independent Black filmmaking industry by co-opting its most marketable genres and poaching its talent and requiring they sign noncompetition agreements. Furthermore, Hollywood used many of these aggressive tactics, including forming powerful lobbies, to dominate international markets and undermine national cinemas in countries like Mexico.[5]

The film cultures described in *Transpacific Convergences* faced a similar if not interrelated fate, although it is impossible to definitively know the precise details of their eventual demise given the dearth of archival remains. Nevertheless, in considering the contemporary milieu, we may ask, how do we account for the media worlds that have been lost to us? Shambu has written that "representations are a kind of wealth — an asset that is accumulated by certain groups or identities over time while being denied to others."[6] Looking to our current media moment, how then do we account for these accumulated disparities? Asian American critics have argued that the desire "to be seen" teaches us to understand our value within the market logic of capitalism.[7] The representational politics of visibility seemingly offer a salve for marginalization, yet what is truly gained in such a call? Herein *Transpacific Convergence*'s methods for reading the past are the lessons for the present. To look beyond the screen is to demand so much more than representation. It is to seek redistribution rather than inclusion. It is not only to reimagine our histories but also to reformulate the possibilities for our futures.

Acknowledgments

The road to completing this book was long and took many detours. I relish the time that I have now to express my gratitude to the many scholars, mentors, archivists, colleagues, and friends and family who have supported my work over the years.

At key stages of writing, I received critical feedback from presentations given at the Cinema and Media Studies Graduate Colloquium at UCLA; the Reischauer Institute of Japanese Studies at Harvard; and the annual meetings of the American Studies Association, the Association for Asian American Studies, and the Society for Cinema and Media Studies. The Faculty Workshop Series at the Center for Humanities, Culture and Society provided a lively forum of scholarly exchange with invited respondent Daisuke Miyao and University of Massachusetts Boston colleagues. Aaron Lecklider and Sari Edelstein deserve thanks for convening us.

I was awarded a faculty fellowship at the Charles Warren Center for the Study of American History at Harvard to complete the book and participate in the workshop Past, Present, and Future of Ethnic Studies. So many of the conversations and exchanges during this year-long residency sharpened my thinking and commitments. For their brilliance and passion, I thank coconveners Ju Yon Kim and Lorgia García Peña and cofellows Takeo Rivera, Robert Diaz, Anjali Nath, Nicole Guidotti-Hernández, Marisol LeBrón, Umayyah Cable, Allan Isaac, and Jason Ferreira. I was glad to muse about Asian American cinema with Keisha Knight. Thanks also to Walter Johnson, Arthur Patton-Hock, and the staff at the Warren Center.

I was fortunate to participate in the first inaugural Japanese Diaspora Initiative Workshop at Stanford University's Hoover Institute. I am grateful for the engagement from Kayoko Takeda, Eiichiro Azuma, Greg Robinson, David Yoo, Meredith Oda, Chrissy Yee Lau, Brian Hayashi, and Robert Hegwood. Thanks to Kay Ueda and the staff for organizing the forum. At Yale University, the Ethnicity, Race, and Migration Postdoctoral Fellowship, which I held in the Film and Media Studies Program, provided the funding for a manuscript workshop at a crucial time in the genesis of this project. I am grateful to Stephen Pitti for critical feedback, to the staff at Yale, and to the workshop participants who provided an engaging forum for my initial ideas: Jacqueline Stewart, Mary Lui, Gary Okihiro, and Charles Musser.

I may have never conceived of this project if I had not found a graduate program that encouraged me to envision, study, and value the sorts of media histories detailed herein. Yen Le Espiritu guided me throughout graduate school from the first day I stepped onto the University of California San Diego campus. She continues to inspire me, serving as a guiding light for my own aspirations as a scholar and educator. Nayan Shah advised this project from its inception and taught me so much about reimagining the past. His mentorship and friendship continue to enliven all that I do. For their inspiring teaching, I would like to acknowledge George Lipsitz, Natalia Molina, Lisa

Yoneyama, Jack Halberstam, Ramón Gutiérrez, Ross Frank, Lesley Stern, David Pellow, and Denise Ferreira da Silva. I had the good fortune to meet K. Scott Wong while a dissertation fellow at Williams College and extend my thanks for his support and mentorship.

Though leaving California for the New England winter has been challenging, I am immensely glad to work alongside my colleagues in the American Studies Department at the University of Massachusetts Boston. Aaron Lecklider, Lynnell Thomas, Marisol Negrón, Rachel Rubin, Bonnie Miller, Jeffrey Melnick, and Judith Smith have enthusiastically engaged my work and inspired my thinking. Shauna Lee Manning keeps everything running. I am also fortunate to work with students and colleagues in the Cinema Studies Program, Asian American Studies Program, and the Critical Ethnic and Community Studies Program. For their collegiality and support, I would like to acknowledge Sofya Aptekar, Chris Barcelos, Elora Chowdhury, Loan Dao, Alex Des Forges, Sari Edelstein, Brian Halley, Andres Henao-Castro, Sara Hoang, Terry Kawashima, Sarah Keller, Peter Kiang, Andrew Leong, Katharina Loew, Shannon McHugh, Denise Patmon, Tri Quach, Heike Schotten, Wenhua Shi, Eve Sorum, Rajini Srikanth, Thea Quiray Tagle, Shirley Tang, Paul Watanabe, Cedric Woods. I would also like to recognize and send gratitude to the late David Terkla.

I had the benefit of colleagues who offered constructive feedback on the entire manuscript. Gordon H. Chang provided me with astute comments to strengthen each of the chapters and the book's overall argumentation. Judith Smith shared her expertise in media history and offered detailed criticism. Ryan Cook, Joshua Glick, and Nayan Shah all took the time to read the manuscript in its entirety and provide essential feedback to me at critical stages of the book's development. Jeff Melnick also read and gave me comments on early portions of the book.

The research that went into this book was extensive, long ranging, and required the efforts of many librarians, archivists, film preservationists, community historians, and colleagues. I would first like to thank Ned Comstock at USC Cinematic Arts Library for helping me locate a print of *The Oath of the Sword*. The George Eastman Museum generously waived fees and granted me the courtesy of reproducing stills from the film. I thank Caroline Yeager at GEM for her support, as well as Sophia Laurent for her work in reproducing the film stills. My research benefitted immensely from the invaluable holdings at the Japanese American National Museum and from the wisdom and support of Karen Ishizuka, Kristen Hayashi, and Jamie Henricks. I also want to acknowledge the librarians, archivists, and staff at UMass Boston's Healey Library, especially Jessica Holden. I am grateful that Jessica enjoys a challenging archival hunt as much as I do. Many institutions and individuals deserve credit and appreciation for their support of my research: Kay Ueda at the Hoji Shinbun Digital Archive, Joshua Lupkin at Harvard's Widener Library, Glenda Pearson at the University of Washington Libraries, Melissa Scroggins at the Fresno County Public Library, Michael Holland at the Los Angeles City Archives, Haley Maynard at the National Archives and Records Administration, Elderina Aldamar at the Oregon Historical Society, Todd Mayberry at the Oregon Nikkei Endowment, the staff at the Wing Luke Asian Museum, Dorothy and Fred Cordova at the Filipino American Historical Society, John Cahoon at the Seaver Center for Western History, Maria Carrillo and Tom Atchley at the Special Collections of A. K. Smiley Public Library, Dawn Webb and Dennis Ogawa at the Hawaii Times Photo Archives Foundation, Mike Okamura at the Little Tokyo Historical Society, and Grant Din at the Angel Island Immigration Station Foundation. I want to express my gratitude to Tom Walsh for sharing his work on Filipino films with me and to Homer Yasui for sharing his family stories and memories of Toyoji Abe.

Financial support was provided to me by UMass Boston's College of Liberal Arts Dean's Office and the AANAPISI (Asian American and Native American Pacific Islander–Serving Institutions) Initiative. The latter provided me funding support to hire student researchers. I would like to thank the following students for their work: Vanessa Yee, Vicki Szeto, Yujin Kim, and Ping Zhou. Shay Park and Kai Uchida also provided important research assistance. Yuki Sakurai and Toshikuni Kawashima provided translation support. Ryan Cook shared his expertise on Japanese cinema and worked on the especially challenging task of identifying Japanese film titles and production credits. Erik Steiner produced the maps included in the introduction.

The University of North Carolina Press has been ideal to work with. I express deep appreciation to Mark Simpson-Vos, who believed in this project and provided me with the guidance and encouragement to cross the finish line. I am thankful to the two anonymous readers for scrupulous criticism that sharpened the book's arguments and interventions. Thanks also to María García and the extraordinary team at UNC Press for shepherding the book to completion.

I express my gratitude to the editors at *Pacific Historical Review* for permission to republish an early version of chapter 4, which originally appeared as "'Filipinos Are the Dandies of the Foreign Colonies': Race, Labor Struggles, and the Transpacific Routes of Hollywood and Philippine Films," *Pacific Historical Review* 81, no. 3 (August 2012): 371–403.

Without the support of my family, I may have never completed this book nor seen any of its promise and possibility. It is from my father, Chin, whom I inherited my cinephilia. I grew up watching him watch cowboy westerns and kung fu films, and now, looking back, I see its formative influence. My mother, Margaret, always cheered me on and taught me to persevere against all odds. Nayana and Hemant welcomed me into their family with open arms. Rose inspires me with her art and beauty. Victor lifts me up when most needed. I continue to be bolstered by the love and support of Mona, Ashay, Cindy, Puja, Sneh, Akasha, Michel, Gabe, and our family's growing brood of children. For boundless friendship, I send gratitude to Diana Aram.

The only person who has been with this project for as long as me is Benita. She read each word on these pages and took all the detours with me. That road ends now, and the next adventure begins. With our kids, Surya and Eshaan, in tow, onward!

APPENDIX I

Japanese American–Produced Films before World War II

The Oath of the Sword (1914)

- Produced by Japanese American Film Company

Nami-Ko (1917)

- Produced by Fujiyama Feature Film Company
- Directed by Frank A. Thorne

Chijiku o mawasuru chikara (1930)

- Produced by Hollywood Nippon Talkie Company
- Directed by James Wong Howe

Taichi ni shitashimu (1933)

- Produced by Hollywood Japanese Picture Association
- Directed by Yujin Takamatsu

Nisei Parade (1934)

- Directed by Ikuo and Seuo Serisawa

Iminchi no haha (1936)

- Produced by Hollywood Japanese Picture Association
- Directed by Jack Matsumoto

Nobiyuku Nisei (1937)

- Produced by Hollywood Japanese Picture Association
- Directed by Yujin Takamatsu

Yume ni yaburarete (date unknown)

- Produced by Hollywood Japanese Picture Association

Benshi in the Continental United States before World War II

Takeshi Ban

Charley Shugetsu Hiyoshigawa

Ken'yu Hokutosai

Taiyo Kawai

Muneo Kimura

Kido Kunimoto

Suimin Matsui

Henry Miwa

Kazuomi Tamae

Herbert Terakawa

Namiemon Tochuken

Notes

Introduction

1. Johnson, "Places You'll Know," 24–50; See also Toulmin and Loiperdinger, "Is It You?," 7–18.

2. Ogihara, "Exhibition of Films," 81. More recently, Fumiaki Itakura expands this work in a Japanese-language publication *Eiga to imin: zaibei Nikkei imin no eiga juyō to aidentiti*.

3. Bean, Kapse, and Horak, *Silent Cinema*, 2.

4. Keil and Stamp, *American Cinema's Transitional Era*, 2.

5. Elsaesser, *Film History*, 73.

6. For a cogent exhibition review, see Glick, "Exhibition Review."

7. For a review of the series *Asian Americans*, see Okada, "Representation, Recognition"; see also the interview with the filmmaker in Khor, "History."

8. The screening series featured a virtual event with the filmmakers Roddy Bogawa, Shu Lea Cheang, Richard Fung, Jon Moritsugu, Spencer Nakasako, and Rea Tajiri. See Sentient.Art.Film, "My Sight Is Lined with Visions," accessed September 12, 2021, https://www.sentientartfilm.com/my-sight-is-lined-with-visions.

9. Contributing authors include Josslyn Luckett, Oliver Wang, Viola Lasmana, Lan Duong, and Melissa Phruksachart. See Hu and Rich, "Dossier."

10. Luckett, "Searching for Betty Chen"; other scholars like Klavier Wang look to new archives for reexamining the community-based multilingual media practices of Asian CineVision (ACV). Wang reidentified and helped process for NYU archives over 380 tapes made in the 1970s by the Manhattan-based media organization. Wang, "Awakening Immigrant Voices: Chinese Cable Television in 1970s–1980s New York Chinatown," paper presented at the Orphan Film Symposium, virtually, May 28, 2020.

11. For accounts of post-1968 Asian American cinema, see Xing, *Asian America*; Feng, *Identities in Motion*; Mimura, *Ghostlife of Third Cinema*; Okada, *Making Asian American Film*.

12. James, *Most Typical Avant-Garde*.

13. Gunckel, *Mexico on Main Street*.

14. Gerow, *Visions of Japanese Modernity*, 113.

15. Kitamura, *Screening Enlightenment*; see also Walsh, "'No Place'"; Itatsu, "Japan's Hollywood Boycott Movement."

16. Serna, *Making Cinelandia*.

17. Azuma, *Between Two Empires*; see also Yoneyama, "Toward a Decolonial Genealogy."

18. Miyao, *Sessue Hayakawa*; Liu, "When Dragon Ladies Die"; Chan, *Perpetually Cool*; Wang, "Anna May Wong"; Chung, *Hollywood Asian*.

19. Stewart, *Migrating to the Movies*, 6.

20. Altman, *Sound Theory, Sound Practice*.

21. Bernardi, *Birth of Whiteness*, 6; in addition to Bernardi's work, scholars have produced a significant body of scholarship on African American connections to the circulation of kung fu and martial arts films in the United States during the 1970s. To name a few, see Desser, "Kung Fu Craze"; Ongiri, "'Just like Bruce Lee'"; Cha-Jua, "Black Audiences"; for another comparative perspective focused on early Hollywood, see Marez, "Pancho Villa."

22. The scholarship on Afro-Asian connection centered on Japan and Japanese Americans includes Kurashige, *Shifting Grounds of Race*; Mullen, *Afro-Orientalism*; Onishi, *Transpacific Antiracism*; Schleitwiler, *Strange Fruit*; Horne, *Facing the Rising Sun*.

23. The phrase "families of resemblance" comes from Lipsitz, "Cruising around the Historical"; for a related concept in media studies, see Shohat, "Ethnicities-in-Relation"; Shohat and Stam, *Unthinking Eurocentrism*.

24. Tajima-Peña, "Moving the Image"; Mimura, *Ghostlife of Third Cinema*; Luckett, "Toward a More Perfect."

25. Kishi, "Final Mix: Unscheduled."

26. Smoodin, "As the Archive Turned," 100.

27. Field, *Uplift Cinema*, 26.

28. The Media History Digital Library has recently begun to expand its holdings into non-English-language sources.

29. King, "Early Hollywood," xi.

30. For a discussion of Japanese American print media, see Robinson, *Pacific Citizens*; Yoo, "'Read All about It.'"

31. Azuma, "Hoji Shinbun Digital Collection."

32. The database is an unparalleled resource containing over 145 titles from the continental United States, Hawaii, and across the Japanese global diaspora. Sources like the San Francisco–based newspapers *Japanese-American News* and *New World Sun* began English-language sections as early as the 1910s. The majority of my sources were focused on the English-language sections and in newspapers produced in California and Washington.

33. Moore, "Ephemera as Medium," 136.

34. I would like to acknowledge the work of the primary participants involved in the restoration of *The Oath of the Sword* (via the grant proposal from the National Film Preservation Foundation), especially Caroline Yeager and Anthony L'Abbate, from the George Eastman Museum, and Karen Ishizuka, Thomas Gallatin, and Kristen Hayashi, from the Japanese American National Museum. Thanks also to Dan Streible for his continual support, and to Stephen Gong for his mentorship.

35. Arthur Dong also published a collection of his archival research on early Chinese American film history wherein he chronicles the discovery of *The Curse of Quon Gwon*. For a discussion of his restoration work, see Dong, *Hollywood Chinese*.

36. Lau, "Marion E. Wong."

37. For scholarship on early Chinese American filmmaking, see Kar, Bren, and Ho, *Hong Kong Cinema*; Curry, "Part One"; Curry, "Part Two"; Wang, "Alter-Centering Chi-

nese Cinemas"; Gruenewald and Wang, "East-West Flows"; Gow, "Performing Chinatown"; Fahlstedt, *Chinatown Film Culture*.

38. *Golden Gate Girls*, directed by Wei Shiyu (2013); Seid, "Forever Her Chinatown."

39. In 2008, Milestone released a DVD of the restored film *The Dragon Painter* along with supplemental materials.

Chapter One

1. Ichioka, "Japanese Associations."

2. Kurashige, *Shifting Grounds of Race*.

3. Azuma, *Between Two Empires*.

4. The Supreme Court's decision rested on the question of race. In its 1922 landmark decision, the court ruled that Ozawa was not "white" because he was not "Caucasian" (which was defined by the pseudoscience of racial taxonomy) and therefore ineligible for naturalized citizenship. For background on the case, see Ichioka, "Early Japanese Immigrant Quest."

5. Ichioka, "Japanese Associations," 409–437.

6. Palmquist, "Asian Photographers."

7. Sueyoshi, "Mindful Masquerades"; see also Sueyoshi, *Discriminating Sex*.

8. Lupack, *Early Race Filmmaking*, 7; scholars and historians such as Thomas Cripps and Pearl Bowser conducted pioneering archival work on the history of race films. The scholarship on the race film industry, its filmmakers and film productions, is vast and includes Cripps, "Birth of a Race"; Bowser, Gaines, and Musser, *Oscar Micheaux*; Gaines, *Fire and Desire*; Stewart, *Migrating to the Movies*; Caddoo, *Envisioning Freedom*; Field, *Uplift Cinema*.

9. Miyao, *Sessue Hayakawa*, 24–27.

10. Miyao, 27.

11. "Protest Referred," *Los Angeles Herald*, January 27, 1916; "Proposal to prevent the celebration of [the] anti-Japanese motion picture," January 1, 1916, in Gijiroku [characters] [Minutes of meetings]. Japanese American Research Project (Yuji Ichioka) collection of material about Japanese in the United States (Collection 2010), Library Special Collections, Charles E. Young Research Library, UCLA [translated by Toshikuni Kawashima].

12. "Japanese Seek to Halt Film 'The Cheat': Censorship Board See the Opera House Picture and Approves It," *San Bernardino Daily Sun*, January 22, 1916, 5; "Japanese Protest Photoplay Exhibition," *Los Angeles Herald*, January 22, 1916.

13. *Moving Picture World*, February 19, 1916, 1114.

14. "Japanese Paper Makes Objection to Play of Local House," *Honolulu Star Bulletin*, May 23, 1916, 5.

15. Miyao, *Sessue Hayakawa*, 28.

16. Cripps, *Slow Fade to Black*; Rogin, "'Sword Became a Flashing.'"

17. Fields, *Uplift Cinema*, 151–184.

18. *Motion Picture News*, February 19, 1916, 992.

19. "Japanese Seek to Halt Film," 5.

20. Birchard, *Cecil B. DeMille's Hollywood*.

21. Yasutaro Soga, "Race Problems and Moving Pictures," *Nippu Jiji*, October 6, 1920, 1.

22. S. Tasaka, "The Film in Question," *Nippu Jiji*, April 21, 1924; "'Clansman' to Be Shown in Hawaii," *Nippu Jiji*, April 20, 1924, 1.

23. "Club Formed by Japanese Players," *Motography*, November 3, 1917, 919; "Jap Photoplayers Club," *Moving Picture Weekly*, October 20, 1917, 16; "Japanese Players Organize," *Motion Picture World*, October 13, 1917, 244; "Photoplayers Club Formed by Japanese Players," *Moving Picture World*, November 3, 1917, 679.

24. See Lopez, *Asian American Media Activism*.

25. With Aoyama's death in 1939, his legacy as an Issei pioneer in Hollywood was commemorated in the Japanese American press. See "Death Claims, Aoyama, Hollywood Issei Film Pioneer's Career Told," *Rafu Shimpo*, December 17, 1939, 3; "Aoyama, Former Screen Actor, Expires in L.A.," *New World Sun*, December 18, 1939.

26. Miyao, *Sessue Hayakawa*, 28.

27. Hayakawa, *Zen Showed Me*, 146.

28. While the Yamato Graph Motion Picture Company has been largely unacknowledged within historiographical accounts of early American film companies, it is mentioned in Kishi, "Final Mix: Unscheduled."

29. Ichioka, *Issei*, 146.

30. Azuma, *In Search*; see also Azuma, *Between Two Empires*.

31. For a discussion of the Yamato Colony, see Matsumoto, *Farming the Home Place*; Noda, *Yamato Colony*.

32. Matsumoto.

33. "California Movies," *Japan Weekly Mail*, December 6, 1913, 737; "Immigrants in 'Movies,'" *Japan Weekly Mail*, December 11, 1913, 755.

34. "California Movies"; "Immigrants in 'Movies.'"

35. "California Movies," 737.

36. "California Movies," 737.

37. "Immigrants in 'Movies,'" 755.

38. Fumiaki, *Eiga to imin*.

39. "California Movies," 737.

40. "Activities in Hawaii Will Be Shown in Film," *Nippu Jiji*, July 26, 1919, 1; "Japanese in the U.S. Are Earnest in Big Exposition," *Nippu Jiji*, July 23, 1919; "Coast Japanese Decide to Take Part in Tokyo Fair," *Nippu Jiji*, June 16, 1919.

41. Orgeron, Orgeron, and Streible, *Learning with the Lights*.

42. Homer Yasui, interview with author, January 14, 2017; Azuma, "History of Oregon's Issei."

43. Harrison, *Japanese Newspaper and Magazine*.

44. Ichioka, *Issei*, 205.

45. "Japanese-American Film Company: Organization Number Forty Japanese Players and Is Located at Los Angeles—Has Made Successful Pictures," *Moving Picture World*, October 17, 1914, 314.

46. *Motography*, February 7, 1914, 168; County of Los Angeles, "Articles of Incorporation of the Japanese American Film Manufacturing Company," 1913, California State Archives.

47. "Japanese-American Film Company," 314.

48. Waller, "Japan on America's Screens."

49. Browne, "Undoing of the Other."

50. Browne.

51. Miyao, *Sessue Hayakawa*, 56.

52. *Moving Picture World*, October 10, 1914, 139.

53. "Jap Films by Jap Actors," *Moving Picture World*, October 10, 1914, 199; "Japanese-American Film Company," 314.

54. Rev. E. Boudinot, "Katana, the Oath of the Sword: An Unusually Refreshing Story of Japanese Life Portrayed by Real Japanese People," *Moving Picture World*, October 10, 1914, 200.

55. Field, *Uplift Cinema*.

56. Edwin M. La Roche, "The Oath of the Sword," *Motion Picture Magazine*, January 1915, 90.

57. Stewart, *Migrating to the Movies*, 191.

58. Azuma, *Between Two Empires*, 25.

59. Ichioka, *Issei*, 24.

60. Uzawa, "Will White Man."

61. Kirihara, "Accepted Idea Displaced."

62. La Roche, "Oath of the Sword," 92.

63. Gaines, *Within Our Gates*.

64. "Sawyer with Two New Companies," *Moving Picture World*, October 10, 1914, 202.

65. "Jap Films by Jap Actors," 199.

66. "A Japanese Producing Firm," *Motion Picture News*, July 25, 1914, 58.

67. Yellowface had its heyday in the classical Hollywood era with films like *Bitter Tea of General Yen* (1933) and *The Good Earth* (1937), although it was also in play at the industry's inception with films like *Chinese Laundry Scene* (Edison, 1894). As Karla Rae Fuller notes, "Implicit in the practice of Asian impersonation by Caucasian actors in Hollywood is the assumption that the Caucasian face provides the physically normative standard onto which an ethnic inscription can take place." As industry practice, yellowface by white actors has long shaped the racial politics of casting and served as barriers for Asian and Asian American actors in Hollywood. See Fuller, *Hollywood Goes Oriental*, 1.

68. "Noted Actress and Actor Form Film Company," *Nippu Jiji*, October 20, 1919, 1; "Noted Actor Now Newspaper Writer," *Nippu Jiji*, March 27, 1920, 8.

69. "Americans and Japanese Plan Film Company," *Nippu Jiji*, October 2, 1919, 1.

70. "Fresno, Cal., as Studio Site," *Motion Picture News*, March 24, 1917.

71. Grace Kingsley, "Japan to Be Exploited as Film Location Field," *Los Angeles Times*, October 13, 1916, II3.

72. *Picture Play Magazine*, September 1916.

73. "Fujiyama Feature Films Are to Be Produced in City," *Redlands Daily Review*, September 12, 1916.

74. For a discussion of the novel, see Ito, "Family and the Nation," 490.

75. "Japan as Setting: Unique Film Production to Be Made in Far East by Nipponese Company," *Los Angeles Times*, December 3, 1916, A22.

76. Kingsley, "Japan to Be Exploited," II3.

77. *Moving Picture World*, October 21, 1916, 504.

78. "Film Star to Be First Japanese Woman to Fly," *Los Angeles Herald*, September 23, 1916.

79. "Japan as Setting," A22; "Plan Nippon Feature: Fujiyama Film Company Soon to Sail across Pacific," *Los Angeles Times*, March 18, 1917, III16.

80. *Moving Picture World* (October 1912–December 1912), 1312; Yamatograph Co. Articles of Incorporation #17666, Oregon State Archives; *Polk's Portland (Oregon) city directory*, Portland, OR: R. L. Polk & Co., 1914; *Polk's Portland (Oregon) city directory*, Portland, OR: R.L. Polk & Co., 1915.

81. "'Oath of the Swords' Innovation in Films," *Oregon Daily Journal*, October 18, 1914, 35; the exhibition of the film in Wisconsin and Indiana is mentioned in Waller, "Japan on America's Screens," 142; the film also had several screenings in California at the Majestic Theatre in Los Angeles and the Elmo Theatre in San Luis Obispo. See *Morning Tribune*, January 22, 1915, 2; *San Pedro News Pilot*, June 8, 1916.

82. Ward, "Price of Independence."

83. Miyao, *Sessue Hayakawa*, 153–167.

Chapter Two

1. Clarence Iwao Nishizu, oral history interview by Arthur A. Hansen, June 14, 1982, Honorable Stephen K. Tamura Orange County Japanese American Oral History Project.

2. "The Kinmon Gakuen Show Goes 'Over the Top,'" *Japanese-American News*, October 25, 1925.

3. Waller, "Locating Early Non-Theatrical Audiences," 85.

4. Acland and Wasson, *Useful Cinema*.

5. Field and Gordon, *Screening Race*, 1.

6. Dym, *Benshi, Japanese Silent Film*; Dym, "Benshi and the Introduction."

7. According to newspapers, the Japanese proprietor had operated the Bison and Electric Theaters in Seattle for fifteen years prior to the Atlas Theater's grand opening in 1918. Yamada was co-owner of the Atlas Theater. See "Yamada and Kaita Open the Atlas," *Moving Picture World*, December 14, 1918, 1225.

8. Ito, *Issei*.

9. Mason and McKinstry, *Japanese of Los Angeles*.

10. Ogihara, "Exhibition of Films," 82.

11. "Japanese Theater," *Sacramento Union*, July 15, 1908.

12. *City directories of the United States, 1902–1935, Sacramento, CA*. Woodbridge, CT: Research Publications.

13. Walker, "History of Theatrical Activity."

14. "Japanese to Banzai in Own Theater: Orientals to Build Show House at Fresno," *San Francisco Call*, January 9, 1911; "New Japanese Theater Opens," *Fresno Herald*, December 23, 1912.

15. "Japanese Buying Smaller Theaters," *Moving Picture World*, January 18, 1919, 332.

16. Koszarski, "Flu Season."

17. "Notes on Washington Theaters," *Moving Picture World*, July 20, 1918, 428; "New Seattle Theatre for Japanese Patrons," *Exhibitors Herald*, December 2, 1918; "Yamada and Kaita Open the Atlas," *Moving Picture World*, December 7, 1918; "Yamada and Kaita Open the Atlas," *Moving Picture World*, December 14, 1918, 1225.

18. Merritt, "Nickelodeon Theaters, 1905–1914"; Musser, *Emergence of Cinema*.

19. Film scholars had a robust debate over ethnic immigrants and film exhibition and spectatorship, especially related to New York City. See Allen, "Motion Picture Exhibition"; Singer, "Manhattan Nickelodeons"; Allen, "Manhattan Myopia"; Uricchio and Pearson, "Manhattan's Nickelodeons"; Mullins, "Ethnic Cinema"; Thissen, "Beyond the Nickelodeon."

20. Fuller, *At the Picture Show*.

21. Lee, *Claiming the Oriental Gateway*, 33.

22. Ito, *Issei*, 136.

23. Kurashige, *Shifting Grounds of Race*.

24. Caddoo, *Envisioning Freedom*, 70.

25. Lassiter, "De Jure/De Facto Segregation."

26. For an extended discussion of Japanese Americans and racial segregation in California, see Kurashige, *Shifting Grounds of Race*; Brooks, *Alien Neighbors, Foreign Friends*.

27. Jensen, "Apartheid: Pacific Coast Style"; Chacon, "Beginnings of Racial Segregation"; McClain, "In Re Lee Sing."

28. Frank Miyamoto, oral history interview by Stephen Fugita, March 18, 1998, Densho Digital Archive.

29. Frank Miyamoto, oral history interview.

30. Heitaro Hikida, interview cited in Ito, *Issei*, 97.

31. Sakigake Hideyoshi, interview cited in Ito, *Issei*, 373.

32. For a discussion of African American racial segregation in southern film theaters, see Regester, "From the Buzzard's Roost"; Gue, "'It Seems That Everything'"; Turner and Kennedy, "Exclusion, Ejection, and Segregation."

33. *Polk-Husted directory co.'s Fresno and Coalinga City and Fresno County directory*. 1910. Sacramento, Calif: Polk-Husted Directory Co.

34. "Yamada and Kaita open Atlas," *Moving Picture World*, December 14, 1918, 1225.

35. Florence Eng, oral history interview by Ron Chew, November 15, 1990, Wing Luke Asian Museum, Seattle, Washington.

36. "Theater, Not Dive, Says Police Chief," *Sacramento Union*, March 20, 1911.

37. "The Yellow Peril," *Moving Picture World*, February 25, 1911, 418.

38. *Proceedings of the Asiatic Exclusion League of San Francisco February*, 1908. Forgotten Books, 275; see also "Japs May be Deported: H. Iwata of Fresno Jailed for Being Illegally in Country," *San Francisco Call*, August 13, 1913; "Iwata and Wife Will Escape Deportation," *Fresno Morning Republican*, September 27, 1913, 6; "To Deport Iwata by November 15," *Fresno Morning Republican*, October 16, 1914, 14; "Year of Delay Is Gained by Iwata," *Fresno Morning Republican*, October 4, 1915, 12; "Seeks By Law to Avoid Deportation," *Los Angeles Herald*, December 7, 1914.

39. "Theater, Not Dive, Says Police Chief."

40. "Japanese Buying Smaller Theaters," *Moving Picture World*, January 18, 1919, 332.

41. Frank, *Purchasing Power*, 230.

42. "Japanese Buying Smaller Theaters," 332.

43. Ogihara, "Exhibition of Films," 82.

44. "Japanese to Banzai in Own Theater."

45. "New Seattle Theatre for Japan Patrons," *Exhibitors Herald*, December 21, 1918, 43.

46. *Moving Picture World*, April 28, 1923, 916.

47. Ogihara, "Exhibition of Films," 87.

48. "Coast Japanese Shot by Gunmen," *Nippu Jiji*, June 9, 1931, 1.

49. Kitamura, *Screening Enlightenment*, 14.

50. U.S. Bureau of the Census, *Foreign Commerce and Navigation*.

51. Bernardi, "Catching a Film Audience," 290.

52. Swan wrote about popular films, Hollywood actresses, film fashion, and other topics for a female readership. Swan's Across the Silver Sheet resembled columns like the *New World Sun*'s Dear Deidre, which was an advice column intended for Nisei women. See Matsumoto, "Desperately Seeking."

53. "The Kinmon Gakuen Show Goes 'Over the Top,'" *Rafu Shimpo*, October 25, 1925.

54. Alfred "Al" Miyagishima, oral history interview by Tom Ikeda, May 13, 2008, Densho Digital Archive.

55. "Japan Talkies," *New World Sun*, July 19, 1935.

56. George Uchida, oral history interview by Richard Potashin, April 9, 2009, Densho Digital Archive.

57. "Fresno YWBA to Commemorate 15th Anniversary with Pictures," *New World Sun*, September 26, 1935.

58. "Fresno YMWBA To Sponsor Benefit," *New World Sun*, May 16, 1936, 2.

59. "WCTU Plans Movie Show," *Japanese-American News*, January 5, 1930, 1.

60. "Berry Exchange to Give Florin Movies," *New World Sun*, July 7, 1937.

61. Groening, "'We Can See Ourselves,'" 34–58.

62. "Long Beach to Show Educational Film," *Rafu Shimpo*, October 31, 1933, 6.

63. "Local Y to Hold Movies Two Nights," *Japanese-American News*, September 14, 1928, 1; "Japanese Movie Packs Kinmon Hall," *New World Sun*, January 18, 1932, 8.

64. "Japanese-American News Gives Free Exhibition of Davis Cup Film," *Japanese-American News*, July 5, 1926, 8.

65. "Komako Sunada Film to Be Shown in S.F. Wed.," *Japanese-American News*, April 25, 1927, 8.

66. "Amusement Firm to Show Weekly Movies in S.F.," *New World Sun Daily*, April 8, 1940, 1.

67. "Bride-Widow Told in Film Tale," *Rafu Shimpo*, October 29, 1939, 9.

68. "Citizens' League Sponsors Benefit Movie This Month," *Rafu Shimpo*, May 5, 1932, 5.

69. Fujiki, "Benshi as Stars," 71.

70. Gerow, *Visions of Japanese Modernity*, 148.

71. Itakura, *Eiga to imin*.

72. "Namiemon Presents Three-Night Movies," *New World Daily News*, December 20, 1933, 8.

73. Nori Masuda, Masako Inada, Fumi Nakajima, and Setsu Hirasuna, interview with Sayoko Taira, January 25, 1980, Fresno West Side, CSU Japanese American Digitization Project, California State University, Dominguez Hills, Archives and Special Collections.

74. Tetsuo Ted Ishihara, oral history interview by Natsuye Bernice Endow, October 2, 1997, and January 19, 1998, JACL/CSUC Oral History Project.

75. Musser, *High-Class Moving Pictures*, 6.

76. Azuma, *Between Two Empires*, 177.

77. Takeshi Ban Papers, 96.5.200, Japanese American National Museum, Los Angeles, CA.

78. Azuma, *Between Two Empires*, 177.

79. "Professor Ban to Show Picture at Nippon Kan," *Great Northern Daily News*, August 29, 1934, 1.

80. Azuma, *Between Two Empires*, 177.

81. Takeshi Ban Papers, 96.5.200, Japanese American National Museum, Los Angeles, CA.

82. "Japan's Blood Superior; Ban," *New World Daily News*, January 19, 1934, 1.

83. Azuma, *Between Two Empires*, 177.

84. "The Fourth Lecture of the Japanese Racial Culture," July 1937–June 1938, Takeshi Ban Papers, 96.5.200, Japanese American National Museum, Los Angeles, CA; "Culture Lectures to Begin in L.A. under Prof. Ban," *New World Sun*, July 1, 1937, 1.

85. Pacific Society of Religious Education, letter from Pacific Society of Religious Education to W. E. B. Du Bois, November 4, 1936, W. E. B. Du Bois Papers (MS 312), Special Collections and University Archives, University of Massachusetts Amherst Libraries.

86. Pacific Society of Religious Education, letter from Pacific Society of Religious Education to W. E. B. Du Bois, June 30, 1937, W. E. B. Du Bois Papers (MS 312), Special Collections and University Archives, University of Massachusetts Amherst Libraries.

87. Onishi and Shinoda, "Paradigm of Refusal"; these ideas interconnecting Japan were also taken up by pro-Japan Black nationalists, who saw the utility of Japanese imperialism ("Asia for Asians") in conceiving Black self-determination. See Lipsitz, "'Frantic to Join'"; Ernest, "When Japan Was."

88. Segrave, *Foreign Films in America*.

Chapter Three

1. "Foreign-Born Film Actors See Handwriting on the Wall, Retreat before Onslaught on 'Talkies,'" *San Bernardino Sun*, February 4, 1929, 3.

2. Gomery, *Coming of Sound*.

3. Melnick, *American Showman*.

4. Scholarship on the sound transition in the American context includes Crafton, *Talkies*; Lastra, *Sound Technology*; Abel and Altman, *Sounds of Early Cinema*; Eyman, *Speed of Sound*.

5. Freiberg, "Transition to Sound."

6. Iwamoto, "Sound in the Early."

7. "First Japanese Engaged as Fox Talkie Scenario Writer," *New World Sun*, August 31, 1931, 1.

8. "Gaynor Farrell Picture Heard in Successful L.A. Japanese Preview," *Japanese-American News*, October 29, 1931, 1.

9. "Japanese Version of Talkies Made for Distribution," *Rafu Shimpo*, September 11, 1932, 7.

10. Durovicová, "Translating America," 138–153.

11. Nornes, *Cinema Babel*.

12. Vincendeau, "Hollywood Babel"; Maltby and Vasey, "International Language Problem."

13. Nornes, *Cinema Babel*, 149; See also Yasar, *Electrified Voices*, 176–177.

14. "Gaynor Farell Picture Heard," 1; "Film with Japanese Talking Now Shown," *Rafu Shimpo*, November 28, 1931, 6.

15. Higson and Maltby, *"Film Europe"*; Latham, "Selling Hollywood," 60–63.

16. "Many Tongues Being Used in Sound Films," *Los Angeles Times*, February 9, 1930, B21; see also "Japanese Shorts"; "Foreign Production Department"; "Kembu Goes Talkie, Too," *Rafu Shimpo*, September 15, 1930, 1; "Japanese Tots in Movietone Parasol Dance," *Rafu Shimpo*, June 15, 1930, 1; "Talkie Takes Japanese Tots in Movie at Terminal Island," *Japan-California Daily News*, March 14, 1932.

17. "First Year of Japanese Talkies Marked in Meet," *Japanese-American News*, April 21, 1931, 1.

18. "Talkie Gets Katsuben to Synchronize," *Rafu Shimpo*, June 9, 1930, 1. For more coverage of Matsui's role in the film, see also "American Talkie to Employ Japanese as Explainer for Film," *Japanese-American News*, May 21, 1930, 1; "Hollywood Talkie Made in Japanese Is Sent to Japan," *Japanese-American News*, July 31, 1930, 1; "Paramount Completes Japan Talkie," *Rafu Shimpo*, July 28, 1931, 1.

19. "Benshi Given New Role," *Japanese-American News*, September 26, 1933, 1.

20. Buddy Uno, "Mr. Suisei Matsui," *Rafu Shimpo*, August 13, 1933, 6; "Beach Party Fetes Paramount Actor," *New World Daily News*, August 14, 1933, 1.

21. "A Benshi of the Films: Preparing a Version of 'Paramount on Parade' Is but One of His Problems," *New York Times*, August 2, 1930, 97. Other mainstream articles include "Leading Actor of Japan Here," *Los Angeles Times*, August 8, 1933.

22. "Byrd-Paramount on Parade Program," 15.

23. "First Year of Japanese Talkies Marked in Meet," *Japanese-American News*, April 21, 1931, 1; additionally, pocket-sized books featuring accompanying English-Japanese translations, or "dialogue textbooks," were circulated at some of Paramount's sound film exhibitions in Japan. As one source noted, this was done "to enable Japanese picturegoers to understand Paramount talkies better and, at the same time, help familiarize them with the English language." See "Japanese Posters Are Colorful Ad Sales," *Paramount Around the World* vol. 3 no. 1 (January 1, 1930).

24. Kinoshita, "Benshi Track."

25. Layton and Pierce, *King of Jazz*, 204.

26. In the *Kinema Junpo* article, Komai describes how *King of Jazz* was shot hastily over the course of two days. Komai, along with Iris Yomokai, was cast as a "host" for the film and also asked to translate. Komai found the task of translation especially challenging. "The script flows well in English, but much of it won't make sense in Japanese," Komai complained. "All the fine nuances would disappear as if I were to translate it as it is." Consequently, Komai "freely adapted the script" with translation help from Kisaku Ito. When the shooting began, Komai had "no time to rehearse" and the "Japanese lettering on the scrapbook was attached upside down." Moreover, because the film was shot in Technicolor, "the lighting was three times as strong as in a regular film shoot," and Komai had to "redo make-up every two minutes." The account is reproduced in Layton and Pierce, 206.

27. Stoever, *Sonic Color Line*.

28. Chung, "From 'Me So Horny,'" 172; see also Pao, "False Accents."

29. An outtake recording of Sojin Kamiyama's performance as host for *Happy Days* (1929) is held at the Moving Image Research Collections at the University of South Carolina.

30. "Manifest Good Points," *Nippu Jiji*, April 28, 1929, 2.

31. Bell, "Talkie Voices."

32. Beltrán, "Dolores Del Rio."

33. Bell, "Talkie Voices."

34. Bell, "Talkie Voices."

35. Stoever, *Sonic Color Line*, 13.

36. Maurice, "'Cinema at Its Source.'"

37. Larry Tajiri, "Meet the Japanese . . . in Hollywood," *Japanese-American News*, January 1, 1937, 5.

38. "As Comedy Relief," *Rafu Shimpo*, August 20, 1933, 6; "Trio Given Movie Bits,' *Japanese-American News*, August 22, 1933, 1; in a cleverly titled column called Mebbe You Know Better, Roku Sugahara quipped, "Eddie Holden, of Frank Watanabe fame, is teaching Tokio star Matsui how to speak pidgin English. Seems that there should be local lads who could help Matsui much more." *Japan California Daily News*, August 24, 1933, 8.

39. T. John Fujii, "Nippon Nisei-Logue," *New World Sun*, July 3, 1935, 8.

40. "First Japanese Talkie to Star Sojin Kamiyama," *Nippu Jiji*, December 23, 1929, 1; by 1931, Shochiku signed Kamiyama and celebrated his return by producing an over-the-top star vehicle *Ai yo jinrui to tomo ni are* (Love, be with humanity, 1931). The film was directed by Yasujiro Shimazu and epic in length at an astonishing 200,000 feet of film negative. It featured 30 stars and employed 80,000 extras. While *Ai yo jinrui to tomo ni are* was a silent film, Kamiyama worked on a few early sound pictures with Sho-chiku, including *Satsueijo romansu renai annai* (1932) and *Kanraku no yo wa kukete* (1934). From the 1930s until 1954, Kamiyama continued to work in the Japanese film industry, appearing in at least thirty Japanese films.

41. Gunckel, *Mexico on Main Street*; Gunckel, "War of the Accents."

42. Kitamura, *Screening Enlightenment*.

43. "Sessue Hayakawa Film Entry and Exit," *Rafu Shimpo*, March 29, 1936, 5.

44. "Sessue Hayakawa Visits Japan Soon," *Nippu Jiji*, January 9, 1929, 3.

45. "S. Hayakawa to Return; Will Produce Pictures Here with U.S. Folk in the Cast," *Nippu Jiji*, November 1, 1929, 2.

46. "Hayakawa, Japanese Movie Star, to Sail for Japan Saturday," *Japanese-American News*, March 29, 1930, 1.

47. "Hayakawa Plans Costly Studio," *Nippu Jiji*, April 2, 1930, 1; "Hayakawa, Japanese Movie Star," 1.

48. "Keep Off Sessue Hayakawa, Cry of Labor in Japan," *Nippu Jiji*, April 7, 1930, 1.

49. "Hayakawa Not on Board Chichibu," *Nippu Jiji*, August 15, 1930, 1.

50. Rainsberger, *James Wong Howe: Cinematographer*, 16; Commenting on film changing from a chemical enterprise to an electrical one with the coming of sound, Wong remarked, "They always had to have this big boom with a microphone hanging and that really interfered with lighting. Sometimes where we wanted the key light, the boom would be there and if we changed the key light, when they moved the boom from one actor to another, you had to be careful you didn't see the shadows. It [sound filming] restricted our lighting." Scott, *Five American Cinematographers*, 67. In an interview with Alain Silver, Howe also noted that when sound came in, "things had changed. . . . The cameras were different, there were new lenses, the lights were different, so people were afraid." Silver, *Camera Eye*, 103.

51. Regev, *Working in Hollywood*.

52. "Howe's Jap Talkers," *Variety*, January 15, 1930, 7.

53. "This Will Be Try-Out House for Spanish Made Pictures," *Hollywood Filmograph*, March 22, 1930, 14; "Latin Films Only," *Film Daily*, March 23, 1930, 1.

54. "Howe's Jap Talkers," *Variety*, January 15, 1930, 7.

55. Marez, "Pancho Villa Meets Sun Yat-Sen."

56. Battat, *Ain't Got No Home*.

57. Chang, "Deployments, Engagements, Obliterations"; Lui, "Rehabilitating Chinatown."

58. *Close-Up* briefly noted a studio described as the "Teruo Mayeda Company, composed wholly of Japanese." *Close-Up* 6 no. 3 (March 1930), 241.

59. Higa, "Hidden in Plain Sight," 36; Archie Miyatake, interview by Martha Nakagawa, August 31–September 1, 2010, Courtesy of Densho.

60. Reed, "Wind Came."

61. "The Tragedy of Life," *Hollywood Filmograph*, June 21, 1930, 20.

62. "First American-Made Japanese Picture to be Shown," *Hollywood Filmograph*, April 12, 1930, 17.

63. "First American-Made Japanese Picture," 17.

64. "New Venture May Presage Big Future," *Rafu Shimpo*, December 2, 1929, 1.

65. "All Nippon-Talkie Near Completion," *Rafu Shimpo*, April 28, 1930, 1.

66. "First American-Made Japanese Picture," 17.

67. "The Tragedy of Life," 20.

68. "The Trajedy of Life," 20; "First Japanese Road Film by America," *Variety*, July 9, 1930, 7; "Talkie Well Received by Many Critics," *Rafu Shimpo*, June 16, 1930, 1; Larry Tajiri, "Film Fun," *Japanese-American News*, October 30, 1930, 1.

69. Itakura, *Eiga to imin*.

70. "All-Nippon Talkie Near Completion," *Rafu Shimpo*, April 28, 1930, 1.

71. "Complete Chinese Talker," *Motion Picture News*, April 26, 1930, 38.

72. "First Japanese Talkie," *Japanese-American News*, June 15, 1930, 1.

73. "Nippon Talkie on Screen at Hongwanji Soon," *Rafu Shimpo*, September 22, 1930, 1; "Japanese 'Talkie' Soon to Be Shown," *Rafu Shimpo*, September 22, 1930, 3.

74. "All Japanese Talkie to Be Shown Twice," *Rafu Shimpo*, October 3, 1930, 8.

75. "First Japanese Road Film."

76. "First Japanese Road Film."

77. "Talkie with All Japanese Cast Made on Coast," *Nippu Jiji*, February 16, 1930, 1.

78. "Talkie Well Received by Many Critics," *Rafu Shimpo*, June 16, 1930, 1.

79. Tajiri, "Film Fun," 1.

80. Jacobs, "James Wong Howe," 219.

81. Tepperman, *Amateur Cinema*.

82. "Hollywood Motion Picture Men Start New Movie Club," *Japanese-American News*, February 3, 1931, 8 (italics added).

83. "Movie Club Is Organized Here," *New World Sun Daily*, May 29, 1938, 7.

84. "Sacramento Camera Club," *New World Sun*, March 2, 1937, 2.

85. Larry Tajiri, "Nisei Life Etched on Celluloid," *Japanese-American News*, December 10, 1934, 1.

86. "Nisei Parade Depicts Life: Photographed against Variegated Scenes of Japanese Life in California," *New World Daily News*, March 14, 1934, 8.

87. For more about the Serisawa brothers, see Higa, "Hidden in Plain Sight"; Robinson, "Great Unknown."

88. "Nisei Parade Depicts Life," 8; Tajiri, "Nisei Life Etched," 1; "A.S.C. Extends Honorable Mention to Amateurs," *American Cinematographer*, February 1935.

89. "Nisei Film to Be Released Through YMCA Sponsorship," *Rafu Shimpo*, December 28, 1934, 6; "Nisei Parade Soon to Be Shown Again," *Rafu Shimpo*, January 20, 1935, 6; "Long Beach to See Nisei-Made Picture," *Rafu Shimpo*, February 2, 1935, 8; "Nisei Parade Tells Story of California Life: To Show Silent Opus in San Francisco on Saturday," *Japanese-American News*, March 13, 1935, 1; "Nisei Parade on Alameda ME Screen March 30," *New World Daily*, March 21, 1935, 1; "Second Generation Life Shown as S.F. Audience Sees Picture," *Japanese-American News*, March 19, 1935, 1; "Wintersburg C.E. Show Nisei Parade," *Rafu Shimpo*, March 28, 1935, 6; "Nisei Parade, Film of California, to Be Screened Saturday at S.F. Hall," *Japanese-American News*, June 7, 1935, 1.

90. According to my research, Hollywood Japanese Association produced the following films: *Taichi ni Shitashimu* (Love of the soil), *Yume ni Yaburarete* (Broken dreams), *Nobiyuku Nisei* (The growing Nisei), *Iminchi no Haha* (Mother of the immigrant soil), and another film, briefly mentioned by newspapers as, *Too Mean Girls*.

91. "Second Nisei Film Casting to Begin," *Rafu Shimpo*, October 28, 1934, 6; "Nisei Lives Depicted in Film," *Rafu Shimpo*, February 16, 1935, 6; "Film to Make Debut in Lil' Tokio Soon," *Rafu Shimpo*, October 7, 1934, 7; "*Taichi ni Shitashimu* Will be Shown at L.A. Union Church," *New World Daily News*, October 10, 1934, 1; "Newly Completed Japanese Film Booked for Union Church Hall This Week-end," *Rafu Shimpo*, October 10, 1934, 6; "Movies on Program of Garden Grove," *Rafu Shimpo*, November 22, 1934; "San Gabriel See Film by Nisei," *Rafu Shimpo*, February 2, 1935, 8; "Films of Lil'

Tokio to Be Previewed," *Rafu Shimpo*, October 2, 1934, 6; "Encinitas to Hold Benefit Movie Show," *Rafu Shimpo*, April 23, 1936, 6.

92. Eiichiro Azuma looks at *Nobiyuku Nisei* as a film that "dramatized major aspects of the Nisei problem from the Issei standpoint" and propagated the back-to-the-farm movement. See Azuma, *Between Two Empires*, 116.

93. Waller, "Projecting the Promise."

94. "Japanese Movie Men Plan Second Film," *Rafu Shimpo*, November 13, 1934, 6.

95. Covered extensively in the Japanese American press and circulating widely across nontheatrical exhibition venues, *Iminchi no Haha* (Mother of the immigrant soil) was a six-reel film based on Los Angeles's Shonien, a Japanese American orphanage, and featured Nisei first-time actors Lily Arikawa, Kay Kawachi, and Lucy Kinoshita. See "Release New Nisei Film Based on Shonien, *Rafu Shimpo*, August, 6, 1935, 6; "Shonien's Film Show Dates Set for City Sites," *Rafu Shimpo*, July 12, 1936, 2; "Shonien Film to Be Shown in L.A. Soon," *Rafu Shimpo*, July 6, 1936, 6; "Southland Nisei Prepare Third Annual Campaign to Boost Shonien Work," *Rafu Shimpo*, February 23, 1936, 7; "City Leaders Prepare for Shonien Film," *Rafu Shimpo*, July 9, 1936, 7.

96. "Nobite Yuku Nisei," *New World Sun*, July 20, 1937, 2.

97. "Reedley Bussei Pick Delegates," *New World Sun*, June 28, 1941, 2.

98. Ogihara, "Exhibition of Films," 87.

99. Drew, *Last Silent Picture Show*, 141.

100. Young, "Synchronized Sound"; Crafton, *Talkies*.

101. Kraft, "'Pit' Musicians"; Fones-Wolf, "Sound Comes"; Kraft, *Stage to Studio*.

102. Jenkins, "'Shall We Make It.'"

103. Anderson, *Japanese Film*, 76.

104. "J.A.U. Swim Meet Film Now Showing at Fuji Theatre," *Rafu Shimpo*, September 13, 1933, 6.

105. Iwamoto, "Sound in the Early."

106. "California Theatre Shows Japan Talkie," *Rafu Shimpo*, December 16, 1931, 6; "Japanese Film at California," *Los Angeles Times*, December 20, 1931, B19; "Japanese Film for Release in America," *Film Daily*, August 14, 1931, 1.

107. Larry Tajiri, "Village Vagaries," *Japanese-American News*, January 25, 1935; Larry Tajiri, "Furusato," *Japanese-American News*, May 26, 1937, 4.

108. Steve Taneyoshi, "Kleig Lights in Nippon: Japanese Lack International Appeal for Her Cinematic Output," *Japanese-American News*, April 21, 1935, 1.

109. *Motion Picture Herald*, January 2, 1932, 39.

110. "New Japanese Film," *Nippu Jiji*, February 9, 1934, 2.

111. "Japanese Talkie," *Nippu Jiji*, April 29, 1933, 8.

112. "Preview of Fumi Kawabata's Film Shown to Critics," *Rafu Shimpo*, June 7, 1935, 6.

113. James T. Hamada, "Noboru Kiritachi is Sylvia Sidney in First Talkie," *Nippu Jiji*, May 30, 1936.

114. "Japanese Movies Wins Praise in N.Y. Premiere," *Nippu Jiji*, April 17, 1937, 3; "'Kimiko' in New York," *New World Sun*, April 10, 1937, 2.

115. *Japanese-American News*, October 11, 1935, E2.

116. *Japan-California Daily News*, April 4, 1932.

117. "Japan Talkies."

118. "Japanese Talkie Will Be Shown in Dinuba," *New World Sun*, July 14, 1935, 8.

119. Nornes, *Cinema Babel*, 133.

120. According to Peter B. High, *Gonin no sekkohei* was derided by Japanese government officials for portraying the war in China as depressing and the Japanese soldiers as weak and suffering. Others embraced the film as a "defense of humanistic values" as well as its depiction of "true military spirit." High, *Imperial Screen*, 200.

121. "Award Movie Set in Newcastle, Monterey," *New World Sun*, July 26, 1938, 8; "Suisun Show," *New World Sun*, July 26, 1938, 7; "Nippon Movies to Be Shown in Oakland," *New World Sun*, September 29, 1938, 7; Nippon Movies to Be Shown in Lodi," *New World Sun*, October 27, 1938, 8.

122. James T. Hamada, "'Gonin No Sekkohei,' Japanese War Drama, Is Well Produced," *Nippu Jiji*, February 15, 1938, 3.

123. "Outstanding Nippon Film to Be Shown at Monterey Hall," *Japanese-American News*, July 29, 1938, 2.

124. "'Nakamura' Is New Japan War Picture," *Japanese-American News*, March 2, 1932, 8.

125. Anderson, *Japanese Film*; High, *Imperial Screen*.

126. "Police in Bellingham Release Two S.F. Japanese after Attempt to Show Nazi Film at Send-Off Party," *New World Sun*, April 12, 1941, 7; "Two S.F. Men Held up North: Films Taken by Police," *Japanese-American News*, April 12, 1941, 7.

127. "San Jose JACL Presents Benefit Movies, Fri., Sat.," *New World Sun*, October 2, 1941, 8.

128. "Woodland YPA Benefit Picture Set for Nov. 12," *New World Sun*, November 6, 1941, 8.

129. Anderson, *Japanese Film*; High, *Imperial Screen*, 92–96; Daniels, "Japanese Domestic Radio."

130. "Salinas Show," *Japanese-American News*, August 26, 1937, 2; "Japanese Movie in Turlock Friday," *New World Sun*, November 3, 1937, 8.

131. "French Camp Camera Club Offer Movie," *New World Sun*, October, 1, 1937, 8.

Chapter Four

1. Palermo v. Stockton Theatres, Inc., 32 Cal. 2d 53 (1948).

2. "Stockton Theatres, Inc. v. Emil Palermo," Supreme Court of the State of California, no. 6243, California State Archives, Sacramento.

3. Strong, *Japanese in California*, 289.

4. Azuma, "Racial Struggle, Immigrant Nationalism," 165.

5. Anderson, *Imagined Communities*.

6. McWilliams, *Factories in the Field*.

7. *Philippine Examiner*, July 30, 1938, 2.

8. Ngai, *Impossible Subjects*, 96–126; Baldoz, *Third Asiatic Invasion*.

9. De Witt, "Watsonville Anti-Filipino Riot"; España-Maram, "Brown 'Hordes'"; Parrenas, "'White Trash'"; Fujita-Rony, "Empire and the Moving Body: Fermin Tobera, Military California, and Rural Space."

10. Mariano Angeles, oral history interview by Cynthia Mejia, 1976.

11. Roces, "'These Guys Came Out.'"

12. Mabalon, *Little Manila*; Yu, "Filipino Migration."

13. Lasker, *Filipino Immigration*; Melendy, "Filipinos in the United States."

14. For a discussion of Japanese immigration and the 1924 law, see Hirobe, *Japanese Pride, American Prejudice*.

15. De Vera, "'Tapia-Saiki Incident.'"

16. Azuma, "Racial Struggle, Immigrant Nationalism."

17. The Star Theatre was first leased in 1930 to three Japanese by the names of Y. Terai, B. Yamada, and S. Tamura. The lease of the theater was transferred twice to corporations of Japanese stockholders, first to the Santa Rosa Theatres in 1934 and second to Stockton Theatres in 1935.

18. *Stockton (San Joaquin County, Calif.) City directory 1933*. S. El Monte, Calif: R. L. Polk; *Stockton (San Joaquin County, Calif.) City directory 1942–1943*. S. El Monte, Calif: R. L. Polk; *Nichi-Bei jūshoroku=The Japanese American directory 1939*. San Francisco: Nichi-Bei Shinbunsha; *Nichi-Bei jūshoroku=The Japanese American directory 1941*. San Francisco: Nichi-Bei Shinbunsha.

19. "Hayashino Shigeaki," report filed by Edgar Bernhardt, Nov. 16, 1944, Records of the War Relocation Authority, record group 210, National Archives, Washington, DC.

20. *Philippine Examiner*, March 31, 1945.

21. *Philippine Examiner*, October 15, 1938.

22. *Philippine Examiner*, October 15, 1938.

23. Jamero, *Growing Up Brown*, 52; this passage is also noted in Mabalon, *Little Manila*.

24. Potamianos, "Hollywood in the Hinterlands."

25. Leavold, "Early Pinoy Films."

26. "Filipino Talkies Showing," *Philippine Examiner*, June 15, 1937, 1.

27. There is one mention in 1932 of the Manila Pictures Company in the American trade publication *Hollywood Filmograph*. Additionally, articles of incorporation for the Manila Pictures Company were filed with the city of San Francisco on August 15, 1932, by a board of directors, including Festo G. Aspre, Vicente B. Asprer, Teodoro E. Estonilo, Amado J. Lloren, Melecio H. Jacaban, Roman A. Estonilo, and Mauricio R. Mabutas. The company's address was listed as 2350 California Street.

28. Tom Walsh, email correspondence with author, January 31, 2016.

29. "O'Brien, Mary Brian on Screen Tomorrow," *Santa Maria Times*, May 25, 1934, 6.

30. "Film Head Accused of Theft in Warrant," *Oakland Tribune*, September 27, 1934, 3; "Filipino Sought in 1st Talkie Theft," *New World Daily News*, September 29, 1934, 1.

31. Del Mundo, *Native Resistance*; Reyes, *Notes on Philippine Cinema*; Yeatter, *Cinema of the Philippines*; for scholarship on contemporary film culture in the Philippines, see Trice, *City of Screens*.

32. Rafael, "Taglish."

33. Salumbides, *Motion Pictures*.

34. *Maui Record*, June 23, 1939, 1.

35. For *Zamboanga*'s discovery in the archives, see Loughney, "American Moving Image Diaspora."

36. Deocampo, *Film*, 263–311.

37. Deocampo, 263–311.

38. P. C. Morantte, "Reviews of Two Filipino Films," *Filipino Pioneer*, July 1, 1938, 6.

39. *Philippine Examiner*, May 31, 1945.

40. For scholarship on historical segregation practices in movie theaters, see Turner, "Exclusion, Ejection, and Segregation"; Conard, "Privilege of Forcibly Ejecting"; Dale, "'Social Equality'"; Regester, "From the Buzzard's Roost."

41. "It's in the Bag, Boys! Watch M-G-M," *Film Daily*, September 4, 1929, 3; "White Theatres Book Sack's 'Two-Gun Man,'" *Boxoffice*, July 23, 1938, 110; "Wow Negro Show Treated as Confidential in Tex.," *Variety*, November 28, 1933, 53; "An Injunction Suit over Negro Showing Waits," *Boxoffice*, August 26, 1939, 84; see also "Black House out of Red," *Motion Picture Herald*, April 30, 1932, 34; "Negroes Movie-Conscious; Support 430 Film Houses," *Motion Picture Herald*, January 24, 1942, 33; "800 Negro Theatres in 32 States Point to Growing Demand," *Motion Picture Herald*, August 15, 1936, 27.

42. Interview with Johnny Latosa, who was the president of the Filipino Community of Stockton, is cited in Hemminger, "Little Manila," 28.

43. These accounts of racial discrimination in Stockton's cinemas are documented in a compilation of oral history interviews conducted by the Filipino Oral History Project and published in *Voices* (Stockton: Filipino Oral History Project, 1984).

44. Felix Zamora, oral history interview by Pearl Ancheta, 1981, National Pinoy Archives, Seattle.

45. De la Ysla v. Publix Theatres Corporation, 82 Utah 598 (1933). The courts asserted that the movie theater was not considered a "public accommodation" that bore the long-established common-law "duty to serve." Rather, a theater was regarded as a private establishment immune from the burdens of equal protection. In addition, the Utah court acknowledged that, while many western states had civil rights statutes that would guarantee equal protection, the state of Utah had "here no application since we have no such statute." De la Ysla v. Publix Theatres Corporation, Third District Court of the State of Utah, no. 48827, Utah State Archives, Salt Lake City.

46. *Philippines Bataan Herald*, August 17, 1945; *Philippine Examiner*, May 31, 1945.

47. I would like to thank José B. Capino for encouraging me to think about prewar Filipino films as "heritage films" and for the reference to Higson, "Re-Presenting the National Past."

48. Maram, *Creating Masculinity*; Fujita-Rony, *American Workers, Colonial Power*.

49. Chin, *Seattle's International District*, 49.

50. See Ellen Kiyomizu, "Kokusai: 60 Years of Asian Films," *International Examiner*, November 15, 1980; John Hart, "Two Seattle Theatres Present Wide Range of Japanese Movies," *Seattle Times*, October 29, 1981.

51. Linda Maram also notes a similar dynamic with Chinatown gambling dens, which offered temporary housing and a meal for Filipino patrons during the Depression. The interview with Chris Mensalves is cited in Maram, *Creating Masculinity*, 33.

52. Stockton Theatres, Inc. v. Emil Palermo, Court of Appeal, 3 Civ 8139, California State Archives, Sacramento.

53. "Hayashino Shigeaki," report filed by Edgar Bernhardt, November 16, 1944, Records of the War Relocation Authority, record group 210, National Archives, Washington, DC.

54. Taylor also notes that months before evacuation, the government closed "enemy owned" banks, leaving many Japanese with little access to financial resources. In Sacramento, officials encouraged city banks to loan money to Japanese on blocked accounts. Bank of America refused to cooperate. In addition to "protecting" evacuee property, agents of the FRB also oversaw internees' continual payment on insurance premiums and taxes. See Taylor, "Federal Reserve Bank," 23.

55. "Japanese Lease on Building is Fought," *Stockton Record*, June 8, 1944, 13.

56. "Hayashino Shigeaki," report filed by Edgar Bernhardt.

57. "Hayashino Shigeaki," report filed by Edgar Bernhardt.

58. Feria, "Status of Filipino Immigrants"; Wong, *Americans First*.

59. Palermo v. Stockton Theatres, Inc., 32 Cal. 2d 53 (1948).

60. The Treaty of Commerce and Navigation between the United States and Japan, signed on February 12, 1911, accords citizens of both nations "liberty to enter, travel and reside in the territories of the other to carry on trade." See "Treaty of Commerce and Navigation between the United States and Japan." *American Journal of International Law* 5, no. 2 (1911): 100–106.

61. Sei Fujii v. California, 38 Cal. 2d 718 (1952).

Epilogue

1. On the development of U.S. counterintelligence and their surveillance of Japanese American communities in California, see Loureiro, "U.S. Counterintelligence against Japan"; for a discussion of the international context, see Everest-Phillips, "Reassessing Pre-War Japanese Espionage."

2. Kumamoto, "Search for Spies."

3. Ruoff, *Imperial Japan*, 1.

4. World War II Alien Enemy Detention and Internment Case File, Toyoji Abe, Department of Justice (RG 60), 146-13-2-11–51, box 100, College Park, MD, National Archives.

5. U.S. Department of the Navy, Office of Naval Intelligence, "Japanese Tokyo Club Syndicate with Interlocking Affiliations," December 24, 1941, in ONI Reports RG 38, box 222, College Park, MD, National Archives.

6. W. T. Tarrant to Chief of Naval Operations, February 1, 1935, in ONI Reports RG 38, box 226, College Park, MD, National Archives.

7. World War II Alien Enemy Detention and Internment Case File, (Rev., Dr.) Takeshi Ban, Department of Justice (RG 60), 146-13-2-12–33, box 154, College Park, MD, National Archives.

8. World War II Alien Enemy Detention and Internment Case File, Muneo Kimura, Department of Justice (RG 60), 146-13-2-1589, box 194, College Park, MD, National Archives.

9. Sodetani, "Benshi and Me," 44.

10. Gondo, "Viewing Post-War Japanese Movie," 139–148.

11. "N.Y. Buddhist Church to Sponsor Benefit Movies," *Utah Nippo*, July 5, 1946, 4.

12. "Newly Acquired Japanese Movies to Be Shown during MISLS Open House," *Utah Nippo*, June 23, 1947, 4.

13. "Ogden Bussei Sponsor Japanese Movies," *Utah Nippo*, November, 7, 1947, 4; "Y.B.A. Sponsors Japanese Movies on April 12," *Utah Nippo*, April 10, 1946, 4; "Japanese Movies!!," *Utah Nippo*, August, 16, 1944, 6; "Bowles YBA to Sponsor Japanese Movies," *Utah Nippo*, December 17, 1947, 4; "Ogden Bussei Sponsor Japanese Movies," *Utah Nippo*, October, 29, 1947, 4; "Japanese Movies to Be Shown in Syracuse," *Utah Nippo*, June 14, 1946, 4; "Japanese Movies Scheduled July 20, 21," *Utah Nippo*, November 7, 1947, 4; "JACL Intermountain District Council Meet in Salt Lake City Jan. 13," *Utah Nippo*, January 7, 1946, 4; "Shina No Yoru to Be Shown at Fort Douglas Theatre," *Utah Nippo*, November 28, 1947, 4.

14. "Resettlers Group Program Features Two Attractions," *Chicago Shimpo*, January 19, 1952, IE.

Coda

1. Hennefeld, "Work of Art."

2. Nancy Wang Yuen, Stacy L. Smith, Katherine Pieper, Marc Choueiti, Kevin Yao, and Dana Dinh, "The Prevalence and Portrayal of Asian and Pacific Islanders across 1,300 Popular Films," USC Annenberg Inclusion Initiative (May 2021); Yuen presented the findings of the report for a virtual event hosted by Amazon Studios, VOICES: Asian & Pacific Islander Representation in Film and Media, May 20, 2021.

3. The box office success of *Crazy Rich Asians* was bolstered by a targeted marketing strategy encouraging Asian American celebrities, media professionals, nonprofits, and community organizations to buy out entire theaters on opening weekend and use the hashtag #GoldOpen. News media reporting about the film often mentioned the hashtag and described Asian American fans prepared to visit theaters multiple times and spend upward of $1,500 to $5,000 to support the film. As a national campaign, the strategy led to 350 theater buyouts across the country. See Lopez, "Excessively Asian."

4. Shambu, "Rethinking Film Evaluation."

5. Caddoo, "Hollywood's Diversity Problem."

6. Shambu, "Rethinking Film Evaluation."

7. Chong, "What Is Asian American Cinema?"; Phruksachart, "Bourgeois Cinema."

Bibliography

Archives and Manuscript Collections

Asian American Film Ephemera Collection, Harvard Film Archive, Fine Arts Library, Harvard College Library, Cambridge, MA.

Japanese American Research Project, Library Special Collections, Charles E. Young Research Library, University of California, Los Angeles.

Record Group 38 (RG 38): *Records of the Office of the Chief of Naval Operations*, Office of Naval Intelligence, U.S. National Archives, College Park, MD.

Record Group 60 (RG 60): *World War II Alien Enemy Detention and Internment Case File*, Department of Justice, U.S. National Archives, College Park, MD.

Takeshi Ban Papers, Japanese American National Museum, Los Angeles, CA.

Yoshio Kishi and Irene Yah-Ling Sun Collection, Fales Library and Special Collections, Elmer Holmes Bobst Library, New York University.

Digital Archives

California Digital Newspaper Collection
Densho: The Japanese American Legacy Project
Hoji Shinbun Digital Archive
Media History Digital Library

Selected Newspapers and Periodicals

Chicago Shimpo [Shikago Shinpō / シカゴ新報], Chicago, IL
Great Northern Daily News [Taihoku Nippō / 大北日報], Seattle, WA
Japan-California Daily News [Kashū Mainichi Shinbun / 加州毎日新聞], Los Angeles, CA
Japanese-American News [Nichibei Shinbun / 日米新聞], San Francisco, CA
The New World [Shin Sekai / 新世界], San Francisco, CA
New World Daily News [Shin Sekai Nichinichi Shinbun / 新世界日日新聞], San Francisco, CA
New World Sun [Shin Sekai Asahi Shinbun / 新世界朝日新聞], San Francisco, CA
Nippu Jiji [Nippu Jiji / 日布時事], Honolulu, HI
The North American Times [Hokubei Jiji / 北米時事], Seattle, WA
Rafu Shimpo [Rafu Shinpō / 羅府新報], Los Angeles, CA
Utah Nippo [Yuta Nippō / ユタ日報], Salt Lake City, UT

Secondary Sources

Abel, Richard, and Rick Altman. *The Sounds of Early Cinema*. Bloomington: Indiana University Press, 2001.

Acland, Charles R., and Haidee Wasson, eds. *Useful Cinema*. Durham, NC: Duke University Press, 2011.

Allen, Robert C. "Manhattan Myopia; or, Oh! Iowa! Robert C. Allen on Ben Singer's 'Manhattan Nickelodeons: New Data on Audiences and Exhibitors.'" *Cinema Journal* 35, no. 3 (1996): 73–103.

———. "Motion Picture Exhibition in Manhattan 1906–1912: Beyond the Nickelodeon." *Cinema Journal* 18, no. 2 (1979): 2–15.

Altman, Rick, ed. *Sound Theory, Sound Practice*. New York: Routledge, 1992.

Anderson, Benedict. *Imagined Communities: Reflections on the Origin and Spread of Nationalism*. London: Verso, 2006.

Anderson, Joseph L. *The Japanese Film: Art and Industry*. Princeton, NJ: Princeton University Press, 1982.

Azuma, Eiichiro. *Between Two Empires: Race, History, and Transnationalism in Japanese America*. Oxford, UK: Oxford University Press, 2005.

———. "A History of Oregon's Issei, 1880–1952." *Oregon Historical Quarterly* 94, no. 4 (Winter 1993/1994): 315–367.

———. "The Hoji Shinbun Digital Collection: Possibilities and Limitations." In *Roots of the Issei: Exploring Early Japanese American Newspapers*, vol. 8. Palo Alto, CA: Hoover Institution Press Publication, 2018.

———. *In Search of Our Frontier: Japanese America and Settler Colonialism in the Construction of Japan's Borderless Empire*. Berkeley: University of California Press, 2019.

———. "Racial Struggle, Immigrant Nationalism, and Ethnic Identity: Japanese and Filipinos in the California Delta, 1930–1941." *Pacific Historical Review* 67, no. 2 (1998): 163–199.

Baldoz, Rick. *The Third Asiatic Invasion: Empire and Migration in Filipino America, 1898–1946*. New York: New York University Press, 2011.

Battat, Erin Royston. *Ain't Got No Home: America's Great Migrations and the Making of an Interracial Left*. Chapel Hill: University of North Carolina Press, 2014.

Bean, Jennifer M., Anupama P. Kapse, and Laura Evelyn Horak, eds. *Silent Cinema and the Politics of Space*. Bloomington: Indiana University Press, 2014.

Bell, Caroline. "Talkie Voices on Dress Parade." *Picture Play Magazine* 32, no. 1 (March 1930): 68–70.

Beltrán, Mary. "Dolores Del Rio, the First 'Latin Invasion,' and Hollywood's Transition to Sound" *Aztlan* 30, no. 1 (January 2005): 55–81.

Bernardi, Daniel, ed. *The Birth of Whiteness: Race and the Emergence of U.S. Cinema*. New Brunswick, NJ: Rutgers University Press, 1996.

Bernardi, Joanne R. "Catching a Film Audience Abroad." *Japan Quarterly* 32, no. 3 (1985): 290–295.

Birchard, Robert S. *Cecil B. DeMille's Hollywood*. Lexington: University Press of Kentucky, 2004.

Bowser, Pearl, Jane Gaines, and Charles Musser, eds. *Oscar Micheaux and His Circle: African-American Filmmaking and Race Cinema of the Silent Era*. Bloomington: Indiana University Press, 2001.

Brooks, Charlotte. *Alien Neighbors, Foreign Friends: Asian Americans, Housing, and the Transformation of Urban California*. Chicago, IL: University of Chicago Press, 2009.

Browne, Nick. "The Undoing of the Other Woman: Madame Butterfly in the Discourse of American Orientalism." In *The Birth of Whiteness: Race and the Emergence of U.S. Cinema*, edited by Daniel Bernardi, 227–256. New Brunswick, NJ: Rutgers University Press, 1996.

"Byrd-Paramount on Parade Program: A Record-Wrecker in Three Day and Date Tokyo Theatres." *Paramount around the World* 3, no. 1 (January 1, 1930).

Caddoo, Cara. *Envisioning Freedom: Cinema and the Building of Modern Black Life*. Cambridge, MA: Harvard University Press, 2014.

Chacon, Ramon D. "The Beginnings of Racial Segregation: The Chinese in West Fresno and Chinatown's Role as Red Light District, 1870s–1920s." *Southern California Quarterly* 70, no. 4 (Winter 1988): 371–398.

Cha-Jua, Sundiata Keita. "Black Audiences, Blaxploitation and Kung Fu Films." In *China Forever: The Shaw Brothers and Diasporic Cinema*, edited by Poshek Fu, 199–223. Champaign-Urbana: University of Illinois Press, 2008.

Chan, Anthony B. *Perpetually Cool: The Many Lives of Anna May Wong (1905–1961)*. Lanham, MD: Rowman & Littlefield, 2003.

Chang, Gordon H. "Deployments, Engagements, Obliterations: Asian American Artists and World War II." In *Asian American Art: A History, 1850–1970*, edited by Gordon H. Chang, Mark Johnson, and Paul Karlstrom, 111–139. Palo Alto, CA: Stanford University Press, 2008.

Chin, Doug. *Seattle's International District: The Making of a Pan-Asian American Community*. Seattle, WA: International Examiner, 2001.

Chong, Sylvia. "What Is Asian American Cinema?" *Cinema Journal* 56, no. 3 (2017): 130–135.

Chung, Hye Seung. "From 'Me So Horny' to 'I'm So Ronery': Asian Images and Yellow Voices in American Cinema." In *Film Dialogue*, edited by Jeff Jaeckle, 172–191. New York: Columbia University Press, 2003.

———. *Hollywood Asian: Philip Ahn and the Politics of Cross-Ethnic Performance*. Philadelphia, PA: Temple University Press, 2006.

Conard, Alfred. "The Privilege of Forcibly Ejecting an Amusement Patron." *University of Pennsylvania Law Review and American Law Register* 90 (1942): 809–823.

Crafton, Donald. *The Talkies: American Cinema's Transition to Sound, 1926–1931*. Vol. 4. Berkeley: University of California Press, 1999.

Cripps, Thomas. "The Birth of a Race Company: An Early Stride toward a Black Cinema." *Journal of Negro History* 59, no. 1 (1974): 28–37.

———. *Slow Fade to Black: The Negro in American Film, 1900–1942*. Oxford, UK: Oxford University Press, 1977.

Curry, Ramona. "Benjamin Brodsky (1877–1960): The Transpacific American Film Entrepreneur—Part One, Making a Trip through China." *Journal of American–East Asian Relations* 18, no. 1 (2011): 58–94.

————. "Benjamin Brodsky (1877–1960): The Trans-Pacific American Film Entrepreneur—Part Two, Taking a Trip through China to America." *Journal of American-East Asian Relations* 18, no. 2 (2011): 142–180.

Dale, Elizabeth. "'Social Equality Does Not Exist among Themselves, nor among Us': *Baylies vs. Curry* and Civil Rights in Chicago, 1888." *American Historical Review* 102 (1997): 311–339.

Daniels, Gordon. "Japanese Domestic Radio and Cinema Propaganda, 1937–1945: An Overview." *Historical Journal of Film, Radio and Television* 2, no. 2 (1982): 115–132.

Del Mundo, Clodualdo. *Native Resistance: Philippine Cinema and Colonialism, 1898–1941.* Manila, PH: De La Salle University Press, 1998.

Deocampo, Nick. *Film: American Influence on Philippine Cinema.* Manila, PH: Anvil, 2011.

Desser, David. "The Kung Fu Craze: Hong Kong Cinema's First American Reception." In *The Cinema of Hong Kong: History, Arts, Identity,* edited by Poshek Fu and David Desser, 19–43. Cambridge, UK: Cambridge University Pres, 2000.

De Vera, Arleen. "'The Tapia-Saiki Incident': Interethnic Conflict and Filipino Responses to the Anti-Filipino Exclusion Movement." In *Over the Edge: Remapping the American West,* edited by Valerie Matsumoto and Blake Allmendinger, 201–214. Berkeley: University of California Press, 1990.

De Witt, Howard. "The Watsonville Anti-Filipino Riot of 1930: A Case Study of the Great Depression and Ethnic Conflict in California." *Southern California Quarterly* 61 (Fall 1979): 223–238.

Dong, Arthur. *Hollywood Chinese: The Chinese in American Feature Films.* Santa Monica, CA: Angel City, 2019.

Drew, William M. *The Last Silent Picture Show: Silent Films on American Screens in the 1930s.* Lanham, MD: Scarecrow, 2010.

Durovicová, Natasa. "Translating America: The Hollywood Multilinguals 1929–1933." In *Sound Theory/Sound Practice,* edited by Rick Altman and Robert Altman, 138–153. New York: Routledge, 1992.

Dym, Jeffrey A. "Benshi and the Introduction of Motion Pictures to Japan." *Monumenta Nipponica* 55, no. 4 (2000): 509–536.

————. *Benshi, Japanese Silent Film Narrators, and Their Forgotten Narrative Art of Setsumei: A History of Japanese Silent Film Narration.* Lewiston, NY: Edwin Mellen, 2003.

Elsaesser, Thomas. *Film History as Media Archaeology: Tracking Digital Cinema.* Amsterdam, NL: Amsterdam University Press, 2016.

Ernest, Allen. "When Japan Was the 'Champion of the Colored Races': Satokata Takahashi and the Flowering of Black Messianic Nationalism." *Black Scholar* 24 (Winter 1994): 23–46.

España-Maram, Linda. "Brown 'Hordes' in McIntosh Suits: Filipinos, Taxi Dance Halls, and Performing the Immigrant Body in Los Angeles, 1930s–1940s." In *Generations of Youth: Youth and Youth Cultures in Twentieth-Century America,* edited by Joe Austin and Michael Willards, 118–135. New York: New York University Press, 1998.

Everest-Phillips, Max. "Reassessing Pre-War Japanese Espionage: The Rutland Naval Spy Case and the Japanese Intelligence Threat before Pearl Harbor." *Intelligence and National Security* 21, no. 2 (April 2006): 258–285.

Eyman, Scott. *Five American Cinematographers*. Metuchen, NJ: Scarecrow, 1987.

———. *The Speed of Sound: Hollywood and the Talkie Revolution 1926–1930*. New York: Simon & Schuster, 2015.

Fahlstedt, Kim. *Chinatown Film Culture: The Appearance of Cinema in San Francisco's Chinese Neighborhood*. New Brunswick, NJ: Rutgers University Press, 2020.

Feng, Peter X. *Identities in Motion: Asian American Film and Video*. Durham, NC: Duke University Press, 2002.

Feria, R. T. "War and the Status of Filipino Immigrants." *Sociology and Social Research* 31 (1946): 48–53.

Field, Allyson Nadia. *Uplift Cinema: The Emergence of African American Film and the Possibility of Black Modernity*. Durham, NC: Duke University Press, 2015.

Fones-Wolf, Elizabeth. "Sound Comes to the Movies: The Philadelphia Musicians' Struggle against Recorded Music." *Pennsylvania Magazine of History and Biography* 118, no. 1 (1994): 3–31.

"Foreign Production Department Concentrating on Making Variety of Short Subjects." *Paramount around the World* 3, no. 1 (January 1, 1930).

Frank, Dana. *Purchasing Power: Consumer Organizing, Gender, and the Seattle Labor Movement, 1919–1929*. Cambridge, UK: Cambridge University Press, 1994.

Freiberg, Freda. "The Transition to Sound in Japan." *History on/and/in Film* (1987): 76–80.

Fujiki, Hideaki. "Benshi as Stars: The Irony of the Popularity and Respectability of Voice Performers in Japanese Cinema." *Cinema Journal* 45, no. 2 (2006): 68–84.

Fujita-Rony, Dorothy B. *American Workers, Colonial Power: Philippine Seattle and the Transpacific West, 1919–1941*. Berkeley: University of California Press, 2003.

———. "Empire and the Moving Body: Fermin Tobera, Military California, and Rural Space." In *Making Empire Work: Labor and United States Imperialism*, edited by Daniel E. Bender and Jana K. Lipman, 208–226. New York: New York University Press, 2015.

Fuller, Karla Rae. *Hollywood Goes Oriental: CaucAsian Performance in American Film*. Detroit, MI: Wayne State University Press, 2010.

Fuller, Kathryn H. *At the Picture Show: Small-Town Audiences and the Creation of Movie Fan Culture*. Charlottesville: University of Virginia Press, 2001.

Gaines, Jane. *Fire and Desire: Mixed-Race Movies in the Silent Era*. Chicago, IL: University of Chicago Press, 2001.

———. "*Within Our Gates*: From Race Melodrama to Opportunity Narrative." In *Oscar Micheaux and His Circle: African-American Filmmaking and Race Cinema of the Silent Era*, edited by Pearl Bowser, Jane Gaines, and Charles Musser, 67–80. Bloomington: Indiana University Press, 2001.

Gerow, Aaron. *Visions of Japanese Modernity: Articulations of Cinema, Nation, and Spectatorship, 1895–1925*. Berkeley: University of California Press, 2010.

Gomery, Douglas. *The Coming of Sound*. New York: Routledge, 2004.

Gondo, Chie. "Viewing Post-War Japanese Movie Showings in Honolulu through the Activities of Hawaii Nichibei Kinema." *Ritsumeikan University Art Research Center Bulletin* 4 (March 2004): 139–148.

Gow, Will. "Performing Chinatown: Hollywood Cinema, Tourism, and the Making of a Los Angeles Community, 1882–1943." PhD diss., University of California, Berkeley, 2018.

Gruenewald, Tim, and George Chun Han Wang. "East-West Flows: Cinematic Currents between China and the United States." *Asian Cinema* 29, no. 1 (April 1, 2018): 3–14.

Gue, Randy. "'It Seems that Everything Looks Good Nowadays, as Long as It Is in the Flesh and Brownskin': The Assertion of Cultural Difference at Atlanta's 81 Theatre, 1934–1937." *Film History* 8, no. 2 (1996): 209–218.

Gunckel, Colin. *Mexico on Main Street: Transnational Film Culture in Los Angeles before World War II*. New Brunswick, NJ: Rutgers University Press, 2015.

———. "The War of the Accents: Spanish Language Hollywood Films in Mexican Los Angeles." *Film History* 20 (2008): 325–343.

Harrison, Scott Edward. *Japanese Newspaper and Magazine Publishing in the Pacific Northwest 1894–2006*. Seattle, WA: University of Washington Press, 2006.

Hayakawa, Sessue. *Zen Showed Me the Way . . . to Peace, Happiness, and Tranquility*. Indianapolis, IL: Bobbs-Merrill, 1960.

Hemminger, Carol. *Little Manila: Filipino Stockton Prior to World War II*. Stockton, CA: University of the Pacific, 1980.

Hennefeld, Maggie. "The Work of Art in the Age of Flexible Inclusion Criteria." *Film Quarterly* (September 2020), https://filmquarterly.org/2020/09/30/the-work-of-art -in-the-age-of-flexible-inclusion-criteria/.

Higa, Karin. "Hidden in Plain Sight: Little Tokyo between the Wars." In *Asian American Art: A History 1850–1970*, edited by Gordon H. Chang, Mark Johnson, and Paul Karlstrom, 30–53. Palo Alto, CA: Stanford University Press, 2008.

High, Peter B. *The Imperial Screen: Japanese Film Culture in the Fifteen Years' War, 1931–1945*. Madison: University of Wisconsin Press, 2003.

Higson, Andrew. "Re-presenting the National Past: Nostalgia and Pastiche in the Heritage Film." *Fires Were Started: British Cinema and Thatcherism*, edited by Lester D. Friedman, 109–129. New York: Wallflower, 1993.

Higson, Andrew, and Richard Maltby. *"Film Europe" and "Film America": Cinema, Commerce and Cultural Exchange, 1920–1939*. Exeter, UK: University of Exeter Press, 1999.

Hirobe, Izumi. *Japanese Pride, American Prejudice: Modifying the Exclusion Clause of the 1924 Immigration Act*. Palo Alto, CA: Stanford University Press, 2001.

Horne, Gerald. *Facing the Rising Sun: African Americans, Japan, and the Rise of Afro-Asian Solidarity*. New York: New York University Press, 2018.

Hu, Brian, and B. Ruby Rich. "Dossier: Asian American Film at Fifty." *Film Quarterly* 73, no. 3 (2020): 28–33.

Ichioka, Yuji. "The Early Japanese Immigrant Quest for Citizenship: The Background of the 1922 Ozawa Case." *Amerasia Journal* 4, no. 2 (1977): 1–22.

———. *The Issei: The World of the First Generation Japanese Immigrants, 1885–1924*. New York: Free Press, 1988.

———. "Japanese Associations and the Japanese Government: A Special Relationship, 1909–1926." *Pacific Historical Review* 26, no. 3 (August 1977): 409–437.

Itakura, Fumiaki. *Eiga to imin: zaibei Nikkei imin no eiga juyō to aidentiti (Cinema and Immigration)* [映画と移民 : 在米日系移民の映画受容とアイデンティティ]. Tokyo: Shin'yosha, 2016.

Itatsu, Yuko. "Japan's Hollywood Boycott Movement of 1924." *Historical Journal of Film, Radio, and Television* 28, no. 3 (2008): 353–369.

Ito, Kazuo. *Issei: A History of Japanese Immigrants in North America*. Seattle, WA: Executive Committee for Publication, 1973.

Ito, Ken. "The Family and the Nation in Tokutomi Roka's Hototogisu." *Harvard Journal of Asiatic Studies* 60, no. 2 (2000): 489–536.

Iwamoto, Kenji. "Sound in the Early Talkies." In *Reframing Japanese Cinema: Authorship, Genre, History,* edited by Arthur Nolletti and David Desser, 312–327. Bloomington: Indiana University Press, 1992.

Jacobs, Jack. "James Wong Howe: Evolved a Photographic Style by Striving for Dramatic Realism." *Films in Review* 12, no. 4 (April 1961).

Jamero, Peter M. *Growing Up Brown: Memoirs of a Filipino American*. Seattle: University of Washington Press, 2006.

James, David E. *The Most Typical Avant-Garde: History and Geography of Minor Cinemas in Los Angeles*. Berkeley: University of California Press, 2005.

"Japanese Posters Are Colorful Ad Sales." *Paramount around the World* 3, no. 1 (January 1, 1930).

"Japanese Shorts." *Paramount around the World* 3, no. 1 (January 1, 1930).

Jenkins, Henry. "'Shall We Make It for New York or for Distribution?': Eddie Cantor, Whoopee, and Regional Resistance to the Talkies." *Cinema Journal* 29, no. 3 (1990): 32–52.

Jensen, Joan M. "Apartheid: Pacific Coast Style." *Pacific Historical Review* 38, no. 3 (August 1969): 335–340.

Johnson, Martin L. "The Places You'll Know: From Self-Recognition to Place Recognition in the Local Film." *Moving Image* 10, no. 1 (2010): 24–50.

Kar, Law, Frank Bren, and Sam Ho. *Hong Kong Cinema: A Cross-Cultural View*. Lanham, MD: Scarecrow, 2004.

Keil, Charlie, and Shelley Stamp, eds. *American Cinema's Transitional Era: Audiences, Institutions, Practices*. Berkeley: University of California Press, 2004.

Khor, Denise. "Dangerous Amusements: Hawaii's Theaters, Labor Strikes, and Counterpublic Culture, 1909–1934." In *The Rising Tide of Color: Race, State Violence, and Radical Movements across the Pacific,* edited by Moon-Ho Jung, 102–125. Seattle: University of Washington Press, 2015.

———. "'Filipinos are the Dandies of the Foreign Colonies': Race, Labor Struggles, and the Transpacific Routes of Hollywood and Philippine Films, 1924–1948." *Pacific Historical Review* 81, no. 3 (2012): 371–403.

———. "History before and behind the Camera: An Interview with Renee Tajima-Peña." *Film Quarterly* 74, no. 1 (Fall 2020): 21–29.

King, Rob. "Early Hollywood and the Archive." *Film History* 26, no. 2 (2014): vii–xiv.

Kinoshita, Chika. "The Benshi Track: Mizoguchi Kenji's *The Downfall of Osen* and the Sound Transition." *Cinema Journal* 50, no. 3 (2011): 1–25.

Kirihara, Donald. "The Accepted Idea Displaced: Stereotype and Sessue Hayakawa." In *The Birth of Whiteness: Race and the Emergence of the U.S. Cinema*, edited by Daniel Bernardi, 81–102. New Brunswick, NJ: Rutgers University Press, 1996.

Kishi, Yoshio. "Final Mix: Unscheduled." In *Moving the Image: Independent Asian Pacific American Media Arts*, edited by Russell Leong, 165. Los Angeles: UCLA Asian American Studies Center Press, 1992.

Kitamura, Hiroshi. *Screening Enlightenment: Hollywood and the Cultural Reconstruction of Defeated Japan*. Ithaca, NY: Cornell University Press, 2010.

Koszarski, Richard. "Flu Season: 'Moving Picture World' Reports on Pandemic Influenza, 1918–19." *Film History* 17, no. 4 (2005): 466–485.

Kraft, James P. "The 'Pit' Musicians: Mechanization in the Movie Theaters, 1926–1934." *Labor History* 35, no. 1 (1994): 66–89.

———. *Stage to Studio: Musicians and the Sound Revolution, 1890–1950*. Baltimore, MD: Johns Hopkins University Press, 2020.

Kumamoto, Bob. "The Search for Spies: American Counterintelligence and the Japanese American Community, 1931–1942." *Amerasia Journal* 6, no. 2 (1979): 45–75.

Kurashige, Scott. *The Shifting Grounds of Race: Black and Japanese Americans in the Making of Multiethnic Los Angeles*. Princeton, NJ: Princeton University Press, 2008.

Lassiter, Matthew. "De Jure / De Facto Segregation: The Long Shadow of a National Myth." In *The Myth of Southern Exceptionalism*, edited by Matthew Lassiter and Joseph Crespino, 25–48. Oxford, UK: Oxford University Press, 2009.

Lastra, James. *Sound Technology and the American Cinema: Perception, Representation, Modernity*. New York: Columbia University Press, 2000.

Latham, James. "Selling Hollywood to the World: US and European Struggles for Mastery of the Global Film Industry, 1920–1950." *Film Quarterly* 57, no. 2 (2003): 60–63.

Lau, Jenny Kwok Wah. "Marion E. Wong." In *Women Film Pioneers Project*, edited by Jane Gaines, Radha Vatsal, and Monica Dall-Asta. New York: Columbia University Libraries, 2013.

Layton, James, David Pierce, and Michael Feinstein. *King of Jazz: Paul Whiteman's Technicolor Revue*. Severn, MD: Media History, 2016.

Leavold, Andrew. "How the Early Pinoy Films Found a Second Home in Hawaii and Ignited an Industry." *ABS-CBN News*, September 22, 2019. https://news.abs-cbn.com/ancx/culture/movies/09/22/19/how-the-early-pinoy-films-found-a-second-home-in-hawaii-and-ignited-an-industry.

Lee, Shelley. *Claiming the Oriental Gateway: Prewar Seattle and Japanese America*. Philadelphia, PA: Temple University Press, 2010.

Lipsitz, George. "Cruising around the Historical Bloc: Postmodernism and Popular Music in East Los Angeles." *Cultural Critique* 5 (1986): 157–177.

———. "'Frantic to Join . . . the Japanese Army': The Asia Pacific War in the Lives of African American Soldiers and Civilians." In *The Politics of Culture in the Shadow of Capital*, edited by Lisa Lowe and David Lloyd, 324–353. Durham, NC: Duke University Press, 1997.

Liu, Cynthia W. "When Dragon Ladies Die, Do They Come Back as Butterflies? Re-imagining Anna May Wong." In *Countervisions: Asian American Film Criticism*, edited by Darrell Hamamoto and Sandra Liu, 23–39. Philadelphia, PA: Temple University Press, 2000.

Lopez, Lori Kido. *Asian American Media Activism: Fighting for Cultural Citizenship*. New York: New York University, 2016.

———. "Excessively Asian: Crying, Crazy Rich Asians, and the Construction of Asian American Audiences." *Critical Studies in Media Communication* 38, no. 2 (2021): 1–14.

Loughney, Patrick. "The American Moving Image Diaspora: The Archaeology of US Movies in International Archives." *American Studies International* 42, no. 2–3 (June–October 2004): 149–156.

Loureiro, Pedro Anthony. "U.S. Counterintelligence against Japan in Southern California, 1933–1941." Master's thesis, San Francisco State University, 1987.

Luckett, Josslyn. "Searching for Betty Chen: Rediscovering the Asian American Filmmakers of UCLA in the Seventies." *Film Quarterly* 73, no. 3 (2020): 34–40.

Lui, Mary Ting Yi. "Rehabilitating Chinatown at Mid-Century: Chinese Americans, Race, and US Cultural Diplomacy." In *Chinatowns in a Transnational World: Myths and Realities of an Urban Phenomenon*, edited by Vanessa Kunnemann and Ruth Mayer, 89–108. New York: Routledge, 2012.

Lupack, Barbara Tepa. *Early Race Filmmaking in America*. New York: Routledge, 2016.

Mabalon, Dawn. *Little Manila Is in the Heart: The Making of the Filipina/o American Community in Stockton, California*. Durham, NC: Duke University Press, 2013.

Maltby, Richard, and Ruth Vasey. "The International Language Problem: European Reactions to Hollywood's Conversion to Sound." In *Hollywood in Europe: Experiences of a Cultural Hegemony*, edited by Daniel W. Ellwood and R. Kroes, 78–79. Amsterdam, NL: Vu University Press, 1994.

Maram, Linda. *Creating Masculinity in Los Angeles' Little Manila: Working-Class Filipinos and Popular Culture, 1920s–1950s*. New York: Columbia University Press, 2006.

Marez, Curtis. "Pancho Villa Meets Sun Yat-Sen: Third World Revolution and the History of Hollywood Cinema." *American Literary History* 17, no. 3 (2005): 486–505.

———. "Subaltern Soundtracks: Mexican Immigrants and the Making of Hollywood Cinema." *Aztlan: A Journal of Chicano Studies* 29, no. 1 (2004): 57–82.

Mason, William H., and John A. McKinstry. *The Japanese of Los Angeles*. Los Angeles: History Division, Los Angeles County Museum of Natural History, 1969.

Matsumoto, Valerie. "Desperately Seeking 'Deidre,': Gender Roles, Multicultural Relations, and Nisei Women Writers of the 1930s." *Frontiers: A Journal of Women's Studies* 12, no. 1 (1991): 19–32.

———. *Farming the Home Place: A Japanese American Community in California, 1919–1982*. Ithaca, NY: Cornell University Press, 1993.

Maurice, Alice. "'Cinema at Its Source': Synchronizing Race and Sound in the Early Talkies." *Camera Obscura* 17, no. 1 (February 1, 2002): 1–71.

McClain, Charles. "In Re Lee Sing: The First Residential Segregation Case." *Western Legal History* 3 (1990).

McWilliams, Carey. *Factories in the Field: The Story of Migratory Farm Labor in California.* Berkeley: University of California Press, 2000.

Melendy, H. Brett. "Filipinos in the United States." *Pacific Historical Review* 43 (1974): 520–547.

Melnick, Ross. *American Showman: Samuel "Roxy" Rothafel and the Birth of the Entertainment Industry, 1908-1935.* New York: Columbia University Press, 2012.

Merritt, Russell. "Nickelodeon Theaters, 1905-1914." In *Hollywood: Critical Concepts in Media and Cultural Studies,* edited by Thomas Schaetz, 25–41. New York: Routledge, 2004.

Mimura, Glen M. *Ghostlife of Third Cinema: Asian American Film and Video.* Minneapolis: University of Minnesota Press, 2009.

Miyao, Daisuke. *Sessue Hayakawa: Silent Cinema and Transnational Stardom.* Durham, NC: Duke University Press, 2007.

Moore, Paul S. "Ephemera as Medium: The Afterlife of Lost Films." *Moving Image* 16, no. 1 (2016): 134–139.

Mullen, Bill. *Afro-Orientalism.* Minneapolis: University of Minnesota Press, 2004.

Mullins, Patrick. "Ethnic Cinema in the Nickelodeon Era in New York City: Commerce, Assimilation and Cultural Identity." *Film History* 12, no. 1 (2000): 115–124.

Musser, Charles. *The Emergence of Cinema: The American Screen to 1907.* New York: Scribner, 1990.

———. *High-Class Moving Pictures: Lyman H. Howe and the Forgotten Era of Traveling Exhibition, 1880-1920.* Princeton, NJ: Princeton University Press, 1991.

Ngai, Mae. *Impossible Subjects: Illegal Aliens and the Making of Modern America.* Princeton, NJ: Princeton University Press, 2004.

Noda, Kesa. *Yamato Colony: 1906-1960 Livingston, California.* Livingston, CA: Livingston-Merced JACL Chapter, 1981.

Nornes, Abe Mark. *Cinema Babel: Translating Global Cinema.* Minneapolis: University of Minnesota Press, 2007.

Ogihara, Junko. "The Exhibition of Films for Japanese Americans in Los Angeles during the Silent Film Era." *Film History* 4, no. 2 (1990): 81–87.

Okada, Jun. *Making Asian American Film and Video: History, Institutions, Movements.* New Brunswick, NJ: Rutgers University Press, 2015.

———. "Representation, Recognition, and the Possibility of a Radically Transformed Future: The Asian American Series." *Film Quarterly* 41, no. 1 (2020): 11–20.

Ongiri, Amy. "'He Wanted to Be Just like Bruce Lee': African Americans, Kung Fu Theater and Cultural Exchange at the Margins." *Journal of Asian American Studies* 5, no. 1 (2002): 31–40.

Onishi, Yuichiro. *Transpacific Antiracism: Afro-Asian Solidarity in 20th-Century Black America, Japan, and Okinawa.* New York: New York University Press, 2014.

Onishi, Yuichiro, and Toru Shinoda. "The Paradigm of Refusal: W. E. B. Du Bois' Transpacific Imagination of the 1930s." In *Citizen of the World: The Late Career and Legacy of W. E. B. Du Bois*, edited by Phillip Luke Sinitiere, Gary Murrell, and David Levering Lewis, 13–36. Evanston, IL: Northwestern University Press, 2019.

Orgeron, Devin, Marsha Orgeron, and Dan Streible, eds. *Learning with the Lights Off: Educational Film in the United States*. Oxford, UK: Oxford University Press, 2012.

Palmquist, Peter E. "Asian Photographers in San Francisco 1850–1930." *Argonaut: Journal of the San Francisco Historical Society* 9 (1998): 87–88.

Pao, Angela Chia-yi. "False Accents: Embodied Dialects and the Characterization of Ethnicity and Nationality." *Theatre Topics* 14, no. 1 (March 2004): 355–372.

Parrenas, Rhacel Salazar. "'White Trash' Meets the 'Little Brown Monkeys': The Taxi Dance Hall as a Site of Interracial and Gender Alliances between White Women and Filipino Immigrant Men in the 1920s and 1930s." *Amerasia Journal* 24 (1998): 115–134.

Phruksachart, Melissa. "The Bourgeois Cinema of Boba Liberalism." *Film Quarterly* 73, no. 3 (2020): 59–65.

Potamianos, George. "Hollywood in the Hinterlands: Mass Culture in Two California Communities, 1896–1936." PhD diss., University of Southern California, 1998.

Rafael, Vicente L. "Taglish, or the Phantom Power of the Lingua Franca." *Public Culture* 8, no. 1 (October 1995): 162–189.

Rainsberger, Todd. *James Wong Howe: Cinematographer*. San Diego, CA: A. S. Barnes, 1981.

Reed, Dennis. "The Wind Came from the East: Asian American Photography, 1850–1965." In *Asian American Art: A History 1850–1970*, edited by Gordon H. Chang, Mark Johnson, and Paul Karlstrom, 141–168. Palo Alto, CA: Stanford University Press, 2008.

Regester, Charlene B. "From the Buzzard's Roost: Black Movie-Going in Durham and Other North Carolina Cities during the Early Period of American Cinema." *Film History: An International Journal* 17, no. 1 (June 2005): 113–124.

Regev, Ronny. *Working in Hollywood: How the Studio System Turned Creativity into Labor*. Chapel Hill: University of North Carolina Press, 2018.

Reyes, Emmanuel. *Notes on Philippine Cinema*. Manila: De La Salle University Press, 1989.

Robinson, Greg. *Pacific Citizens: Larry and Guyo Tajiri and Japanese American Journalism in the World War II Era*. Champaign: University of Illinois, 2012.

Roces, Mina. "'These Guys Came Out Looking like Movie Actors': Filipino Dress and Consumer Practices in the United States, 1920s–1930s." *Pacific Historical Review* 85, no. 4 (2016): 532–576.

Rogin, Michael. "'The Sword Became a Flashing Vision': DW Griffith's The Birth of a Nation." *Representations* 9 (Winter 1985): 150–195.

Ruoff, Kenneth J. *Imperial Japan at Its Zenith: The Wartime Celebration of the Empire's 2, 600th Anniversary*. Ithaca, NY: Cornell University Press, 2010.

Schleitwiler, Vince. *Strange Fruit of the Black Pacific: Imperialism's Racial Justice and Its Fugitives*. New York: New York University Press, 2017.

Segrave, Kerry. *Foreign Films in America: A History*. Jefferson, NC: McFarland, 2004.

Seid, Danielle. "Forever Her Chinatown: Where Is My Grandmother in Chinese American Feminist Film History?" *Feminist Media Histories* 5, no. 1 (January 1, 2019): 141–167.

Serna, Laura Isabel. *Making Cinelandia: American Films and Mexican Film Culture before the Golden Age*. Durham, NC: Duke University Press Books, 2014.

Shambu, Girish. "Rethinking Film Evaluation." *Film Quarterly* (March 2020), https://filmquarterly.org/2020/03/11/rethinking-film-evaluation/.

Shohat, Ella. "Ethnicities-in-Relation: Toward a Multicultural Reading of American Cinema." *Unspeakable Images: Ethnicity and the American Cinema*, edited by Lester B. Friedman, 215–250. Champaign, IL: University of Illinois Press, 1991.

Silver, Alain. *James Wong Howe: The Camera Eye; A Career Interview by Alain Silver*. Self-published, CreateSpace, 2011.

Singer, Ben. "Manhattan Nickelodeons: New Data on Audiences and Exhibitors." *Cinema Journal* 34, no. 3 (1995): 5–35.

Smoodin, Eric. "As the Archive Turned: Writing Film Histories without Films." *Moving Image* 14, no. 2 (2014): 96–100.

Sodetani, Naomi. "Benshi and Me." In *A'ala: The Story of a Japanese Community in Hawaii*, edited by Michael Okihiro, 44. Honolulu, HI: Japanese Cultural Center, 2003.

Stewart, Jacqueline Najuma. *Migrating to the Movies: Cinema and Black Urban Modernity*. Berkeley: University of California Press, 2005.

Stoever, Jennifer Lynn. *The Sonic Color Line: Race and the Cultural Politics of Listening*. New York: New York University Press, 2016.

Strong, Edward K. *Japanese in California: Based on a Ten Percent Survey of Japanese in California and Documentary Evidence from Many Sources*. Palo Alto, CA: Stanford University Press, 1933.

Sueyoshi, Amy. "Mindful Masquerades: Que(e)Rying Japanese Immigrant Dress in Turn-of-the Century San Francisco." *Frontiers: A Journal of Women's Studies* 26, no. 3 (2005): 67–100.

Tajima-Pēna, Renee. "Moving the Image: Asian American Independent Filmmaking 1970–1990." In *Moving the Image: Independent Asian Pacific American Media Arts*, edited by Russell Leong, 10–33. Los Angeles: UCLA Asian American Studies Center, 1991.

Taylor, Sandra C. "The Federal Reserve Bank and the Relocation of the Japanese in 1942." *Public Historian* 5, no. 1 (Winter 1983): 9–30.

Tepperman, Charles. *Amateur Cinema: The Rise of North American Moviemaking, 1923-1960*. Berkeley: University of California Press, 2014.

Thissen, Judith. "Beyond the Nickelodeon: Cinemagoing, Everyday Life and Identity Politics." *Audiences: Defining and Researching Screen Entertainment Reception*, edited by Ian Christie, 45–65. Amsterdam, NL: Amsterdam University Press, 2012.

Toulmin, Vanessa, and Martin Loiperdinger. "Is It You? Recognition, Representation and Response in Relation to the Local Film." *Film History* 17, no. 1 (2005): 7–18.

Trice, Jasmine. *City of Screens: Imagining Audiences in Manila's Alternative Film Culture.* Durham, NC: Duke University Press, 2021.

Turner, Max, and Frank R. Kennedy. "Exclusion, Ejection, and Segregation of Theater Patrons." *Iowa Law Review* 32 (1946): 625–658.

Uricchio, William, and Roberta E. Pearson. "Manhattan's Nickelodeons New York? New York! William Uricchio and Roberta E. Pearson Comment on the Singer-Allen Exchange." *Cinema Journal* 36, no. 4 (1997): 98–102.

U.S. Bureau of the Census. *Foreign Commerce and Navigation of the United States.* Washington, DC: U.S. Government Printing Office, 1928 and 1938.

Uzawa, Yoshiko. "'Will White Man and Yellow Man Ever Mix?': Wallace Irwin, Hashimura Togo, and the Japanese Immigrant in America." *Japanese Journal of American Studies* 17 (2006): 201–222.

Vincendeau, Ginette. "Hollywood Babel: The Coming of Sound and the Multiple-Language Version." In *"Film Europe" and "Film America": Cinema, Commerce and Cultural Exchange, 1920-1939,* edited by Andrew Higson and Richard Maltby, 207–224. Exeter, UK: University of Exeter Press, 1999.

Walker, Phillip Nathaniel. "A History of Theatrical Activity in Fresno, California, from Its Beginnings in 1872 to the Opening of the White Theatre in 1914." PhD diss., University of Southern California, 1972.

Waller, Gregory. "Japan on America's Screens, 1908–1915." In *Early Cinema and the "National,"* edited by Richard Abel and Rob King, 139–152. Bloomington: Indiana University Press, 2008.

———. "Locating Early Non-Theatrical Audiences." In *Audiences,* edited by Ian Christie, 81–95. Amsterdam, NL: Amsterdam University Press, 2012.

———. "Projecting the Promise of 16mm, 1935–45." In *Useful Cinema,* edited by Charles R. Acland and Haidee Wasson, 125–148. Durham, NC: Duke University Press, 2011.

Walsh, Michael. "'No Place for a White Man': United Artists' Far East Department, 1922–1929." *Asian Cinema* 7, no. 2 (Winter 1995): 18–33.

Wang, Yiman. "Alter-Centering Chinese Cinemas: The Diasporic Formation." In *A Companion to Chinese Cinemas,* edited by Yingjin Zhang, 535–551. Hoboken, NJ: Blackwell, 2012.

———. "Anna May Wong: A Border-Crossing 'Minor' Star Mediating Performance." *Journal of Chinese Cinemas* 2, no. 2 (2008): 91–102.

Ward, Richard. "The Price of Independence: The Rolin Film Company's Quest for Distribution." In *Networks of Entertainment: Early Film Distribution 1895-1915,* edited by Frank Kessler and Nanna Verhoeff, 157–166. Bloomington: Indiana University Press, 2008.

Wong, K. Scott. *Americans First: Chinese Americans and the Second World War.* Cambridge, MA: Harvard University Press, 2005.

Xing, Jun. *Asian America through the Lens: History, Representations, and Identity.* Walnut Creek, CA: Rowman Altamira, 1998.

Yeatter, Bryan L. *Cinema of the Philippines: A History and Filmography, 1897-2005.* Jefferson, NC: McFarland, 2013.

Yoneyama, Lisa. "Toward a Decolonial Genealogy of the Transpacific." *American Quarterly* 69, no. 3 (2017): 471–482.

Yoo, David. "'Read All about It': Race, Generation, and the Japanese American Ethnic Press, 1925–41." *Amerasia Journal* 19, no. 1 (1993): 69–92.

Young, Paul. "Synchronized Sound Comes to the Cinema." In *The Wiley-Blackwell History of American Film*, edited by C. Lucia, R. Grandmann, and A. Simon, 115–130. Hoboken, NJ: Wiley, 2011.

Yu, Elena S. H. "Filipino Migration and Community Organizations in the U.S." *California Sociologists* 3 (1980): 76–102.

Index

Page numbers in *italics* refer to images.